Pre-Views:

"Re. *Maxwell's Passion and Power*—who can describe that wonderful man? A riveting speaker; man of deep compassion, side-splitting humor, and an unswerving determination to follow his God!"

—**Elisabeth Elliot**, author, conference speaker

"Our country's history is marked by risk-taking visionaries who see in their waking hours what most dare not dream in the night. L. E. Maxwell was one. He changed the course of our nation's church history, and heaven will forever rejoice in his sojourn of faith."

—**Brian C. Stiller**, President, Tyndale College & Seminary

"Re. *Maxwell: Passion and Power*—he was a pioneer of tremendous vision and bold faith. His 'Prairie Vision' brought great blessing to…every continent—even Inland China. The mark of the people Maxwell mentored was their commitment to Christ, love for the Word, heart for the world, and servant spirit."

—**James Hudson Taylor III**, OMF (formerly China Inland Mission)

"Historians assessing Canadian prairie Christianity…will have to account for L. E. Maxwell's influence. This memoir by a former student of his who became a missions statesman will be an invaluable resource. For those who remember Maxwell, it will stir deep memories—and quicken our own passion for God."

—**Maxine Hancock**, Author, Broadcaster, Regent College Professor

"Many of those involved in the early days of Trinity Western University's miracle studded history gave testimony to the tremendous influence both Prairie Bible Institute and L. E. Maxwell had in their lives…The account of 'passion and power,' produced by one of Maxwell's grandsons, Mark Maxwell (TWU '81), and authored by W. Harold Fuller, helps us understand the vibrant spirit of the co-founder of Prairie."

—**R. Neil Snider,** President, Trinity Western University

"L. E. Maxwell and PBI had a unique impact on SIM. The man with his zest for life and strong victorious message challenged young people to serve well the missionary enterprise. The remarkable expansion of the Church around the world in those years is a tribute to God's blessing on a life and ministry. Fuller has done well to tell this story in *Maxwell's Passion and Power*."

—**Ian M. Hay**, General Director Emeritus, SIM

"Clearly captures the ethos of LE. Tackles some of the tough theological questions, shows courage and clarity in developing what my father taught."

—**Paul T. Maxwell**, Director, International Students Inc. (Canada); former President, PBI

i

"When the story of a legend you've known and admired all your life is written by a recognized storyteller, you've got a treat in store! Through firsthand accounts of encounters with L. E. Maxwell, you'll laugh, you'll be astonished, and maybe even be changed as you feel the heartbeat of one of the twentieth century's giants in biblical education."
—**Robertson McQuilkin**, President Emeritus, Columbia Bible College and Theological Seminary

"Clear and convincing, focussing on the message of union with Christ which formed generations of students spiritually and equipped them for life's responsibilities and relationships."
—**Ted S. Rendall**, President and Chancellor Emeritus, PBI

"In a masterful way the author has captured the dynamism of this man of zest and Spirit-filled forthrightness. From these pages LE emerges—still a blessing and a challenge!"
—**Mel Donald**, early Director of IVCF, Canada; author, pastor, missionary

"Captures the exciting, dynamic life of the Founder of Prairie. We see him through the eyes of students, missionaries, associates, and precious family— and relive the inspiration of this great man of God."
—**Henry & Inger Hildebrand**, Founders of Briercrest Family of Schools

"In a highly readable narrative style, Harold Fuller gives us personal glimpses of Prairie Bible Institute and its founder, seen through the eyes of students and staff from across the years. . .effectively capturing the passions of the great heart of L. E. Maxwell."
—**Audrey Dorsch** ('74/'01), Director, Exchange Publishing; former editor *Faith Today*

"Refreshing, challenging, informative. Readers in general and theological academics will be blessed by LE's message, so clearly enunciated and elucidated."
—**George M. Foxall**, International Council of Evangelical Theological Education

"A very readable book! Harold Fuller captures Prairie's rigorous training in self-denial and simple lifestyle—all very attractive to Chinese Christians in Hong Kong in the 1960s. No wonder so many came to Prairie in ensuing decades—attracted by L.E. Maxwell's emphasis on spiritual discipline as well as foreign missions!"
—**Lena Lau**, former lecturer, Hong Kong University; Prairie Board ('92-98)

"L.E. Maxwell and my father Ernest C. Manning (then Premier of Alberta) were contemporaries at a time when the Canadian prairies blazed with the spiritual fire of renewal and the political fire of prairie populism. The ministry and passion of Mr. Maxwell were a blessing to the West, to Canada, and to the world. That blessing lives on through Fuller's engaging tribute to this disciplined soldier of Christ. As the husband of a Prairie alumna, I personally am conscious of Maxwell's indelible mark on the lives of tens of thousands of students."
—**Preston Manning**, M.P., House of Commons, Ottawa

Maxwell's Passion & Power

By W. Harold Fuller

No heart is pure that is not passionate;
no virtue safe that is not enthusiastic.

—-J. R. Seeley[1]

Maxwell Foundation
Huttonville, ON

2002

---

[1] From *What is a Living Church?* by J.S. Whale (London: Edinburgh House Press, 1938), p.59

Maxwell's Passion and Power
ISBN 1-930285-05-1

Copyright ©2001 Mark L Maxwell
       Text written by W Harold Fuller
       Typesetting and Layout by Alma Turnbull
       Front Cover Design by Julie M. Bentson, Allegra
       Published by The Master Design
             in cooperation with Master Design Ministries
             PO Box 17865
             Memphis, TN 38187-0865
      bookinfo@masterdesign.org
      www.masterdesign.org

Additional copies of the book may be purchased from:
       Prairie Book Room
       319 - 5th Ave. N.
       Three Hills, AB, T0M 2N0
         Email: bookroom@pbi.ab.ca
         Tel: 403-443-5519

       Mark L. Maxwell
       2 Ostrander Blvd.,
       Huttonville, ON L6V 3N2 Canada
         Email: maxwellfoundation@rogers.com

       Olford Ministries International
       P.O. Box 757800
       Memphis, TN 38175-7800
         Email: OMI@Olford.org Website: www.Olford.org
         Tel: 901-757-7977

Unless otherwise noted, Scripture quotations are taken from the HOLY BIBLE, NEW INTERNATIONAL VERSION ©1973, 1978, 1985 by the International Bible Society, used by permission of Zondervan Publishing House.

Printed in the USA by Bethany Press International

*To the memory of
Leslie and Pearl Maxwell,
whose vibrant lives helped shape ours,
and whose spiritual legacy lives on in
Prairie Bible Institute's schools
and in hearts around the world.*

CONTENTS:

Contents

FOREWORD

By Stephen F. Olford

IT IS A DISTINCT HONOR to write a Foreword to this story of the life and work of Leslie E. Maxwell. I like the title, *Maxwell's Passion and Power*, because it descriptively images the man, the message, and the ministry as we all knew him.

From head to toe he was a man! *Physically*, he was a rare specimen of fitness. I vividly recall the litany of procedures he shared with me on how to keep fit. He was engaged in all manner of "workouts," including mountain climbing, hunting, fishing, and running. I once asked him why he ran from one building to another between classes and faculty meetings. His simple reply was, "To keep fit and show the student body that time is precious and that the work of the Lord 'requires haste.'"

Mentally, his mind was razor sharp! In debate and repartee he was extraordinary. He was also a voracious reader of the Word of God, theological books, and Christian literature. *Spiritually*, he exuded the presence of Christ because he walked with God and exhibited the "fruit of the Spirit."

As this volume affirms, L. E. Maxwell was a man with a message. Of course, he taught "the whole counsel of God," but his core message was "Jesus Christ and him crucified" (1 Cor. 2:2), and "I am crucified with Christ" (Gal. 2:20). He taught that Christ was crucified FOR us to save us from the guilt of sin; but, just as surely, we are crucified WITH Christ to save us from the grip of sin. What Christ did for us, the Holy Spirit makes real in us, as we count on him in dependent faith.

The key text LE used was Romans 8:13—"If you live according to the flesh [sinful nature], you will die; but if by the Spirit you [continually] put to death the [misdeeds] of the body, you will live." LE always saw the cross as the prelude to life, even the resurrection life of Jesus realized in us by the Holy Spirit.

This is a message seldom preached or practiced in evangelical circles today, so I urge you to read carefully and prayerfully Chapters 10-13 of this book. Also get hold of Maxwell's *Born Crucified.*[1] It is a classic!

This Foreword would be incomplete without mention of LE's ministry, which inevitably flowed out of his message. Prairie Bible Institute is an eloquent reminder of his teaching and training philosophy. I have met graduates from this school all over the world. They are usually known for two distinctive Christian qualities—spirituality and stickability.

Living in strange countries, cultures, and circumstances truly tests spirituality. Without the moment-by-moment application of the Cross to the self-life, relationships are strained and resentments are stirred to explosive proportions. This, in turn, can lead to alarming defections from the mission field. When this takes place men and women with spirituality and stickability stand out! This caliber of missionary was the result of Maxwell's unique ministry through his example, preaching, teaching, and writing.

All this and more, Harold Fuller has insightfully chronicled for us and generations to come. It only remains for me to add that the greatest honor L. E. Maxwell ever conferred on me was his personal request to conduct his funeral. What a day of celebration and consecration it turned out to be! Thousands attended and hundreds responded to the challenge to serve "anywhere, at any time, at any cost." This is how LE wanted it and this is how God ordered it—as the choir, accompanied by the orchestra, sang "The Hallelujah Chorus"!

Maxwell's Passion & Power is more than a biography. It is a blueprint for victorious living. For those with an inner longing to "live no longer for themselves, but for him who died for them and rose again," this book is a reading must!

—Stephen F. Olford, Founder and Senior Lecturer,
The Stephen Olford Center for Biblical Preaching, Memphis, Tennessee

---

[1] L.E. Maxwell, *Born Crucified.* Chicago, Moody Press, 1945. Reprinted edition available from Prairie Book Room, Three Hills, Alberta, Canada.

MISSIONS FOREWORD
By George Verwer

WHEN GOD GAVE US the concept of getting Christian literature into the hands of people all over the world, Operation Mobilization set up a network with men and women of many nationalities, missions, and churches. It was interesting to note that among our most dedicated workers were graduates of a school called Prairie Bible Institute.

While I was a student at Moody Bible Institute, I came across the book written by L.E. Maxwell—*Born Crucified,* and it became one of the key titles we distributed on our ship, the *Logos*. Later I met Mr. Maxwell and resonated with his passion for the world's unevangelized, and with the power of his message. I've seen that same passion in his children and grandchildren—Don who served with OM, and Mark, who has chaired our Canadian board.

I'm glad author Harold Fuller, whose own literature work was an inspiration in the early years of OM, has set out to capture *Maxwell's Passion and Power*. LE's message of the Cross in the life of the believer is basic to fulfilling Christ's Commission. Yet I find it a missing message as I travel the world. Fuller not only introduces us to the vibrant Maxwell we remember, but also shows the process of the Cross in the life of the believer, through graphic pilgrimages—those of L. E. Maxwell, his own family, the author, and others.

"We're engaged in a spiritual war for the souls of men, women, and children!" I've challenged students at Prairie's missionary conferences, and this has been my burden when speaking at InterVarsity's Urbana and elsewhere. I'm concerned as I see today's churches centering on self-fulfillment, rather than fulfilling Jesus' commands. OM and other missionary agencies are looking for committed disciples who demonstrate the Lordship of Christ in their own lives.

I know that was Maxwell's concern in his day, and I trust that God will use *Maxwell's Passion and Power* to stir us all afresh. This world has never been in greater spiritual need!

—George Verwer, International Director,
Operation Mobilization, Bromley, Kent, UK

PREFACE

By Ted S. Rendall

HOW DID A YOUNG SCOTSMAN, born and raised in Edinburgh (scene of so much evangelical history), come into contact with Leslie E. Maxwell and in time become a close associate of the dynamic leader of Prairie Bible Institute?

I'd met several Prairie graduates and was impressed with the emphasis on "the crucified life." So I arrived in Three Hills as a student in 1953. My "gratis"[1] assignment in 1955 was with the *Prairie Overcomer*, writing "The Young Overcomer," a feature for young people.

As Harold Fuller mentions in this book, my early editorial assistance led to further involvement with Mr. Maxwell and PBI. In 1956 I joined the staff as editorial resource person to LE, and eventually joined the faculty. When I became vice-Principal in 1960 and later Principal and President, I had a unique opportunity of getting to know this Spirit-anointed man.

Although I never called him "mentor," that is truly what he was to me. Eventually when my office was moved next to his, I had full access to him any time he was alone. He answered my questions, lent me books, and pointed to underlined statements in his books. In return I brought him materials that I had read and marked. He would read to me the articles he'd written for the magazine's feature, "The World of Today," and we'd set them out in the sequence he wanted for the magazine.

LE loved the apt quotation, the appropriate illustration, and the timely joke. As preacher and teacher he had a great sense of humor. His witticisms poured forth in a constant stream. Teaching one day in a Bible class he referred to people who were biblically mixed up: "as confused as a chameleon on a piece of Scotch plaid!"

---

[1] Student work that helped defray expenses.

There is a sense in which LE led the Institute by the power of his example and his Spirit-anointed ministry. Since he didn't really like administration, it wasn't long before he asked me to chair various Institute committees on his behalf. He trusted us younger colleagues to carry out our responsibilities faithfully. This was one of his greatest leadership traits—delegating responsibilities to his officers and letting them get on with the job.

When LE resigned as Senior Pastor of the Prairie Tabernacle Congregation in 1975, PTC asked me to become Pastor of Preaching. For me, this was a difficult decision, for he'd been preaching to the campus church folk since the beginning. And our preaching style was so different! To crown it all, he would be sitting in the audience Sunday by Sunday! But I accepted the position and he accepted me. It was surely a mark of his greatness that he could sit at my feet and listen to my expositions of the Word on a regular basis.

This was LE's attitude toward the men and women of God who came to speak at Prairie conferences—and what a galaxy of evangelical preachers came! I think of Alan Redpath, Stephen Olford, Mary Morrison (now Peckham), Harold Wildish, Ian Thomas, Elisabeth Elliot, Arthur Mouw, and Helen Roseveare. He took notes of a speaker's sermon and then wove comments from the message into his closing appeal (which sometimes became a sermon in itself!).

LE was truly a man of passion and a man of power—a man of power because he was a man who passionately loved his Lord and Master, his calling to lead Prairie Bible Institute, the staff and students God brought to campus, and people around the world who had not heard the good news of Christ.

I count the privilege of working with him as one of the most significant aspects of my Christian heritage. When I became President of the Institute, someone commented about my filling his shoes. "No—not filling his shoes but following his steps," I corrected. I can hear him saying to all of us who have studied or served at Prairie, "Follow my example, as I follow the example of Christ" (1 Cor. 11:1).

Now my friend, Harold Fuller, has introduced LE for a new generation. His sketch is clear and convincing, focussing on the message of union with Christ. That message formed generations of students spiritually and equipped them for life's responsibilities and relationships. When the definitive history of Prairie Bible Institute is written, it will show that what was planted on these prairies in the plan of the all-wise God was what Charles J. Mellis calls "a committed community"—and God has used this community to bless all nations.

—Ted S. Rendall, Chancellor Emeritus, Prairie Bible Institute

FAMILY'S ACKNOWLEDGEMENTS

By Mark L. Maxwell

From the Maxwell Family

THIS BOOK is not intended to make a hero of L. E. Maxwell but to glorify his God, and to recognize how "LE" was used, making the most of his strengths and weaknesses. As we developed the initial concepts of this somewhat daunting project, we had one over-riding objective: to encourage people in their walk with God, their work for God, and their service to fellow mankind.

Conflicts from around the world reverberate through our televisions, often illustrating the futile efforts by mankind for control of their own lives and those of their neighbors. By comparison, this book about a man with a *passion* for God, who has the *power* to conquer evil, is timely and perhaps timeless. Timeless, not because of the man but because of his God — the one who holds eternity in his hand.

This is the story of a man who went to the western Canadian prairies to teach young men and women the Word of God. As Prairie Bible Institute developed, he was "hoping for nothing," walking humbly, in complete abandonment to his God. His tools were a tireless work ethic, honed by a modest education, sprinkled with quick wit, empowered by solid counselors and the wisdom to take their advice.

In many ways his academic achievements and excellence were the result of intense study and an abiding belief that each person could teach him about the God he loved. The recognition of his achievements is not trophies mounted on shelves or diplomas framed on walls but the productive lives of Christian workers around the world, multiplied in successive generations.

Many of my Grandfather's dearest peers have come together to remember him and the wonderful richness of his life, to remember his

xvi

passion for life and for his fellow man. They have come to honor their good friend, colleague and mentor, and more, to honor the God who worked mightily through him.

When Harold Fuller expressed an interest in telling the story of Grandpa Maxwell, I felt that this was perhaps the greatest compliment that could be given to LE. Here was this outstanding statesman of international missions, graciously giving his time and talents to the memory of L. E. Maxwell and to his God.

Harold's contribution as author is exceptional, both in the quantity of time he has committed to this project and the quality of work he has demanded of himself. Through it all he carried a gracious spirit, putting up with the many versions and "re-versions" of the story that surfaced from the disparate stakeholders.

His attitude was well illustrated when one of the contributing authors, wanting to get Harold properly titled, asked me, "Is he Mr., Rev., Dr. or what?" Harold responded: "As to what to call me— 'missionary' is the highest title you could give me, but for the sake of the article, maybe we should leave it as it is—simply 'Harold Fuller' Someone referred to me in a recently published book as the Rev. Dr. Harold Fuller. That may all be true but it sounds a little horrific, even if honorific!"

Harold, as a family, we want to say "thank-you" for this record of the way God used Grandpa and this reminder of how he can use any one of us. Thank you for the many decades of friendship you have given the Maxwell family as well as Prairie Bible Institute. And on a personal note, I want to thank you for your friendship and good counsel you have "wasted" on me from as far back as high school.

Among the many who are part of this story, we want to be sure to say thank you to:

• Alma Turnbull, for her friendship to Elaine and me over many years. This time it came in the form of professionally typesetting and processing the manuscript to make it camera-ready for printing, a "sweet-smelling offering" to the Lord by one who also sat under LE's mentoring.

• Master Design Ministries of Memphis, Tennessee for their work on the publishing side. MDM is a non-profit organization that helps missionaries and pastors get their books published, a wonderful partner for those of us who know so little about the many details involved in this process.

• David Maxwell and Donald Harbridge, for wise marketing counsel as veterans in the book retailing trade.

• The faculty and staff of Prairie Bible Institute, including Deans and dorm supervisors, who stood with LE and endured the students the author described (even including the members of the Maxwell clan!).

• Alumni, who have carried "Maxwell's Passion and Power" in their own service throughout the world.

• Prairie's faithful constituency, without whom the founders would never have been able to develop the Institute.

• Three Hills townsfolk, who patiently endured the influx of young life on the campus at the north end of town, and who through the years helped to make PBI feel part of the community.

• Parents and children, pastors and other Christian workers, without whom the student body could not have grown as it did.

• The personal friends of the Maxwell Family, who have "stuck closer than a brother" in times of need and stress, as well as in seasons of joy.

• … and the Maxwell clan, who worked with the author adding color and detail, however revealing the truth has been, in order to tell the story honestly and completely—a real family with real challenges and a real God who has been faithful to us through all these decades.

In summary, we would like to take this opportunity to thank the many friends and colleagues who stood with Grandma and Grandpa for several decades. The school has become a landmark on the Canadian prairies for international Christian workers, a beacon that shines, not as a result of this single man but of the entire community that rallied around him and continues to carry the torch.

To all, on behalf of the entire Family (daughters, sons, grandchildren, and great-grandchildren), we say God Bless You—enjoy the story of Daddy/Grandpa/LE in *Maxwell's Passion and Power*.

Mark L. Maxwell
Maxwell Foundation

AUTHOR'S ACKNOWLEDGEMENTS

My deep appreciation to:

- The immediate Maxwell family, who opened their hearts with honesty and love—sometimes with laughter, occasionally with tears. Each could write a similar book from a personal perspective. So could the grandchildren.

- Mark,[1] "main sparkplug" for the project, his hospitable wife Elaine; brother David and his wife Sue, and sister Ruth—all helpful to the "enth." My mentioning them does not overlook the helpfulness of other Maxwell grandchildren but reflects my personal relationship with them ever since childhood, and with their beloved parents, who died in an untimely (to us) way.

- The Prairie Board, the family, the grandchildren, and friends for challenging me to write this story. Living afresh through the memories of Leslie Maxwell (my most significant mentor apart from my parents) and Pearl, has touched my life again with their love, passion, and power.

- Prairie friends Ted and Hester Rendall (who suggested the title), Rick and Naomi Down, Phil and Ramona Callaway— representative of current leadership, faculty, and staff whom I greatly respect and who have encouraged me in this project.

- Long-time friends, such as Margaret Ratzlaff (favorite "adopted aunt" of three Maxwell grandchildren), George and Ruth Foxall, Ben and Marilyn Weber and others who came to my rescue with research details.

---

[1] At half my age, Mark had produced over one thousand professional manuscript pages and several media articles on the financial industry, as well as a series of annual poems. In addition to serving on several boards of Christian organizations, he has been a member of Prairie's Board and is financial consultant to a number of Christian organizations, including Prairie.

- Besides, a host of helpful people who patiently put up with my checking, cross checking, re-checking—and answered questions about improbable details. (Examples: "How far is it from Philadelphia to Three Hills in air miles?" A pilot friend in Virginia sent me the figure by return email. Or, "When is winter wheat planted?" Again, "Why didn't Prairie use local well water?")

- My wife Lorna—excellent manuscript reader, and editor in her own right. Before the correcting stage, she'd already transcribed miles of taped interviews—some barely intelligible because of highway or crowd noises in the background. (Thanks to those who graciously allowed me to poke my pocket recorder in their faces! That included Ruth Dearing, in whose face I saw the reflection of heaven as, shortly before she died, we reminisced for several days about the ones we both highly respected.)

- Busy leaders who took time to scan the manuscript and kindly commented on whether it is worth reading. (See "What Others Say" inside front cover.)

- Authors of source material—published and unpublished (see Bibliography). I purposely wrote the basic "story line" before reading these sources, in order to create a fresh approach. But books, articles, and interviews about Prairie and its Founders later helped me enormously with details and affirmation of my own memories.

In particular, thanks to the books of Roy Davidson, W. Phillip Keller, and Bernice Callaway, the analytical thesis of grandson Steve Spaulding, and an unpublished manuscript by Don Richardson—who years ago vividly recreated the Maxwells' pre-Prairie years. (Several of my quotations about Maxwell appear in LE's own books, the writings of others, or notes recorded by Kathleen "Sandy" Head and Margaret Ewing. But since much is also common in the memories of us who sat under this Master Mentor, in most cases I've not attributed material to any published source.) And thanks to Wentworth Pike for compiling *Quips &*

Quotes,[1] from which I've used a memorable saying at the beginning of each chapter.

- Most of all, the Holy Spirit— the "Alongside One." This is not a cliché. I can only conclude that he came to my rescue, right from the start. A number of times an offhand remark in an entirely different context far away from Three Hills led me to another significant piece of "the picture." I knew family and friends were praying, and many a time I bowed my head and said, "Thank you, Lord! That just fit!"

W. Harold Fuller, Toronto, 2002

---

[1] Pike, Wentworth, *Quips & Quotes* by L. E. Maxwell. Three Hills, Action International Ministries, 1992.

A journalist traces his personal encounter with
L. E. Maxwell and his life-changing message.
Seen through the eyes of those who knew him
best—his family and students—here is the unlikely
drama of a Prairie farmhouse Bible study that grew
into a world-encircling ministry—all expressed in
Maxwell's passion for life and spiritual power.

Maxwell's Passion and Power

Introduction

"CAPTURE THE MAN'S PASSION!"

MAXWELL'S PASSION & POWER? Some who've heard of Leslie E. Maxwell, co-founder of Prairie Bible Institute, had a different opinion of his message—more to do with "dying to self" and "the crucified life," or worms not crowns!

But death and crucifixion weren't the final objectives of the principal's life. Those were only the pathways to what he wanted everyone to find – life, eternal, victorious!

Anyone who knew Maxwell would readily associate "passion" with his name. "Someone needs to capture the passion of the man!" Bob Spaulding, son-in-law of Leslie E. Maxwell, exclaimed to me. Even the man the family call "Daddy" would accept that, I felt. He wrote in *Born Crucified*:[1] "Our [Lord] cries out for . . . the man with a passion that is stronger than death" (p. 125). Again he wrote: "If . . . it is our eternal passion to press on to know Christ, we shall soon discover that the crucified Lord must have crucified followers" (p. 147).

Although we all agree Maxwell bubbled over with spiritual passion, "power" may almost seem contradictory in describing this man who, like the Apostle Paul, shunned all earthly power. That's the point —Maxwell's power was not human, but was at the heart of his life desire "to know Christ and the power of his resurrection . . . ." [2]

"LE," as many of us called him, passionately wanted us students to get past the death march and dance for joy in "all the riches in Christ Jesus." As part of his vibrant spiritual life, he had a zest for, well . . . simply living! That's why we students made the trek from near and far to sit under his teaching.

[1] *Op. cit.*

[2] Philippians 3:10.

1

Maxwell's Peak Years

How did he get that way? How did a careless youth end up as a prophet for his day?

That's what this book is about. It doesn't pretend to be a definitive (as in "exhaustive") history—rather a first-hand opportunity to know L. E. Maxwell's secret of passion and power. Readers expecting a simple biography of LE may wonder at all the stories of student life. I've purposely inserted these as mirrors to reflect life at Prairie and the influence of our Mentor on our lives. They complete the picture of the man by showing how his teachings stood up under the tests of ministry—call them case studies, if you like.

As a journalist, instead of starting with "beginnings," I've chosen to land the reader smack in the midst of LE's peak years of ministry, adding historical details along the way. I've also sought to reveal secrets of his powerful message and passionate life.

"We want a book," Maxwell's grandson Mark told me, "that work-weary people, feeling drained and even thinking of quitting (or readers who know someone like that) will pick up and keep reading until they exclaim (maybe at 2 a.m.), 'I've been through that! . . . He or she is just like me! . . . God can do that for me too!'"

The story of Leslie Earl Maxwell and the Bible school he and Fergus Kirk co-founded has already been told. (See Bibliography at end.) With new research, interviews, and refreshed memories, I hope I've been able to tell it afresh. "Daddy Maxwell" was a prophet for his times, but he'd tell you the most important element of his life and work was not himself or the school, but the message of the Cross worked out in students' lives. He discipled and inspired us so we could carry that message into the market places of our own communities and of countries around the globe.

A Pilgrimage and Paradox

I first arrived at Prairie just out of the Navy, a budding journalist, and fairly skeptical of Maxwell's message. In this story I invite the reader to accompany me and others on our own pilgrimage to the Cross, as the message changed our hearts and worldview. In God's strange plan, I've had the privilege of converging paths unexpectedly with the Maxwell family in their own pilgrimages. Through the drama of all of our lives, you'll see how each has experienced the Cross in passing its message on to others. I guess that's my underlying thesis, true of every disciple of Jesus.

This was L. E. Maxwell's Paradox. Of course it wasn't his paradox; it was the divine paradox of death and resurrection. God used him to re-focus a sorely needed truth of Scripture. Today, as it was to the early disciples, it continues to be a paradox—an apparent contradiction among the menu of formulas for "successful living."

Maxwell's unique presentation of the Cross in the life of the believer has gripped my own heart afresh, alternately bringing laughter and tears. As I realized how little I hear that message these days, and how needed it is, my initial hesitation changed into a burden to put it all down on paper—to tell today's readers about *Maxwell's Passion and Power*.

—W. Harold Fuller ('50), Toronto, Canada, April 2002

Maxwell's Passion and Power

Chapter 1: First Exposure

*"If you have need of nothing, that is what you will get
—in fact, that is what you have already."*—LEM

THE PRAIRIE FIREBALL

A FIREBALL SEEMED TO BURST on to the platform. An electric expectation suddenly filled the cavernous wooden "Tabernacle" (the auditorium of Prairie Bible Institute). Perhaps I was the only skeptic seated on the rudimentary wooden benches. Some thousand men and women had assembled for our first exposure to Principal Leslie E. Maxwell.

His face I recognized from photographs—square jaw, broad forehead, strong mouth lines, easy smile, expressive eyes set deep between kindly crow's-feet. What I wasn't prepared for was the vitality of the man. He seemed to note everything and everyone as we filed in.

Ramrod straight, he strode to the microphone to welcome us, staccato sentences often ending with a chuckle. In contrast to the spartan "Tab," L. E. Maxwell sparkled. At a distance on the rustic platform, he seemed a giant. When I later stood near him, I was surprised how average he was in height—but giant in spirit.

Some students had already heard Mr. Maxwell speak at conferences across North America. They chose Prairie in spite of its isolation, chiefly because of the man and his message. Some, believe it or not, chose it because of its regulated disciplines. They came to hear "the voice of one crying in the wilderness."[1] The rolling prairie of southern Alberta wasn't exactly a wilderness, and the principal of PBI wasn't a prophet in the sense of predicting Armageddon. But many considered

---

[1] John 1.23.

him a prophet on the Prairies proclaiming a life-giving message to a spiritually thirsty world.

A Skeptic's View

His message that first day was simple enough: "Settling in at PBI—Unpack!" But the message he preached most of the time, I didn't yet understand. In fact, shortly after discharge from the Canadian Navy, I'd written to Maxwell to complain about the wimpy image he and his Prairie Bible Institute seemed to project.

"We need to go out weeping, bearing precious seed," Leslie E. Maxwell had written in the school's pocket-sized digest, *The Prairie Overcomer*. He was commenting on the Psalmist's words: "He who goeth forth and weepeth, bearing precious seed, shall doubtless come again with rejoicing."[2] Since childhood I'd been turned off by what I felt were "namby-pamby" Christians. I viewed my Sunday school teacher as almost effeminate, Sunday school papers as insipid, and Christians in general as lacking red blood. Where was the challenge of the gospel?

"We'd do better to face the foe with clear vision, not eyes blurred with tears!" I wrote in my youthful "wisdom." I'm now amazed I had the conceit to write such a letter. I later found the answer at Three Hills, and it wasn't what I expected. I simply hadn't understood the deeper meaning of the Cross—the paradox of strength out of weakness, of life out of death.

Pioneering the West

My father always had *The Prairie Overcomer* in the house and encouraged his six children to read it. I glanced at it only occasionally. Years later I understood Dad's interest in Prairie Bible Institute and its co-founder, L. E. Maxwell. Eight years before Maxwell arrived in Three Hills to teach a handful of young people in a farmhouse, my missionary father had ridden his horse from settler to settler on the Canadian Prairies, preaching the gospel. One of his parish churches was just north

---

[1] Psalm 126.6 AV

of Three Hills at Elnora, where my mother gave birth to my eldest sister, Esther.

Foreseeing increasing liberalism developing in some denominational churches,[3] Father had prayed for a strong Bible-teaching ministry to be raised up in the area. He saw the answer to his prayers in the Bible school that the Kirks, Maxwells, and others developed at Three Hills. And now I was here!

I'd come from serving in the Canadian Navy, immersed in the rough life of wartime on the heaving North Atlantic. As I got off the train in the shadow of the stark grain elevators in Three Hills in 1946, I didn't feel I belonged here.

Whatever Was I Doing Here?

Why should this 21-year-old Navy veteran attend a segregated school where the boys and girls could go into town only on separate days—not together unless married? Where they sat on separate sides in the classrooms, dining room, and auditorium? Why leave the excitement of Toronto's big-city life for an isolated barrack-like campus on a windswept plain more than two thousand miles away?

Whatever views I'd developed of milquetoast Christianity, I had to admit that when I was a child, "Prairie" graduates visiting our home in Toronto had impressed me. They seemed disciplined and purposeful. I joined a boys' prayer group for one graduate heading to Africa as a missionary. Before I joined the Navy, my boyhood goal was to end up there too, and attending "Prairie" seemed to be the logical way to prepare. When the Second World War intervened, I felt I had to do my part to combat Adolph Hitler's drive to dominate the world.

In the Navy I'd been the only known Christian on the ships on which I served. God kept me from the worst excesses of a sailor's life,

---

1 As an itinerant missionary preacher, Wm. A. Fuller served across Canada in churches of the Baptists, Brethren, Congregationalists, Methodists, Presbyterians and (later) United Church of Canada. He gave thanks that in each the Holy Spirit was keeping aflame the light of the gospel, however flickering in some.

but my heart was not spiritually warm. Upon discharge, I discovered that Veterans' Affairs would cover further education, so I decided to fulfill my boyhood commitment and enroll at Three Hills.

But by the time I lined up to register, I was sure I couldn't stick at it more than a few months. I decided to head further west at the first opportunity, to see the world. Maybe sign on to a crew headed from Vancouver for Australia. Little did I know I'd end up in Africa long before seeing Australia!

I did have to admit the exuberant leader on the platform that first day seemed a good example of "red-blooded Christianity." I couldn't have guessed the impact he would have on my life, or how I would eventually be involved with several family members.

I soon discovered there were many other ex-servicemen and women—Canadians and Americans—enrolling that year.[1] The intake of new students was more than the rough wooden dormitories could hold; so about one hundred of us men bedded down in the basement of the high school building. Stowing my sea bag above the wooden locker assigned me, I swung myself on to an upper bunk. Gazing at the white-washed wallboard ceiling, I saw only a blank as I wondered what I had got into!

The quiet student assigned to the lower bunk seemed somewhat fragile, but other young men from the armed forces helped turn that school basement into a boisterous wartime barracks. Maybe I could tolerate this after all—at least until Christmas or Spring break!

Farmhouse Roots

That week, as we launched into classes, we met faculty and staff—and the co-founder of Prairie, J. Fergus Kirk, one of ten children of settlers from Ontario. Andrew, father of Fergus, had been a Presbyterian lay preacher and home missionary. Jack and Mabel (sister of Fergus)

---

[1] Not only Three Hills but also the nation began to notice the burgeoning school. The December 15, 1947 issue of Canada's national montly, *Maclean's*, featured it as "Miracle at Three Hills."

McElheran had come west with them and were also key figures in giving birth to the Bible Institute. It was in their farmhouse that the first classes were held.[1] They all valued their Scottish Presbyterian Bible heritage.

Ordered by his doctor in 1920 to rest from intensive farming, Fergus had started teaching a weekly Bible class in his home. When he exhausted his own repertoire, his sister Hattie suggested he write William C. Stevens, author of a correspondence Bible course she'd studied.[2] Stevens had founded a small Bible Institute named Midland—perhaps he'd know someone who could teach in Three Hills. "Liberal teaching is beginning to enter the church," Kirk wrote to Stevens in Kansas, Missouri. "We'd like a teacher from a Bible school. Can you send us one for a couple of years?"

The once robust farmer (who in our time was president of PBI) was somewhat stooped, but he never tired of telling how a freshly graduated Leslie Earl Maxwell arrived at the farm north of Three Hills in 1922.

"My father was a real man of faith and vision," recalls Doug Kirk, Prairie's radio technician when I was a student. "He expressed solid convictions about the way Prairie should go. Although as president he chaired Board meetings, he also helped with building operations and maintenance on campus."

The Unlikely Team

In time, we'd learn what an unlikely candidate for Bible teacher Leslie had once been. Born July 2, 1895, eldest of nine children, Leslie was raised on the grain plains of Salina, Kansas. Life for his family and neighbors was at subsistence level, and young Leslie had little time for "religion." Instead, as a child he'd dreamed of becoming "monarch of all he surveyed," but by teen years he wondered if he'd ever amount to any-

---

[1] The story of the Kirks, the McElherans, and Leslie and Pearl Maxwell has been told by Bernice Callaway in *Legacy*. Three Hills: MacCall Clan, 1987

[2] Hattie had also studied under W.C. Stevens when he taught at the Missionary Training Institute and Nyack College, NY, before founding Midland in Kansas City.

thing worthwhile.

"I played ball, I played pool, and I played the fool!" was how Maxwell later described his youth. He had godly grandparents, and several traumatic events in childhood made him stop to think. Once he'd nearly drowned, and the tragic death of a younger brother made him and his family think of eternity—briefly. But it was the persistent praying of an aunt, Christina, and the preaching of a Methodist evangelist, which finally brought him, at age 20, to trust in Christ as Savior.

The night he made that decision, he stayed up reading the Scriptures—he was so excited about finding eternal life. His aunt's godly life also set an example for his own spiritual growth. After serving in the US Army in Europe during World War I, he studied at Midland Bible Institute in Kansas City and at one time considered missionary service in Africa.

Even then, no one could have predicted that Leslie would become the fireball leader we got to know as principal of Prairie Bible Institute. In his youth he'd been terrified of public speaking, and he certainly didn't fancy a vocation of teaching. When he arrived in Three Hills at age 27, neither he nor Kirk had planned on opening a Bible school. Maxwell hadn't wanted to be a teacher, and Kirk hadn't wanted to teach or preach. But God used the spiritual needs around them to develop skills neither knew he possessed.

Fergus, besides teaching at a nearby rural church for 27 years, became president of what eventually grew to be Canada's largest Bible school. As principal, Leslie soon found himself leading young people into the Word of God—and he was enjoying it!

Exploding on a Rustic World

So the intended two-year stint lengthened as Maxwell and Kirk formed an "odd-couple" partnership between a shy farmer and a brusque army veteran. Yet these personality traits complemented each other, and the duo's partnership typified Prairie through the years as others from both urban and rural backgrounds joined faculty and staff. They all were bonded by a common purpose: "Training Disciplined Soldiers for Christ."

However, meeting the principal some twenty years after he first arrived in the little grain town, I could only imagine the initial adjustments the quiet, unassuming Kirk family must have had to make as this feisty Bible school grad from America exploded upon their rustic world! He didn't yet have at his side the gracious Pearl Eleanor Plummer, the girl to whom he was engaged. But the Kirks took him into their home and their hearts. Perhaps their common Scottish ancestry and Leslie's childhood on a wheat farm[1] helped overcome some of the inevitable cultural tensions between an idealistic Bible school graduate and a pragmatic farmer. And if there was any tension, the Bible teacher's infectious laugh always saved the day.

In coming to the Canadian Prairies, the single young man had already faced a certain amount of self-denial. He never wanted to live in a cold climate or a rural setting. Now he found himself enduring both—some 1,500 miles from the girl he'd met in Bible school and to whom he'd proposed. Also, he agreed to stay only two years, hoping to go on for further education. But back in Kansas City the Lord had "begun a good work" and now was continuing it in the life of twenty-seven-year-old Leslie.

He and Fergus learned from each other, struggling through the privations of that era. The promised crop wealth of the previous century had evaporated as the virgin top-soil, when cultivated, often blew away, leaving farmers grasping for straws in dust bowls. Many, like the Kirks, coming from Ontario, had to adjust to different soil and climate. The young Bible teacher soon realized the farm families just didn't have the money to pay him.

---

[1] When his father died, he's been left with the care of his mother and siblings and the family farm on the Kansas wheat plains.

Early Crisis

An early crisis drove Leslie to the Cross afresh. After his first winter the young preacher spent the summer pastoring three churches further north, riding horseback 21 miles each Sunday. As a result, a church in Edmonton invited him to be their pastor—an attractive post that would have enabled him to study at the University of Edmonton part time. Leslie wondered if this were God's provision, not only for his own needs but also to help support his widowed mother back in Kansas. He preached a candidate sermon and waited for the church's decision.

It may have seemed like choosing between isolation in a farmhouse or opening up a wide, fruitful urban ministry along with personal development. However, having no peace to leave, he set a deadline to receive the church's firm invitation. When the date passed, Leslie did what he later would advise us students to do: "When you feel God has closed a door, throw away the key!" The next day the invitation arrived, but Leslie had made his decision. He was there to stay. Somehow he would continue his own education through self-study. He could never have imagined what lay ahead as the school grew and he and his message became known worldwide.

"If Leslie had left then, that would have been the end of our little Bible school!" Fergus later said.[1] Meanwhile there was the problem of accepting a monthly salary from families struggling to survive.

"Don't worry," he told them at last. "I'll stay without salary. You just feed me and I'll teach the Word!" They realized Leslie had hoped to save enough to travel back to Iowa to fetch his future bride. It was 1925, three years after Leslie's arrival in Three Hills, before he was able to return to Iowa and marry his sweetheart Pearl. (See Chapter 23, Family Album.)

So teacher and students both knew the meaning of sacrifice. God

---

[1] Maxwell responded to that by stating, "Without Fergus Kirk's workaday dedication to God, Prairie Bible Institute would have forever been Prairie Bible *Destitute!*"

used the privations of those years to bond their hearts and teach them the meaning of dying to self—the Cross in the life of the believer, the core theme of what became Prairie Bible Institute.

Achieving Success

Those years of full reliance on God's provision gave them the founding faith principle of the school: "Hoping for Nothing."[1] They'd be faithful in ministry without looking for personal gain. This was certainly not conventional thinking even in most Christian circles. Hoping for nothing? That was certainly a paradox! Usually one hopes for something, if not everything. "We're children of the King!" brag some Christians in ministry. "We're supposed to be successful!"

"Success" could have different meanings. "Hoping for nothing" was part of Maxwell's paradox. And it was great preparation for the coming decade of The Great Depression. Whatever money came in, after meeting operating costs the principal, faculty, and staff all shared alike.

They also shared alike in lending a hand to help with any task. For instance, guest speakers shared the rudimentary student facilities when dormitories were later built. Sewage disposal was a bucket, with a trap door opening at the back of each unit on ground level. Before the school was hooked up to sewage disposal, early one conference morning a shadowy figure quietly emptied the guests' buckets. A student who discovered that the "volunteer" was none other than the principal, was touched by his servant leadership.[2] That was part of the principal's "success."

---

[1] Luke 6:35.

[2] Cited by grandson Stephen M. Spaulding in an unpublished thesis, *Lion on the Prairies: An Interpretive Analysis of the Life and Leadership of Leslie Earl Maxwell,* May, 1991.

(L) Leslie Maxwell in the 1920s, in Three Hills. (R) "LE" as we knew him at his prime (1950).

(L) Fergus and Jennie Kirk. (R) 1928 Faculty D.R. Miller, Katherine Anderson, L. E. Maxwell, Muriel McElheran

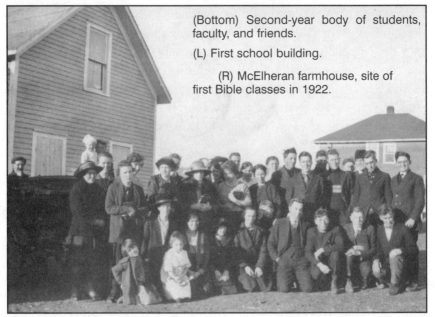

(Bottom) Second-year body of students, faculty, and friends.

(L) First school building.

(R) McElheran farmhouse, site of first Bible classes in 1922.

Chapter 2: Romances

"Our consecration is not to service but to Someone."—LEM

WAS *THAT* HOW PRAIRIE BEGAN?

YOU MEAN A ROMANCE BLOSSOMED in that farmhouse back in 1922? That's what a member of the first class told me. According to her, one of the young men had a crush on her, and when she spurned his romantic attentions, he dropped out. Some things never change! This reportedly led to the imposition of segregation rules.[1]

Only eight met for those first classes in the farmhouse. One had to take time out to handle farm responsibilities, the love-sick student dropped out, and another fellow enrolled to make up the first graduating class of seven—three women and four men—in 1927. (Four were from the initial class; three from a class that began in 1923). Early faculty consisted of L. E. Maxwell, his "Aunt Kate" Anderson, and Dorothy Ruth Miller, one of LE's earlier teachers in Kansas. Sit-in students were the co-founding farmer, Fergus, and his tinsmith brother, Roger.

The Principal Takes a Wife

But the biggest romance story of the early years featured the principal and his new bride.

Pearl Eleanor Plummer had been born into a close-knit family in Boone, Iowa, in 1900. Although the family knew only the simplest of food, her godly parents invited a stream of pastors, missionaries, and other Christian workers to their meal table. They prayed that in time, their daughters would hear God's call to service.

Pearl's awareness of missions and understanding of the Bible grew

---

[1] From the author's interview with Muriel (McElheran) Hanson, member of the class.

as she attended a Christian high school opened in town. At the time, the names of W. C. Stevens and Dorothy M. Miller meant nothing other than that they ran the school. When they left to start Midland Bible Institute 250 miles away in Kansas City, Pearl and the rest of her family were devastated. But Pearl was able to follow them there and enroll at Midland.

As a child Pearl had committed to God her desire to find "Mr. Right," but she hadn't expected to meet him the day she arrived at Midland. At least, her pounding heart told her that Leslie Maxwell, who also had just arrived, was the man God meant for her. But romance was not on this handsome ex-serviceman's agenda, so she "hid these things in her heart."

When Pearl heard that some farmers away off in Canada were asking for a Bible teacher, and the principal had asked Leslie, the only male student, to consider the request, she wondered what God was up to! She felt called to Africa, not Canada. After turning down the request at first, Leslie told Stevens that he'd go for a couple of years.

Pearl still wasn't in the picture for him—until shortly before leaving for Three Hills. Leslie and his Aunt Christina were having a time of prayer together. Out of the blue—or was it out of Heaven?—an unexpected impression came to him: "Pearl Plummer is to be your wife!" Always a man of action, Leslie proposed to Pearl at the first opportunity.

Although the girl from Boone saw her dream being fulfilled, she remembered her "call" to Africa. She asked for time to pray about Leslie's proposal. But back home, the family doctor ruled against her living in the tropics. Green light for lovers! On his way to Alberta, Leslie visited Pearl in Boone. They pledged to wait for God's timing, but neither knew it would be nearly three years before they would see each other again.

A Remarkable Network

Nor could they fully realize how the Lord had linked Pearl Plummer, Leslie Maxwell, and the Kirk clan through common ties with W. C. Stevens and Dorothy Miller. Not even Stevens and Miller would yet realize that. It was an amazing network that the Holy Spirit, not human planning, put together, over the heads of the participants. The result would be the founding of a remarkable work, the birthing of a spiritual family encircling the globe in coming years.

It was 1925 before the prospective groom found the time and money to make the trip from Three Hills. No problem to Pearl that Leslie turned up in Boone without the wedding ring—she finally got the man! While she was confident she had the husband of God's choice, she had little idea what the package included. In a letter[1] to her when he'd proposed in 1922, Leslie forewarned her: "If I may judge from the apparent trials that have come my way to cut me off from his service, the woman who becomes my wife will have no easygoing time of it." She was ready for that, but on the way back to Three Hills she began to find out what marriage to Leslie might be like.

For their honeymoon, the newlyweds traveled by train to Seattle, where they enjoyed visiting their former Bible school principal everyone called "Daddy Stevens." When Midland had closed, Stevens joined the faculty at Simpson Bible College in Seattle.[2] Honeymoon or not, Maxwell spent most of the week ministering to the SBC students.

The new husband also found time to recruit a teacher for his own Bible school in Three Hills—someone he'd known back at Midland. Elmer V. Thompson had been a freshman there, and when the school closed, he went on to SBC and now was about to graduate. He agreed to join Leslie's team in Alberta.

---

[1] Stephen Spaulding, *op.cit.*

[2] Stevens knew the area well from his earlier years as C&MA superintendent for the West Coast.

Although it turned out to be a busy honeymoon, Pearl didn't complain. Long before she married Leslie, she knew he was completely committed to ministering to others. Fortunately she was too.

Honeymoon Over!

What a reception the little group in Three Hills gave Leslie's new bride as the train steamed into Three Hills! It was three years after he'd first arrived in the grain elevator town. Now Leslie brought his Pearl "home." An unusual home it was for a new bride—a small room in the home of a farmer. And the newlyweds' combined wealth amounted to only $20.

"The very next day my new husband left for meetings in Edmonton, over 150 miles away!" Pearl later enjoyed telling busy pastors' and missionaries' wives. "I was in a strange country among people I didn't know—but I knew I was in God's will. Years before, my mother told me that as a girl she'd prayed, 'Let me have no interest in any man except the man of thy choice.' I decided I'd do the same—and God did just that for me, as he'd done for my mother."

During the ensuing summers Leslie was often away speaking at conferences—a help in attracting students. In the winter, classes and students took most of his time. After a dormitory was built, the Maxwells moved in, along with their first child, Eleanor.

"In her first year, Eleanor didn't know who her mother was!" Pearl recalled. "Because I was matron, the students took turns looking after her. When she was a year old, she amused herself playing in a box with spoons and tin lids while I helped other wives can food for the winter."

It was 19 years before Pearl re-visited her hometown. She could have traveled home sooner, when a friend sent her the fare. Instead she put the money toward buying cement for the new dormitory. Another opportunity came when Leslie received a government bonus for his military service—but a greater priority was to purchase 40 acres to meet the needs of the expanding school.

Buying property brought attention to the fledgling school. While it was a home Bible study on a farm, that was OK. But it was a different thing when the school bought two lots on the edge of town. The purchase raised eyebrows. A religious school on the edge of a frontiers-tough town? With teachers and students who believed the Bible and talked about being "born again"? Even the local clergyman who sold the initial two plots (for $10, the taxes he owed on them) changed his mind and tried to regain title.

"It Might Make a Dance Hall!"

"Wish they'd build right in town so we could use it for a dance hall when it folds!" some locals jeered over their beer. Built through personal sacrifice and volunteer labor, the building took shape—rustic and rudimentary but debt free. The little school grew as students arrived for one thing—immersion in the Word.

Prairie was built on sacrificial giving and sacrificial living. In the early years, Fergus Kirk sold his car and the lumber he'd bought to build himself a new home. Donors, whether during conferences or throughout the year, for the most part were not wealthy. They were frugal, hard-working, and dedicated. In place of buying extra comforts, they gave liberally to keep the school going.

Besides that, they gave liberally to support missions to help people in lands they'd never seen.[1] That was nothing new for the Kirks—whose parents had done without butter for a couple of years so they could fulfill their missionary support pledge. In 1923, at the first missionary conference, the little group of farmers pledged $2,000 for missions.[2] Within four years of the first classes, friends had channeled over $10,000 (many times that in today's currency) to foreign missions through the school.

---

[1] Years later I learned what a powerful encouragement this means to struggling believers in other lands. I heard one African church leader tell his people how convicted he was to discover that those who sent out missionaries did so because of the love of Christ—even though they'd never met his people!

[2] $2,000 in 1923 would be $40,000 in today's money!

At the first graduation (1927), conference guests heard of the need for a Bible school in Cuba and took up an offering to help build it.

While most early support came from local farmers, later a larger donation would occasionally arrive from afar.

"Here's a cheque for $1,000, just arrived in the mail!" LE announced at one meeting. It was from a government official in Ottawa, Fred Blair, who had heard about Prairie through Edward Kirk and his wife, still living in Ontario. That was during the Great Depression, when unemployment nationally was 20% and on the prairies was up to 35%!

On another occasion, Anthony Rossi, founder of Florida's Tropicana Orange Juice, generously donated the money that helped build a much-needed residence for women, and to pay PBI's share of a new water system for the town of Three Hills.

"As long as you exist to give and not to get, you'll be all right," W. C. Stevens (who was listed in PBI's first catalogue as Honorary President) told the Board on one of his visits. What was to become Canada's largest Bible school was slowly taking shape with that philosophy.

One of the early grads still on staff when I arrived was Roy L. Davidson.[1] He and his family lived four miles north of the school. Their farmhouse had been a haven for Maxwell when he needed some quiet— and a haircut. Roy took on farm tasks for the school and daily trucked in drinking water from his own well.[2] In those years there was no running water or electricity. Where's the toilet? In the "outhouse" at the back, thank you.

---

[1] Roy's brother Arthur was a member of the first class. He went to Nigeria with SIM. Details about Roy are from his booklet, *God's Plan on the Prairies.* Three Hills: PBI, c.1986

[2] Local well water was high in sodium, a health risk. As the school grew, Roy had to find a more plentiful water supply—14 miles away. In winter, the staff melted snow for the school boiler, to avoid sedimentation.

"I love you" in Swedish

Farmer Roy's accounts of early years proved to us that "the heart of man"—at least the students' capacity for mischief—hadn't changed through the years. Several students had a Swedish background. One of them taught another fellow how to ask, "May I help?" Or so the fellow thought, until he tried it out on the girls washing dishes. They blushed and giggled in his face. When the fellow asked his "language teacher" why they laughed, the Swede told him he'd asked if they loved him.

And talk about circumventing the law! Both boys and girls decided to go skating together one Saturday afternoon. "The boys got permission from Mr. Maxwell," Roy recalled. "And the girls got permission from Miss Anderson. Aunt Kate put two-and-two together when she asked Mr. Maxwell for transport for the girls. The co-ed skating party was cancelled!"

Roy's brother Arthur encouraged Leslie Crawford (both of the cancelled party) to write a poem about school life. One stanza read:

Oh how faithful was our teacher
To enforce the rules so rash;
If he chanced to catch us wooing,
He was on us like a flash!

But Leslie Crawford became a pioneer missionary in Nigeria, and Arthur Davidson joined him after serving on the Prairie Board. Yes—they both got married!

"Mr. Maxwell was full of zeal!" remembered Roy, who also joined the Board and eventually became a Member of the Alberta Legislative Assembly, representing Three Hills. "I remember his preaching on 'putting off the Old Man and his duds'—deeds! He'd pull off his jacket as he quoted the verse. He was a little lively for Presbyterians, but they loved his message and overlooked his antics."

The Rowdy Principal

The Bible teacher's zest for life nearly landed him in hot water one evening when the hallowed quiet of study hour on the men's floor was suddenly shattered. Racing down the hallway, the supervisor located the offending dorm room.

"There's a lot too much noise in here!" he declared, throwing open the door. Suddenly he saw the principal's face looking up at him in surprise. Maxwell had gone to see the student about drawing a cartoon for his publication, and he along with the student and his roommate had become so engrossed in the humorous cartoon they'd forgotten all about study hour!

We got to know another family linked with the early years—the Jacobson brothers. Their father and mother, Helmer and Agnes, had been among the many hardy immigrants from northern Europe who helped to settle Canada's Prairies. When Helmer heard of the Bible study classes in Three Hills, he enrolled in 1926.

Helmer and Agnes had three boys. By the time I reached Three Hills, the eldest, James, was already serving in Nigeria, and the youngest, Ralph, had just graduated and was serving as school baker. Herbert, the middle son, was one of the servicemen who joined our class.

I'll never forget the appetizing smell as Ralph, the school's baker, [1] drew trays of golden-brown rolls out of the oven. Snacking on them on even the coldest winter night made my turn on campus patrol almost a pleasure!

---

[1] Ralph seemed ready to take on any task. Besides becoming a baker, he also became a Bible teacher, missionary, bookshop manager, and broadcaster. In the late 1970s he applied for a license to operate Canada's first full-time Family Radio station, as a channel for Christian and other wholesome programs. The government initally approved his application, but lobbying by certain religious groups forced the reversal, mainly because Ralph's "non-classical religious music" provided a pervasively religious sound and was apparently unacceptable in Canada! But his pioneering efforts laid the basis for later successful applications by Christian broadcasters.

"What I enjoy most!"

"I remember the Maxwells very well from when I was a little boy," Ralph, born in 1923, told me. "What impressed us was their openness and complete lack of hypocrisy. Mr. Maxwell got involved in whatever we were doing. He loved playing baseball at camp.

"While I was on staff, although his teaching load was at its heaviest, I had the nerve to ask if he'd speak at a music night I'd planned in a village schoolhouse. Sure enough, he came—and the place was packed out, even though the village had been snowed in for weeks. Many farmers arrived by horse-drawn sleigh.

"'This is what I enjoy doing most,' he told me afterwards; '— getting out and proclaiming the gospel to people!' We often saw him earnestly leading people to Christ.

"Even though Mr. Maxwell sometimes spoke quite sternly, we always knew he loved us. On several occasions I remember his apologizing for an attitude or speaking too severely. He did this in front of our class and in chapel."

Ralph vividly remembers the principal's talking to him privately about pride in his life. Ralph says he hadn't been conscious of that as a problem, but apparently it showed.

"I knew he did it for my good," Ralph recollects. "Mr. Maxwell always sought to apply Bible study to life—making it practical. He used to say, 'Once your doctrine ceases to be practical, it ceases to be profitable.' That was true of his whole ministry. He didn't waste a lot of time philosophizing or theorizing. The Bible became central to our thinking through the Search Question method: find out what a Scripture actually said, understand its context, and relate it to our need today."

Serving Rotten Eggs

Ralph became a member of the school's Overcomer Quartet, representing the school across Canada and in eastern USA. The year before, while travelling with the Canadian Sunday School Mission quartet north of Edmonton, they were "served" eggs. That is, non-evangelical church members objected to the gospel message and pelted the visitors with rotten eggs.

"That even drove off the dogs!" Ralph remembers.

In 1948 he joined SIM and eventually arrived in Ethiopia as a Bible teacher. "In our home, we Jacobsons grew up on missions!" he says. "We had missionaries at meals as often as not. So it was a matter of where should I go—not whether I should." In Africa he married Prairie high school classmate Doris Bouck.

The rotten egg attack in Alberta was mild compared to the ordeal the Jacobsons, fellow missionaries, and many Ethiopian believers would have to endure in later years. But that's a story for another chapter.

Chapter 3: The "Commune"

*"If you are as dry as dust and know it and admit it,
you qualify for God's filling."—LEM*

BULL PENS AND INK PENS

A COMMUNE IN A FARMHOUSE—that's more or less how PBI began. As enrolment increased, the sense of communal living continued, with students contributing an hour and a half (called "gratis") to the operation and upkeep of the campus, which eventually expanded to 120 acres.

Staff and faculty continued to live communally without salary, sharing school facilities and products from the 1,000-acre farm. Although the school had to take on an academic structure—courses, programs, classes, exams, papers, grades—, at the core of Institute life was the concept of a spiritual retreat, personal spiritual development rather than only academic achievement. More than just classroom learning, Prairie was essentially a growing experience—a place where we could feed on the Word and apply it to our lives.

My "gratis" assignments ranged from digging trenches (for the steam heating pipes from the boiler plant to the buildings on campus), clearing snow, solving electrical problems, butchering, pasteurizing, and marking English essays. (If one of PBI's goals was to help us develop "tools" for future ministry, I chuckled over the practical variety my four years of student work provided: a pickaxe, snow shovel, screwdriver, butcher knife, and marking pen![1]) Most of all, student "gratis" work was one more way of practicing self-discipline. We knew it also helped keep fees low.

There were other advantages. By working alongside staff and

---

[1] Later in Africa, I used all of these tools except a snow shovel (that was for furloughs in Canada!). But the most important tool Prairie helped us all develop was searching the Scriptures.

faculty, we got to know the men and women who sacrificially made it possible for the school to function: apart from teachers, there were plumbers, mechanics, welders, nurses, printers, dairymen, and bakers. Coming from all walks of life, they converged on Prairie to contribute their skills to the development of young lives.

One of our favorite staff was the elderly night watchman, Ernest "Pop" Gowdy. From the perpetual grin he now wore, we'd never guess his sad past. He'd arrived from Chicago at the age of 48 and found campus odd jobs more interesting than classroom studies. Joining the staff, he milked cows and hauled coal. He could handle a team of four horses with one hand!

"Lord, you may be surprised!"

"Pop" always enjoyed a joke, but on one occasion he unintentionally made one. At a Board meeting LE read a request from a seemingly confirmed bachelor on staff to be engaged to one of the spinsters. The principal asked "Pop" to commit them to the Lord.

"This is a real surprise to us, Lord, and no doubt it is to you too!" he prayed disingenuously. He was a loveable teddy bear, without guile. The meeting dissolved in laughter.

Another staff bachelor who found his bride late in life was Ernest Richardson. Alcoholism before his conversion had left its effects, and he'd easily nod off during a service. Once he awoke with a jolt upon hearing his name called from the platform, asking him to pray. Unfazed, he stood up and pronounced the benediction.

The worship leader had only asked him to thank the Lord for the offering—but "Uncle Ernie," as we fondly knew him, hadn't heard that detail.

Another benefit from our "gratis" work was the opportunity to improve practical skills. Because of my experience in the Navy as an electrician, one year I was assigned to the Electric Department under

David Roy Hartt. From the Seattle, WA., area, Roy (as his mother called him) had been a shipyard machinist and electrician during the Second World War. After his eldest son attended Prairie, Roy with his wife Jennie enrolled for studies. A year later the school invited him to head up the Electrical Department.[1]

All of us on the electric crew learned to love "Mr. Hartt"– a cheerful optimist. When anyone asked, "How are you?" his typical reply was, "A lot to be thankful for!" Mr. Fix-it himself, he had a trouble-shooting philosophy: "If man made it, man can fix it!" If some electrical trouble seemed baffling, he'd re-assure us, "There's a reason for everything except a passenger getting off a streetcar backwards!" There was no reason in the statement itself, except to convince us a problem must have some cause, and we could find it if we used our heads! I remember one of our crew's best trouble-shooters was Ernest, eldest Maxwell son, but I couldn't have guessed what kind of problems he and I would work on together, years later on another continent.

"They'd been with Jesus"

Roy Hartt's disposition continued to spread sunshine all over campus even after he and Jennie joined the large retirement community in Three Hills. (The Alberta government and the Three Hills community built an excellent senior extended-care facility and hospital on the edge of town—a great boon to Prairie retirees.) "Daddy Hartt" retained his nimble mind, positive outlook, and vibrant faith right up to the day he died, aged 100 less ten months.

"At his funeral," recalls his son Brad, "more than one nurse told me when they'd pass Dad's room in the mornings, he'd be on his knees by his bed—and often they'd hear him praying for them by name."

That was it! Whatever the staff and faculty's contribution to school

---

[1] Roy Hartt got LE interested in fishing for recreation. The Hartts and the Maxwells became good friends, and Bradford, the Hartts' second son, eventually married Ruth Maxwell. (See Family Reminiscences, Chapter 24.)

operations, we couldn't help noting "they'd been with Jesus." Some faculty members could have commanded top salaries in their professions. At the time, they received only a basic living allowance (sometimes a few dollars a month) and farm products. It's true they also received housing, utilities, medical, dental, and optical care, and children's schooling. But few could afford major appliances or a car—or travel.

Professor Dwight R. Malsbary, Sr., and his wife Pauline were outstanding musicians. They taught instrumental music and he directed the school orchestra. Then in 1947 they announced they were returning as missionaries to Korea, where they had served earlier with the Independent Board for Presbyterian Foreign Missions. That amazed me—such talent, yet leaving behind their grand piano and ministry of music in order to work with Korean churches to proclaim the gospel! And in a country struggling to recover from wave after wave of invaders. It wasn't prosperous as it is now, and the Korean War was looming ahead.

These were real "pros"—red-blooded men and women—who let God use their talents, I concluded.

Putting out the Fleece

As we got to know the team of artisans and other staff, it seemed that only the Holy Spirit could have brought them all to this Prairie grain town. Amazingly, they often arrived in Three Hills without knowing of a need and sometimes without anyone's foreknowledge that they'd be needed! Emil Bruck was one them.

"I want you to come here and be Prairie's toolmaker and machinist!" engineer Emil Bruck heard God tell him during his son's Prairie High School graduation exercises in 1945. Comfortably employed for 18 years as a foreman in a major machine shop in America's North-West, Emil was understandably amazed at what he was hearing. "God," he appealed, "if this is your voice, and you're really asking us to make such a drastic change in our lives, please confirm it by taking care of my job and home!"

God remarkably provided for both of those "fleeces," and the family set off for Three Hills. Emil, aged 50, and his wife, Hazel, enrolled in Bible school (one year Bible was required of all prospective staff at the time—a policy later changed) along with their son Don.[1] The school didn't know they'd be needing a machinist; so for student "gratis" work they assigned Emil to mending chairs.

Emil used $300 of his savings to purchase farmland across from the school, and with Don's help built a little home. That area later came to be called Ruarkville in honor of another staffer and became an extension of Prairie's growing staff community.

Then one cold day the boiler plant broke down. The plant supervisor, Edwin J. Kittridge, asked Emil if he could repair it—and of course he could. When the school realized his skills, they purchased a lathe and set up a machine shop.[2] For the next 25 years Emil saved Prairie thousands of dollars making tools and machine parts. That was before the days of computers, but engineer Bruck was equal to the task of calculating each item with precision. Day or night he answered emergency calls to repair some mechanical breakdown on campus or at the farm.

When Emil died in 1979, his incessantly barking dog led his neighbor Vic Carlson to Emil's basement. The faithful engineer was lying on the floor—a chisel in one hand, a hammer in the other.

Adam's Name Game

People like these were obviously committed men and women. They made us students feel part of the campus family. I was beginning to feel more comfortable being at Prairie. But after the rigors of the Navy—including bouts of land-based studies—I'd become a critical student.

So when I came across what seemed to be circular reasoning and a very weak argument for creation in one of our textbooks, I had the

---

[1] Don ('49, BRE '84), with his wife Vivian (Strickert '48), later served in Japan.
[2] One of his machinists, Arvid McLennan, in retirement became an Alberta-wide celebrity for his "Grandma Moses"–style art, winning awards.

temerity to write the Dean. The text stated that Adam's intelligence was proved by the fact that he gave the creatures names that correctly described them. I noted in Genesis that God gave Adam the task "to see what he would call them, and whatever the man called a living creature, that was its name." The task showed the dominion over the creatures God had given Adam, I felt, not necessarily the accuracy of a name's description. Names, it seemed to me, usually stick by association, not description.

Moreover, in my "superior wisdom," I pointed out there were stronger arguments for man's created intelligence, but the use of questionable logic in the first chapter of the book could undermine its credibility. And this "evidence" could add to the image of fundamentalist anti-intellectualism. Did I lay it on the poor Dean!

I may have been right, but what came across to the Dean was conceit—a freshman criticizing a foundational textbook! What gall! Since Prairie's inception, the school had used the book without question. Besides, the Dean may have thought I was trashing Creation and espousing Darwinian theory.

"I'll reply to your letter after Fall Conference!" the Dean told me after the next class. I had no idea what took place at "Fall Conference," but I assumed the Dean knew it would be good for me.

Revival Fire on Campus

The days shortened, the shadows lengthened across the grain stubble that stretched to the horizon, and Fall Conference was upon us. It was purposely held in October, when farmers would be free from their intensive summer's work. Harvest was in, "winter wheat"[1] planted, and entire families could leave their farms and gather for a week of inspiring

---

[1] Alberta's hard wheat made some of the best bread flour in the world—matched only by wheat grown in the Ukraine, which has similar rich clay soil and climate. Winter wheat is planted in September, begins to sprout, and then lies dormant in sub-zero temperatures until Spring, giving it the maximum growing season.

music, enjoyable fellowship, and outstanding Bible exposition. They drove in from hundreds of miles, some bringing loads of potatoes and other farm products. Cattle ranchers trucked in sides of prime grade Alberta beef.

The school, its clapboard buildings already bulging with its largest enrolment of students (swollen by discharged armed forces personnel), stretched its facilities. Students gave up their rooms to guests and bunked on straw-filled mattresses (appropriately named "ticks") on classroom floors.

For many years the school didn't charge conference guests room and board. LE usually announced that the offerings went towards hospitality expenses and speaker honoraria. Teenager Eleanor Maxwell was disturbed to hear her father say on several occasions, "Where else could you get meals like this for nothing!" He meant it as a reminder, but Eleanor felt it wasn't the way to approach Prairie's loyal friends. So she went to see him in his office between sessions.

"Daddy," she began in fear and trembling, "our guests trust you; they'll give without your reminding them that hospitality is free!"

"My father's humility in accepting this from me, his daughter, really touched me!" Eleanor says. "I was even more impressed when, in the next session, he apologized to everyone with tears. Word of Life founder Jack Wyrtzen was there as main speaker. He threw his arms around Daddy and urged everyone to give generously. A mini revival broke out at that conference as the guests saw my father practice what he often exhorted us all to do: 'Keep close accounts with God.'"

If Fall Conference was the event of the year for Prairie's friends— a spiritual retreat—it was also a launching pad for the school year of studies. A second annual conference took place at graduation time in April,[1] with the main emphasis on missions.

---

[1] The school year started late and ended early so farmers could meet the demands of their fields. In the 1960s, PBI changed to opening early in September, in keeping with changing student needs and other schools.

My first experience of Fall Conference began normally enough with instrumental groups, choirs, and testimonies by visiting missionaries—most of them graduates of Prairie.

Conviction Falls

Mr. Maxwell spoke each day, but he left the main sessions to guest speaker Armin Gesswein, an evangelical Lutheran. Gesswein's low-keyed but powerful Bible teaching on the Holy Spirit had seen much spiritual blessing along America's west coast. Now as he opened the Scriptures to us morning after morning, something happened that no one could have planned.

The Holy Spirit began to convict us of sin and righteousness (which, after all, is what Jesus said the Holy Spirit would do!). At lunchtime, students didn't hurry off as usual to be first in line at the dining room. Many stayed in their seats, praying or talking quietly with each other. Some fell to their knees by their benches. There was a quiet hush in the Tab, broken only by murmurs of prayer or an occasional sob. Back in the dormitories students asked forgiveness of each other, and roommates met together for prayer.

By the second morning, the session leader announced that a few students had asked for time to confess something the Lord had spoken to them about. "I've had a proud, critical spirit!" began one." "I ask the forgiveness of my dorm mates!" said another. Some simply wept, unable to speak. LE would sometimes place an encouraging hand on the student's shoulder or quietly lead us in prayer. More quietly left their seats and lined up for a turn at the microphone.

In prayer meetings, sometimes several would pray at the same time. "Sort them out, Lord, sort them out!" Maxwell would exclaim. After one evening session, students came to the platform and confessed sin in their lives for another hour and a half, until Mr. Maxwell broke in and told us he thought the Lord would be pleased if we all got to bed. We needed a refreshing sleep in preparation for the next day's sessions.

Struggle on the Balcony

The Conference program had no sessions marked "Confession Time," but students and leaders ignored the daily schedule as the spirit of revival broke out across campus. I had never been in such meetings. My usual clinical analysis of preaching style and content turned into self-examination, as I allowed the Holy Spirit to apply his Word to my own life. It all came before me, like a video screen: my childhood subterfuges, my teen-age rebelliousness, my coldness of heart in Navy days—and most of all, my conceit, my pride, and my arrogance.

I recalled my father's last words as I was leaving home for Three Hills. Putting his arm around my shoulder, he said, "Write and tell us when you've given everything to the Lord, Son." I was furious and stomped off without a word. Did he think I had problems? Mother commented, "I wonder if you should have said that, Dear!"

Now I sat in a remote corner of the Tab balcony. Gesswein had just spoken on Romans 6.16: "Don't you know that when you offer yourself to someone to obey him as slaves, you are slaves to the one whom you obey—whether you are slaves to sin, which leads to death, or to obedience, which leads to righteousness?"

The dreadful irony of that question struck me.

Here I was—raised in a Christian home, a follower of Jesus, but not fully yielded to him! If not to him, to whom was I yielded? I was serving self, and self was not of God. The self-life was of the Devil. So I was living a lie!

It was not a theological debate going on in my head—it was a struggle over lordship in my heart. As other students streamed down to the platform and lined the aisles, I stayed in my seat. The contest within was between the Holy Spirit and my will. I didn't need to line up on the platform; I needed Christ to be not only Savior but also Lord of my life. I had proudly run my own life, and I knew I hadn't made it a spiritual success. The self-life didn't need success—it needed to be put on the Cross, to die with Christ and to be raised again with him. Was I ready for that death-to-life experience? Could I trust Christ to fill me with His Spirit and rule my life? There on a rough balcony bench I struggled until sweat broke out on my forehead. Finally I gave in and responded, "Yes, Lord, you take over! No longer I but Christ."

"A Pile of Ashes"

I didn't need a mike to tell anyone that a paradigm shift had taken place in my life. Since boyhood I'd trusted in Jesus as my Savior. I hadn't denied Christ in the Navy—although neither had I lived as positively for him as I should have. But my spirit hadn't been at peace—there was a striving for self instead of submission to God. On that balcony bench I experienced a new calmness—brokenness but also inner strength. It was as if the fever that had wracked my soul suddenly broke, and in the post-fever sweat I could relax. The struggle was over. I had peace.

"Dad, 'Harold Fuller' is no more!" I wrote my father. "He's now a pile of ashes on God's altar!"

Or so I thought. I had no idea that the ashes could easily stand up and take the shape of the self-life once again. The struggle was not over, I would find. That was what the rest of my stay at Prairie would show me, preparing me for a life-long pilgrimage.

Of course I didn't head off to Australia at Christmas break—it would be 36 years later that I would arrive Down Under, as part of my missionary ministry. And the simplistic reasoning about Adam's naming the creatures—the topic of my letter to the Dean before Conference—was no longer worth protesting. If that was circular reasoning, so be it—I didn't need to indulge in it myself. Most of all, I no longer had to prove myself by picking apart a textbook.[1] I could relax and give myself to preparation for whatever God would lead me into. Just a pile of ashes? Maybe!

---

[1] It was later replaced, for whatever reason.

Chapter 4: Discipline

"You need a backbone instead of a wishbone." —LEM

NO CHOCOLATE SOLDIERS

W HY WOULD SO MANY CHINESE want to study at Prairie?" Stephen and Lena Lau[1] wondered. Lecturing at the University of Hong Kong and active in a lot of Christian work, Lena noted the number of students who made the flight across the Pacific in order to study at a Bible institute in the town of Three Hills—barely discernible on the map. "I couldn't understand, until later on I learned what Prairie stood for—a life of discipline and self-denial. That was what appealed to serious-minded Christians of that era. It fit their Chinese ethic and Christian convictions."

For the most part, North Americans who came to the Institute also accepted rules (even if a few didn't seem necessary!) as part of their self discipline—and then got on with life, including a good share of fun. They saw the rugged regimen as part of "training soldiers for Christ."

To Maxwell, campus regulations were a form of self-discipline to embrace, not endure as legalism. A favorite phrase he used was "God doesn't want chocolate soldiers!" Missionaries who spoke at Prairie had lived through the rigors of service in demanding circumstances—whether of climate, primitive conditions, or political and religious intolerance. Some joined the faculty and strongly supported Prairie's lifestyle.

---

[1] Mrs. Lau was Lecturer in Linguistics, University of Hong Kong, and Hon. Secretary of SIM HK Council. Upon moving to Canada, she served as a member of Prairie's Board for six years and, with her husband, has been active in church planting in the Toronto area.

"Students today come to us undisciplined!" Alban Douglas, a veteran of rugged service in China with OMF, told "Homecoming"[1] guests. He taught missions at Prairie for several years and decried the moral relativism of North America. "But one student told me he chose Prairie because of its discipline—the last thing he wanted but what he knew he most needed!"

Although Prairie's regulations seem quaint in today's social context, they were a natural outcome of the culture at the time. The founding families were from strict Scottish Protestant lineage, and early faculty and students reflected Victorian values. Mennonite students felt comfortable at Prairie. More than one member of our class went on to graduate studies at segregated Mennonite colleges. And many who went overseas found themselves in cultures that segregated the sexes and frowned on social contact between unmarried adults.

Skirt Length "ID"

Hair and skirt length became rigid rules—indeed, a mark of identity in town.

LE enjoyed telling about the Prairie student who wanted to cash a money order in town but forgot to bring identification. The postmaster excused himself while he went to another wicket and discreetly peered over the counter to check on the student's skirt length. He returned and accepted her money order without further ID!

During our time as students, games were regulated—Monopoly and Rook were banned but chess and checkers allowed. Use of time was the school's major concern. Often quoted was the couplet: "I've only got a minute, but Eternity is in it!" Although there seemed little difference between Monopoly and chess as to playing time, some considered the former promoted consumerism, while the latter stimulated reasoning.

---

[1] Every few years Prairie's Alumni Department holds a summer conference for alumni, families, and friends.

We could read newsmagazines and daily newspapers, but only with "strong caution and counsel." Comics, Westerns, and detective stories—considered addictive time wasters—were banned. Cosmetics wasted the Lord's money and promoted the values of the world. But when face powder became an issue, LE—himself with growing daughters—defused the debate by reminding staff, "The day may come when we'll be ashamed we let such a little bit of powder be so explosive!"

What about "pink and blue sidewalks"—the rumored symbol of segregated male and female students? (No—the sidewalks weren't really painted pink or blue!) With my new commitment, separation of men and women, along with other institutional rules, was never an issue. I'd had my social friendships in the Navy, and now it was time to concentrate on the purpose of being at Prairie—understanding God's Word and honing the tools I'd need to help others understand.

"Even though the regulations may be difficult for some to understand today," Paul Maxwell comments, "they reflected the intense desire of the PBI community to let nothing detract from wholehearted consecration to the Lord." However, reports of this segregated, regulated school spread far afield, making Prairie seem to some like a kind of monastery or convent.

Maxwell on a Bullhorn

"When I was Inter-Varsity Christian Fellowship's Canadian Secretary in the early 1940s," recalls Melvin Donald;[1] "I invited Mr. Maxwell to be the main speaker for our Ontario Pioneer Camp young peoples' conference. Growing up in Alberta, I'd first heard him speak when I was in high school and was mightily impressed by this dynamo for God—he was full of zest and Spirit-filled forthrightness.

"But staff were apprehensive. They'd heard that such things as mixed bathing were taboo on the prairies at the time, and that Maxwell's

---

[1] Melvin V. Donald, an early Director (then called "Secretary") of Canada's InterVarsity Christian Fellowship, is author of *A Spreading Tree*, the history of IVCF in Canada. He also has been a pastor and with his wife Lola was a missionary with SIM in Ethiopia.

school maintained that culture. How could he fit in with students from mostly secular campuses?"

Their fears vanished when LE did the judging at a regatta held between Bible study sessions. "There he was, bellowing through a bullhorn, fellows and girls in bathing suits crowding around him to see the results!" Mel remembers. "He didn't blink an eye, and from then on no one questioned his ability to communicate with youth in their own context!"

In fact, three years later (1946), IVCF's General Secretary, Stacey Woods, and the IVCF Missions Secretary, Christy Wilson, invited L. E. Maxwell as one of the main speakers at Inter-Varsity's first missions conference, held in Toronto.[1]

"One can easily . . . have many years of service without ever experiencing the enduement of power for service," Maxwell warned the eager college students gathered for that historic first "Urbana." "Only by the deepening of the spiritual life can missions grow with success." Jim Elliot, who would later be among the five "Auca Martyrs," was one of the students attending.[2]

LE was able to move between different cultures and accept them as they were— Prairie students enrolling as "soldiers for Christ" in training, or young people seeking to survive in a secular world. He and his wife often hosted off-campus visitors. On one occasion, a group included a young woman wearing fairly brief shorts (at the time all shorts were banned for Prairie female students). After the visitors left, a student exclaimed, "Did you see what that girl was wearing!"

"I didn't notice," LE replied. The visitor wasn't a Prairie student and hadn't agreed to follow Prairie rules. She was as welcome in his home as anyone, whatever she was wearing!

---

[1] The site of the next conference moved to the University of Illinois and became known as "Urbana," recently attracting 20,000 students from across North America and overseas.
[2] Elisabeth Elliot, who attended Prairie before marrying Jim, tells the story of how vibrant churches later sprang up among the once head-hunting Aucas, in *Through Gates of Splendor*. New York: Harper 1957.

"He listened to me!"

Miriam Charter, born in China of missionary parents, was a student at Prairie in the 1960s, and graduated from Bible school in 1971.

"I didn't easily acquiesce to the regulations—only out of respect for my parents, I suppose," she later recalled. "Mr. Maxwell knew I was a 'silent rebel.' But what thrilled me was he 'listened' to me! He let me process what I was working through and wasn't judgmental. He even liked my boldness! (Maybe I reminded him of his own daughter. He once told me that he also had a Miriam.)

"We discussed the benefits and deficits of growing up at Prairie. Mr. Maxwell was deeply hurt that some people felt the 'unnatural' environment was harmful to their development. As we talked, any fear of this great man vanished, and I loved him as a father."

"That Is Discipline"

LE's own military background gave him an appreciation for self-discipline, for which he found ample support in Scripture. Missionary author Amy Wilson Carmichael was an inspiration to him, and he often quoted from her poem, "That Is Discipline":[1]

> *When I refuse the easy thing for love of my dear Lord,*
>   *And when I choose the harder thing for love of my dear Lord,*
>   *And do not make a fuss or speak a single grumbling word,*
>   *That is discipline. . . .*
>
> *To rule myself and not to wait for others' do and don't,*
>   *That is discipline. . . .*
> *To learn to live according to my Savior's Word, "Deny,"*
> *That is discipline.*

---

[1] Amy Carmichael's verses are from *Born Crucified, op. cit.,* pp. 127, 128, 131. Maxwell's bookshelves held a number of her some 30 books (which included over 560 poems), from which he often quoted.

LE also quoted another classic Carmichael verse:

> *From subtle love of softening things,*
> *From easy choices, weakenings*
> *(Not thus are spirits fortified,*
> >   *Not this way went the Crucified),*
> *From all that dims Thy Calvary,*
> *O Lamb of God, deliver me.*

Each time Maxwell mentioned Amy Carmichael, I thought of my sister Olive working with her in India. Olive had sailed across the Pacific for South India during World War II, while I was sailing the Atlantic. Through the years, she shared insights about this hardy Irish missionary who first served in Japan and then India with the UK-based Church Missionary Society (evangelical Anglican). Discovering the plight of baby girls who were committed to "marry" the gods in temple life (resulting in ritual immorality), Carmichael founded Dohnavur Fellowship (DF) in India. It became a safe commune for children at risk. Her Calvary love touched many a cruel heart determined to wrest from Dohnavur's care some rescued child.

But at the height of activity, she suffered a crippling fall and spent the last 20 years of her life in constant pain. At times, my sister took her turn at her bedside sharing about the joys and sorrows of the children, praying for them by name.

Powerful Message from Weakness

This strong-willed woman, Amy Carmichael, had traipsed across Asia with the gospel, but in Dohnavur was suddenly leveled—literally. She refused to return to her homeland but stayed in the sweaty south of India without furlough.[1] Instead of exhibiting self-pity, she died to self and grasped the spiritual will of her Lord. Although her body lay in a world of affliction, she entered into a universe of spiritual power. By embrac-

---

[1] "Amma" lived in Asia for 53 years with no furlough. After her death (1951), nationals and expatriates shared in leadership of the DF work. When government policy required that Dohnavur name a president, the DF appointed Nesaruthina Carunia, earlier discipled by my sister Olive as well as others.

ing the Cross in her life, she transformed her stretcher-bed into springs of meditation that flowed through her many books into the hearts of men and women all over the world. From her bedroom she inspired the DF members, including my sister, and the staff to continue her vision.

Through her writings, Amma (Tamil for "Mother") touched thousands more than before her injury. One of them was L. E. Maxwell. While W. C. Stevens had immersed Maxwell in the Word of God, Carmichael became his greatest contemporary model of spiritual discipline. In turn, LE passed on to us students Amma's challenge: to embrace the Cross of Christ in our lives. From her weak state came truths that we, in our good health, might otherwise have missed.

"Prairie Bible Institute stands for an unusual ruggedness, discipline, and spiritual emphasis in training," noted Stephen F. Olford.

"The mark of the people Maxwell mentored was their commitment to Christ, love for the Word, heart for the world, and servant spirit," recently commented General Director Emeritus of OMF James Hudson Taylor III, great-grandson of the founder of the China Inland Mission.[1] "Maxwell was a pioneer of tremendous vision and bold faith. His 'Prairie Vision' brought great blessing to Canada and from there to every continent. Inland China shared in this blessing."

Avoiding Bondage

Knowing Prairie's reputation, most students came with their eyes wide open. Many felt their own need to develop self-discipline. In those years, they chose Prairie because of its rigorous study, manual work, and Spartan conditions. This was no place for romancing. Some students quipped about certain Bible schools that were like shoemakers—"mending soles/souls and turning them out in pairs!" Surprisingly, however, a fair number of Prairie grads did find their future spouses at Prairie.[2]

---

[1] Although the fourth generation, he is JHT III because the pioneer's son was named Howard, not Hudson.
[2] Both my brother Dave (with OMF: Overseas Missionary Fellowship) in the Philippines and I (with SIM: Servants in Mission) in Africa married Prairie graduates—but we didn't get to know them at Prairie!

A few students came under bondage to the rules—applying them in a legalistic way. On the way to class, young men and women passed each other with averted eyes, so as not to be guilty of breaking "the rules." I remember the confession of a young fellow, Mortimer, at a prayer meeting: he had looked at a girl sitting across the aisle. "The Bible warns about looking on a woman....'," Mortimer quoted from Matthew 5.28. "I ask God's forgiveness!"

Legalism on the part of such students sent me examining the context and meaning of oft-quoted Scripture texts. Mortimer, I felt, had not lusted after the girl (the problem stated in the verse in Matthew). He'd simply followed a wholesome impulse—admiring a beautiful female—as God had intended when he created male and female.

The student's sense of guilt made me see the importance of a wholesome attitude to the opposite sex—difficult for anyone, surrounded as we all are by the crass immorality of our perverted society. My time in the Navy had made me aware of that. Dying to self ("the lust of the flesh") and becoming alive to righteousness ("walking in the Spirit")—not legalism—was the path to a healthy, scriptural attitude towards sexuality. In those years, however, this topic was "off limits" for most people.

We couldn't help noting that some students were endowed with good looks. Years later I was interested to find that the Prairie grad I married, Lorna Parrott, agreed with me as to the most beautiful girl and the most handsome fellow of our day. Of course as students we kept such beauty-contest opinions to ourselves!

The large number of war-service students made an impact on the social life of the school. The service women and men were older than the average student coming straight from secondary school. We had been accustomed to discipline and regimentation for a cause—to save lives and nations from tyrants. So the Institute's rules did not seem as irksome to us as they proved to be to later generations. Actually, many students found ways to mix acceptably on committees and in other activities (such as choir, orchestra, and student work).

42

"You either become better or bitter"

Prairie may not have seemed suitable for everyone, although men and women came from every type of background. My personality needed the constant emphasis on dying to self. For students arriving with a low self-image, this emphasis could be depressing—unless they listened to what LE was really saying: Self-deprecation was as sinful as self-promotion. Neither glorified God, and both kept the believer from living victoriously.

While in Japan in the 1950s, LE ministered to a group of missionaries—including one who had read *Born Crucified* and misapplied its message.

"This poor man later told me he'd been tied up in knots," recalls Lois (Maxwell) Friesen, serving in Japan at the time. "He said he couldn't open a door without worrying whether he was in God's will. But he gained an entirely new perspective as Daddy showed him the scriptural conclusion to the message of the Cross—the liberty of walking in the Spirit. He was set free."

Maxwell realized that his listeners heard his powerful preaching from different perspectives. He once told his daughter Ruth, who tended to be introspective, that she was "the kind of person who took herself too seriously."

"I preach hard," Ruth remembers his telling her; "and those who ought to listen, let it go in one ear and out the other! Whereas others of you take everything to heart!"

"Whatever It Takes, Lord!"

Daisy Stinson, a member of our class, was one who took "everything to heart." She found it difficult to find freedom from bondage. She was suffering from depression when she graduated, but she didn't realize it was really the result of events in her life before she ever enrolled at Prairie. Daisy had suffered abuse in childhood but didn't link that to her depression. She felt she was failing God. At the time, not many Christians, including pastors, understood depression. Later she told me that years passed before she got the professional and biblical help she needed. Finally she was able to write a hymn, the last stanza and chorus reading:

> *Lord how I thank you for all the past trials,*
> *And though they were hard, you taught me to see*
> *How they were used by thy Holy Spirit*
> *To draw me much closer, yes closer to thee.*
>
>> *Whatever it takes, Lord, whatever it takes;*
>> *Draw my heart closer, whatever it takes.*
>> *You may send trials, suffering and pain—*
>> *But keep me from sin, Lord, whatever it takes!*

There were other students whose church teachings placed them under bondage after graduation. In his book, *Women in Ministry*,[1] LE recounts how one graduate's church forbade women even to sing in public. Although she was a gifted vocalist, she came under bondage to the church's doctrine of "women keeping silent."

Inevitably, there were also students who were hurt by misapplied rules and judgmental statements when they really needed understanding and counsel. "You either become bitter or better through life's experiences," was the way Laura Jacobson ('72), looked at things. "The good influences of Prairie on our lives completely outweighed problems that arose at times."

In spite of PBI's reputation for rigid regimentation, "law" was often tempered by "grace." For instance, Beverley Erickson, who later married my brother, at first turned down a graduate's invitation to spend Christmas break at her home. The place was more than 300 miles away, and that distance was beyond the approved range for a Christmas visit.

---

[1] Maxwell, Leslie, with Ruth Dearing, *Women in Ministry*. Wheaton: Victor Books, 1987, p.99.

(The school had in mind the tiring effect on students travelling long distances in the midst of the school year.) Eventually Bev found courage to approach the Dean of Women, with some trepidation.

"Of course you may go!" replied Ruth Dearing, to Bev's surprise. "Doesn't the Bible say, 'We've been given all things freely to enjoy'?"

While teaching at PBI in the late 1950s, Ted Rendall (who later became principal and eventually president), dated another staff, Norline Norbo. Neither had a car, and at the time there was no student lounge or campus snack bar where they could sit and get better acquainted. The only alternative was to go for walks together along the country road running north from the school to the landmark three hills. As winter's cold increased, Pearl Maxwell, the principal's wife, noticed them passing her house and invited them for dinner one evening. She did that on several occasions, discreetly leaving the room after the meal and closing the door behind her.

"A man all wrapped up in himself
makes a mighty small package."—LEM

THE FALL OF MAN

LIFE AT BIBLE SCHOOL COULD BE SO DULL! Our snow-clearing crew had to clean the sidewalks before class time. Noting that the girls left their water buckets (in 1946 their dorm had no running water) in a snowpile on their way to breakfast, we hard-packed the buckets full of snow. An alternative prank was to wire half a dozen handles together. By the time the students had finished breakfast and tried to fill their buckets, we were shoveling elsewhere in the pre-dawn winter darkness, enjoying the young women's exasperated shouts, "Those boys!"

Of course our men's barracks in the high school basement provided an environment conducive to intensive study. That included (by way of diversion, that is) planning the usual camping gags (knotted bed-sheets, sugar or gravel in beds, and toothpaste tubes refilled with shaving cream). Through research, however, the young men became more innovative.

One night I swung up onto my upper bunk just after "lights out" and found myself hurtling downward into the Abyss. I landed on top of my unfortunate bunkmate, no doubt reducing his life expectancy. At the sound of my unscheduled flight, the lights flipped back on and a dozen "innocent" faces appeared, to check on the cause of the clatter.

"What happened, Fuller?" they inquired solicitously. "Are you hurt?"

"I'm OK," I replied in the calmest voice I could muster. Smarting from my unscheduled "flying trapeze" act, I reconnected the bedsprings someone had unhooked from the metal frame. My friendly roommates had undone all except two, cater-corner from each other. A broomstick set at cross-angles held up the springs and mattress until I jumped on top. "I'll be OK. Thanks for checking!"

This was going too far, I decided – chiefly because it would be difficult to top! (And why should they pick on me?) Since my bruises and scrapes kept me awake anyway, after everyone else was asleep I tiptoed upstairs to a student washroom. I took along my oilpaint box[1] and Navy first aid kit.

Beautiful Shiner

In front of a mirror I painted one eye with the most lurid "shiner" I could imagine. Dark purple around the lids spread outwards to magenta, fuchsia, and avocado, eventually dissipating into bruised lemon that merged with flesh tones. A Band-Aid partly revealed a realistic slash of scarlet pigment alongside the eye. Satisfied with this "medical treatment" (and work of art), I returned to my bunk and slept. I don't remember, but maybe I dreamed about going to medical school. Or else eternally falling into the Abyss.

In the morning my roommates called by, expecting to have a good laugh as they hurried off to breakfast. Instead they were dumbfounded.

"We're so sorry, Fuller!" exclaimed the innocents of the previous evening. "We didn't mean you to get hurt!"

"It's OK," I graciously repeated, quietly noting those who seemed most worried. "Nothing serious. Thanks, anyway!"

I went off to breakfast too, pretending not to notice the whispered comments of my fellow students. Being Saturday morning, there were no classes. I skipped lunch in order to type notes to six students I thought

---

[1] In the Navy, I'd dabbled in oils as a hobby. My paint box and first aid kit always traveled with me.

had "sprung" the bed prank on me, and pinned terse notes to their locker doors: "You are requested to meet in the Dean's office at 2 p.m." (Like
a Philadelphia lawyer, I was careful to tell no lie, not identifying who
made the request, whom they were to meet, or why they were called to
the office. They could assume the worst!)

The appointed hour coincided with an exciting school hockey
game. I went to an upstairs classroom window and watched six hockey
players and their best buddies traipse dejectedly towards the office
building. Half an hour later they returned looking puzzled.

They'd found the office locked. But now they were shocked to find
me sitting on my bunk reading – with no trace of the black eye and gash.
Completely healed!

"Consummate Conceit"

The next year a double men's dormitory, J-K, was completed.
Administration hoped to stem pranks early in the school year by placing
a sign prominently on the men's bulletin board: ***The Thought of
Foolishness Is Sin. Proverbs 24.9*** (AV).

No doubt a plea for moderation was in order, but I wondered about
the appropriateness of the selected Scripture. Several humorless students
believed it meant all levity was out of place for a Christian. (They obviously didn't include LE's humor in that category.) Like good monks, we
should engage ourselves only in serious discourse. The time was too
short for joking; we'd be held accountable for every idle word.

Non-scholar though I was, I was able to check my Bible concor-
dance and Hebrew lexicon.[1] After a little study, I figured the verse might
also be translated, "The thought of the fool is evil." The verse had nothing to do with harmless student pranks or wholesome fun.

---

[1] In that era at Prairie, we didn't have access to contemporary versions, and of course no
commentaries.

Recklessly, I typed my "revised version" on a note, suggesting more appropriate Bible verses that spoke to the problem of excessive or coarse joking. I pinned my thesis to the bulletin board – unsigned, even as the original Scripture notice was unsigned.

Next morning my note was gone, and at lunchtime Mr. Maxwell (who in those years usually presided over lunch hour) had a special announcement for us all.

"Someone placed this note on the men's bulletin board!" he thundered, reading my brief thesis and holding it aloft. "I've never heard of such consummate conceit!"

I hoped the fellows at my table didn't notice my face changing color a few shades. I hadn't thought of my commentary as conceit. If someone had the gall to misquote Scripture (and thereby place students under bondage), I certainly had the temerity to examine the actual meaning and suggest more appropriate verses. Wasn't this a Bible school, and weren't we supposed to "search the Scriptures"? Anyway, that's how I saw it at the time. But I did go to the principal's office and thank LE for the public spanking.

"What spanking?" LE asked.

"I put that note on the men's bulletin board," I explained apologetically.

"Oh," he chuckled; "I had no idea it was you!" And that was the end of it. I guessed that the floor supervisor or men's Dean had looked upon my note as a public challenge to authority, and had presented it to the principal in that light.

As for me, I had to learn once again that although I might be right, my approach might be all wrong. Were Harold Fuller's "ashes" standing up again? Instead of publicly setting administration right, I'd have done better going to the Dean of Men and discussing the appropriateness of the official sign—and its possible effect on introspective students.

49

Was I learning what it meant to be ashes on God's altar? Perhaps my letter to Dad in itself had implied a certain conceit, as if to say, "I've arrived (spiritually) at last!"

I was beginning to learn that incidental things—although fairly harmless in themselves—could reveal "self" attitudes I was unaware of. I'd a sneaking suspicion that God allowed me to do something stupid just to set me up for a fall (and a lesson in humility).

Upon further thought, I had to concede that God didn't need to "allow me" or set me up—I was perfectly capable of stupidity all by myself!

A Bath at Forty Below

While Principal Maxwell knew a lot about our foibles—he accepted us as we were—perhaps remembering his own youthful years. He often came across as "Daddy Maxwell"—such as the time he scolded us all for risking skin if not limb by going outside without proper clothing. Many students were from the warm south, and even Canadian students often were from urban centers, where they could duck from one building to another in winter.

I learned about the rigors of winter on the Prairies when I spent my first Christmas at a German classmate's home. The mercury dropped to minus forty Fahrenheit. Being the guest, on Saturday night I had first dip in the metal bathtub set by the wood stove. A sheet strung across the corner of the kitchen was a concession to privacy. This was the only warm room in the house, so while I splashed away, the family happily chatted around the kitchen table—awaiting their turn (in the same water).

And when we absolutely had to visit the freezing outhouse, we ran across the snowy trail coming and going!

"The air is so dry, you can freeze without feeling it!" back at school LE warned us after several students suffered frostbite. "Wear warm

50

clothing—and put a hat on. If you don't have a hat, wrap a scarf or pull a sock over your head!"

That was all the inspiration another ex-sailor and I needed. Next day we turned up with our long thermal seaman's socks on our heads—after having pinned a poem on the notice board (this time it was OK). Someone gave it to the principal, who entered into the fun and read it to the students in the dining hall:

Ode to a Sock on the Head

While some around here like to mock,
To others the thought is a shock;
        But we have been told
        The weather is cold—
So over our head goes a sock.

Although on the thought we are sold,
There's one thing you should us have told:
        It's easily seen
        That they should be clean –
The socks should not smell very old.

The kids who catch cold in the head
(So nurses all know, 'tis been said)
        Get bouts of chilblains
        In place of their brains –
And wake up to find themselves dead.

The mor'l of this story is clear:
To shun a big frozen right ear,
        Take sock from your feet,
        On head make it neat –
Then brave the fierce cold without fear.

Taking Prairie Seriously or Joyously

Students from different parts of the world—including Africa, Asia, Europe, and Latin America—enriched campus life. Les J. Thompson came from Cuba—where he'd been born of missionary parents.[1] Les was so fluent in Spanish that he found the different syntax of English confusing.

We got to know each other when he joined the electric crew working for Roy Hartt. We also found ourselves as part of the Prairie Male Quartet, singing at campus services and over the radio.

Born in Cuba, Les had grown up on the Cuba Bible Institute's campus. The Cuban cook led him, at age six, to personal faith in Christ. In 1945, aged 15, Les arrived in Three Hills to attend PBI High School, rooming with an uncle, Pringle McElheran, who was attending the Bible school.

"There are two ways to take Prairie," advised Pringle, nephew of Prairie's co-founder Fergus Kirk. "Seriously—reacting against the rules—or joyously—putting up with the rules!" Pringle seemed to take the latter tack, along with a fair share of fun, and Les followed his example.

Prairie High School's voice program developed Les's natural tenor voice. After completing high school in 1948, he enrolled in Bible school, staying with relatives in Three Hills. In the summer of 1949, Kathleen Dearing, Music Director, asked him to join a "summer male quartet" she cobbled together to help provide musical numbers during the school break. (The noted Janz Men's Quartet had done that during the school year, but after graduation had left for Europe with Youth For Christ. Later they formed an evangelistic mission in Germany, The Janz Team.)

The other quartet members were students who had stayed as vol-

---

[1] Les's father, Elmer V. Thompson, an early faculty member at Prairie, married Prairie graduate Evelyn McElheran. Thompson co-founded the West Indies Mission and became its General Director. The McElherans and Kirks were related by marriage.

unteer "summer workers": Jack Lentz (second tenor), George Goudy, (first bass), and I (second base). While Les (first tenor) was the only one with a professionally trained voice, we all seemed to blend well in four-part harmony—thanks to Kathleen's patient coaching. At the end of the summer, she asked us to carry on as the Prairie Male Quartet the following school year.

As we huddled around the microphone (no hand-held individual mikes in those days), Les and I faced each other, being at opposite ends of the foursome semi-circle. Thin, blond, and handsome, Les wore a perpetual smile.

It may have been a smile of joy or of mischief—or both. He'd built a record of mischief during his high school years.

"I came to recognize the heavy footsteps of the dorm supervisor heading for my room!" he remembers. Innumerable times he found himself in the office of Mr. Maxwell himself. "If it weren't that your father is Elmer Thompson," LE once warned him, "you'd be out of here!" Was that privilege, or was it pity (at least consideration) for parents leading a mission far away in the Caribbean? Another time he called Les into his office, looked at him, shook his head, and with a sigh exclaimed, "Let's pray!"

Christmas Eve Party

Les thought he'd arrived at the "out-of-here" point during one Christmas school break. While many other students left for nearby homes, Les and other missionary kids stayed on campus. Their parents were in other lands.

To celebrate Christmas Eve, they planned to stay up all night and play games. When staff announced that because of a Christmas morning service the next day, it would be "lights out" at ten p.m. Christmas Eve, the other MKs came to Les in consternation. "No problem!" Les told his friends, detailing what they'd do.

At breakfast Christmas Day, Les was assigned to wait on the principal's table.

"I hear you stayed up all last night," LE casually remarked, noting Les's heavy eyelids as he placed a bowl of steaming porridge on the head table.

"Yes, that's true," Les replied, trying to look innocent.

"Didn't you hear the announcement that everyone was to be in bed by ten?" LE probed.

"But we were, Mr. Maxwell!" Les protested, beginning to wake up. "We were all in bed with lights out by ten."

And that was true. What Les did not add was that the group of MKs then got up at eleven and met in Les's room. They covered the window with a blanket and played games the rest of the night.

Fortunately, their floor neighbors had gone home for Christmas. But unfortunately, a humorless student in the room below hadn't.

Fortunately he had a hearing problem and had removed his hearing aid. But unfortunately the vibrations of the party games came right through the thin ceiling.

Holding the pocket mike of his "early edition" hearing aid to the ceiling, he was able to identify all the partying students and dutifully informed staff next morning.

When Les told the principal the full story, LE burst into one of his hearty laughs. After breakfast during announcement time, he shared the escapade with the rest of the dining room—then turned Les into an impromptu doctrinal illustration.

"You see," the principal pressed home his point to the assembled students; "this illustrates the difference between keeping the letter of the Law and following the spirit of the Law! Many people religiously try to fulfill the letter of the Law but never live by its spirit. They say, 'I haven't murdered anyone,' but they constantly 'assassinate' others with their tongues. Jesus condemned Pharisees who didn't commit adultery physically but did so in their lustful hearts!"

Les received a lesson in Grace vs. the Law when the school forgave the Christmas Eve romp.

Tempting Offer

In an unusual way, the Holy Spirit finally got through to Les Thompson about doing God's will. Before leaving Cuba, he'd clearly felt a call to missionary service and made a personal commitment at age 13. Later, in his final summer at Prairie, he traveled with a school ministry team, recruiting students. He grew accustomed to churches asking him to come back as their music director, but shrugged off the invitations. The most tempting offer came from a major church in Toronto.

"Our music director's just left to join the Billy Graham team," explained the elders, cornering Les after the service. He told them he had another year to complete at Prairie.

"You can finish your Bible school right here in Toronto," they countered. "We'll provide you a house and a car!"

That was fairly attractive for a "missionary kid" who'd never owned a house or car. When the elders told him the salary, it was beyond any he'd ever expected to receive. But he was adamant in turning down the invitation.

On the flight back to Three Hills Les got to thinking, "That was pretty stupid of you, Thompson! After all, it would be a fulfilling ministry, using God's gifts and your training. It's a natural. Maybe you were mistaken back in Cuba when you were only 13."

He closed his eyes and told himself, "Whatever I said when I was 13, if another offer like that ever comes along, I'll take it!"

The Lost Chords

The next Sunday Les and another student stood on the Tab platform to sing a duet. To everyone's surprise, Les seemed to have lost his voice. While the two men looked uncomfortable, the accompanist played the introduction over again. For some reason, Les still wasn't able to sing. He tried practicing on other occasions but had to give up. His vocal chords didn't produce those violin-like tenor sounds.

"I was the most miserable student on campus for the next six months!" Les later recalled. "I stopped reading my Bible, except for class assignments. I wanted to give up the whole Christian life."

Finally Les realized the Holy Spirit was trying to tell him something—not that a church music director's position was a bad thing for him or that a 13-year-old's commitment was necessarily what God ultimately had in mind.

"My struggle was whether I was fully committed to doing God's will—whatever and wherever that was," says Les. "True, I'd made a childhood commitment, but my heart wasn't into following it through. On the one hand, I couldn't let my parents or myself down in the eyes of others. Yet I was holding back on letting God have everything I was and had and hoped for."

In his dorm room one day Les knelt and earnestly told the Lord, "I belong to you, O God. I live because Christ died, and now I die in Christ to self. I'll do whatever you want me to do!"

The Song Returns

Suddenly the Cross became real in Les's life. He felt such a joy and peace that he stood to his feet and started singing. That tenor voice was his again, because he had given it to God. After graduation, Les headed back to Cuba and married another missionary, Mary Doty ('52). For eight years they led the Cuba radio ministry for West Indies Mission, producing daily programs that were broadcast throughout the island. But while they were on a year's furlough in USA, Mary died giving birth to their third child.

Les returned to Cuba with his three children, living with his brother Allen. A year later Fidel Castro's police expelled him from Cuba for broadcasting "anti-revolutionary" teaching (the gospel). Les moved to Costa Rica to head an intermission organization promoting Christian literature throughout the Spanish world. In 1961 Les remarried, and he and Carolyn had a fourth child. Moving to Miami in 1965, they founded Logoi, Inc., a ministry providing distance theological education for pastors and church leaders throughout Latin America. Through their program over 45,000 have graduated. Today Les spends much of his time in pastors' conferences. In fact, many churches in Colombia and Venezuela call him their "Pastor at Large."

"At Prairie I never achieved more than a B+ in my English classes, struggle as I might for an A," Les remembers. "Ruth Thompson, our teacher, didn't seem to value my Spanish syntax! But she did develop my writing ability so that we've been able to produce Bible study courses and other materials in Spanish."

In 1997 Prairie Alumni Association recognized the work of Les and Carolyn by awarding them the Distinguished Alumnus Award. In 2001, Les received the 2001 Spanish Evangelical Christian Publishers Gold Medallion award for his book *Más que Maravilloso* (More Than Wonderful), a popular study on the greatness of God.

As to the other members of our quartet, Jack Lentz joined Far Eastern Gospel Crusade (which later became SEND International) and served as director of Radio CKXL in South Korea. The station beamed gospel radio programs not only in that nation but also into China, Russia, and other lands. George Goudy became a pastor in the US, and I eventually ended up in Africa. But before that, God had to apply the Cross to my life in other ways.

Out of the Public Eye?

"I don't think I should do mission work this summer," I'd written my father, with whose mission I'd worked the previous summer.[1] "While I enjoyed the experience, it meant being in the lime light, so to speak. I need a time of working and meeting with God out of the public eye."

So that's why I'd stayed on at Three Hills that summer. Since I'd already served on the electric crew, I volunteered for that department— the kind of work that interested me. It came somewhat as a blow, there- fore, when the summer workers' coordinator asked me to switch to the farm crew. It was short staffed, whereas the electric crew was over- staffed for the summer work it had to do.

Raised in the city, I wasn't particularly enamored with barnyards. Besides, it meant getting up at 5.30 a.m. while everyone else was still sleeping, to ride the open farm truck 1fi miles north. At the school farm we milked the cows, pasteurized the milk, and delivered it to staff homes and campus by breakfast time.

Worse still, once a week we had to slaughter and butcher. I didn't let on I'd once worked in a meat packing plant while waiting to go on active service. I'd found the greasy environment of carcasses so objectionable that I walked off the job. In spite of roughing it in the Navy since then, I didn't feel at home in a slaughter house! But now there was no way out.

I died inwardly each time we slaughtered an animal, but as we dis- sected joints, muscles, and organs in the butchering process, I marveled at God's creation. Still, when I'd written Dad about needing to work for the summer away from the public eye, I hadn't expected to meet God in a blood-splattered slaughterhouse. I guess one lesson was that humility wasn't learned only in a cloister.

The irony of the summer was that after sloshing around a dairy

---

[1] Ken Getty ('48) and I had held evangelistic meetings and vacation Bible schools along the north shore of Lake Superior, under my father's Railway Mission of North America (now Christian Transportation Inc.) We'd had to preach, sing, provide the music, make crafts, and almost stand on our heads to keep the attention of unchurched children and their parents!

barn and butcher shop all week, incognito in coveralls and gum boots, I found myself on Sunday singing in the male quartet—all suited-up on the Tab platform. Does God have a sense of humor? As LE would have said, "Serves you right!"

Quartets such as ours were part of Prairie's music program. Professional musicians trained students in voice and instrument. The school's regular services, conferences, radio broadcasts, and summer outreach provided ample opportunity for staff and students to use their musical talents through solos, trios and quartets, choirs, bands, and orchestras. After the Malsbarys left, musician Robert Snyder came with his family to study Bible and stayed on to teach instrumental music and lead the school orchestra. His son Steven later became the school's legal advisor.

LE's elderly Aunt Katherine Anderson was general voice instructor—and a general she was! "Don't sing through the top of your head!" she'd command. "Sing from your diaphragm!" And to make sure we were doing so, she'd come around and place one hand on our abdomens as we practiced scales with a "Ha! Ha! Ha!" In the segregated setting of Prairie, some fellows were embarrassed to have a woman touch them like that. But "Aunt Kate" was harmless—skinny as a blackboard pointer, strict, and brimming with mischief.

Among the singing groups at the time were The Maxwell Sisters. The three eldest made a striking trio, their voices perfectly matched in harmony. As an older sister left school, a younger would make up the third member of the Trio.[1] Seeing them on the platform in their immaculate white blouses and black skirts, many students might think of them as belonging to a special angelic category—but their fellow students knew they were quite human. One or two of them were more mischievous than the others—but each had the usual concerns and joys students experience. (See Family Reminiscences, Chapter 24, for their stories.)

---

[1] As I listened to the Maxwell Sisters, I almost heard my own four sisters, who had sung all over Ontario in The Fuller Sisters' Quartet from childhood on, until different ones left home.

Chapter 6: Missions

"Christians must become convicted and convinced that missions is the first business of the Church."—LEM

"IT'S EASIER TO STEER A MOVING VEHICLE"

WHICH CAME FIRST—CHICKEN OR EGG? Bible school or school of missions? Missionary concern was already in the hearts of the founding families who called for help in training their young people in the Word. It was a natural outcome of Bible study applied to life —commitment to the Savior's call to discipleship and to making disciples—"to the ends of the earth."

Before the school began, Hector, older brother of co-founder Fergus Kirk, had left for Nigeria.[1] His sister Hattie was a missionary in Virginia (later Central America). Their father, Andrew, had been a Presbyterian home missionary. Both Leslie and Pearl Maxwell, before marriage, had wanted to serve in missions. While single, Leslie spent summer months as an itinerant missionary on horseback. Students from the first graduating class became missionaries, forerunners of several thousand graduates to serve at home and overseas. The Maxwells' own children all went on to serve in full-time Christian ministry.

When the fledgling Bible school in Three Hills heard of the need to train pastors in Cuba, three faculty members (3/5 of PBI's teachers that year) headed off to the Caribbean island to help staff Los Pinas Neuvos Bible Institute, founded by the West Indies Mission.[2] Since then

---

[1] In Ontario Hector heard Rowland Bingham's plea for the neglected Sudan. He joined the fledgling Sudan Interior Mission (SIM) in 1917, serving in Nigeria until 1951. He was Field Secretary and deputy Director.

[2] The call to Cuba came through Fergus Kirk's sister Hattie, who earlier served in Costa Rica. West Indies Missions was founded through the shared vision of a Cuban Presbyterian, B.J. Lavastida, and Prairie faculty Elmer V. Thompson. Years later I saw the fruit of their ministry when the annual church conference of Los Pinos Neuvos, the Cuba-wide national churches, invited me to bring the Bible messages.

in lands around the world, graduates have initiated hundreds of Bible studies and schools based on Prairie principles.

Closer to home, graduates formed what became the Alberta branch of the Canadian Sunday School Mission. As Prairie expanded, several missionaries joined the faculty—some on furlough, some on medical leave, and (in the 1940s) some who had been expelled by Communist regimes.

Not a Missionary "Mill"

Yet Prairie was never a "mill" for turning out missionaries. Although Prairie was known for its missionary vision, and our principal kept the need of missions before us, I never felt pressured to become a missionary.[1] That could have become an end in itself and missed LE's more basic focus—to bring us into the resurrection life of Christ. He knew the only path was the way of the Cross.

This was the same emphasis he'd made in 1946 at the first "Urbana," InterVarsity's mission's conference: "Only by the deepening of the spiritual life can missions grow with success." He'd tell us, "The greatest mission is submission."

As LE hammered away at this core message, he knew the Holy Spirit would call us to respond to Jesus' prayer to "Send forth reapers." We students had plenty of opportunities to learn about "the fields ripe to harvest."

He opened his pulpit and classrooms to men and women (many of them Prairie graduates) who had served in missions. They shared with us their burden for rural and urban children, for city missions, for ethnic groups overseas that still didn't have the Scriptures in their own language, or who hadn't heard the gospel. The question was more often where to serve rather than whether to serve.

---

[1] Perhaps I didn't feel pressured because I knew my parents had prayed that their six children would become missionaries at home or abroad. As a child I had imagined going to Africa.

"Get moving, and God will steer you in the right direction!" Maxwell urged as we faced catalogues of opportunities and needs. "Remember, it's easier to steer a moving vehicle than a stationary one." Geography was not the most important factor, but rather being located in God's will. He also reminded us that while God could close a door, it was up to us to knock in the first place.

Most of all, Maxwell believed we were engaged in a global struggle. In *World Missions: Total War*[1] he quoted Francis Steele of what was then North Africa Mission: "[Total warfare] means total commitment with no option and no returns, and past the point of no return."

Many students became involved in home missions between school years, but the great need of lands without the gospel was ever before us. Often we heard William W. Borden's challenge: "If I saw ten men carrying a log, with nine men on one end, I would hurry to help the one man on the other end."[2]

We were haunted by Amy Carmichael's allegory of happy people sitting in a grassy field, peacefully making daisy chains while men, women, and children tumbled over a nearby cliff to their deaths.[3]

A Shallow Grave beside the Trail

Norman and Evelyn Charter were a couple who didn't spend their lives making daisy chains! They went right to the cliff edge in their concern for people who knew not Christ. Although they met at Prairie, graduating in 1937, it was six years later, in 1943, that they married in China, as missionaries of the China Inland Mission. They'd already experienced privations and loneliness, being stationed hundreds of miles apart.

---

[1] Maxwell, L.E., *World Missions, Total War.* Three Hills: Prairie Press, 1977
[2] Usually referred to as "Borden of Yale," William (1887-1913) gave his vast Borden Dairy inheritance to missions and sailed for Cairo to reach Muslims for Christ. Within weeks he died of spinal meningitis, but friends found a scribbled message under his pillow. "No Reserve! No Retreat! No Regrets!"
[3] "Thy Brother's Blood Crieth," from *Things as They Are,* by Amy Carmichael. North Harrow: Dohnavur Fellowship (nd). See Appendix E. page 297.

Just a year after their marriage, near the end of World War II, the Charters along with other foreigners fled from Japanese invaders. Evelyn was expecting her first child. Out of the sky screamed Japanese Zeros, strafing and bombing the lines of struggling refugees. As Norman and Evelyn dived into a ditch, Evelyn felt labor pangs. American soldiers got her to a military first aid unit, but her first-born survived only a few hours. The war-shocked parents scratched out an unmarked grave beside the trail.

After sunset the Charters staggered into a friendly village, only to find the frightened people in shock. The attacking aircraft had killed several villagers. One woman was inconsolable. Evelyn, exhausted and hurting, tried to help her, speaking in her dialect.

"Go away, yellow dog!" screamed the distraught woman through her tears. "You don't understand. I just buried my son!"

"So did I!" wept Evelyn along with her. As Evelyn told about burying her new-born infant beside the trail, the two embraced amid their sobs. A flickering oil-wick lamp cast on to the bamboo wall the shadows of two bereaved mothers—cultures apart, but bonded by a common grief and finding solace in a message that transcended anger and race and war. The village woman grasped Evelyn's arm, listening to the only story that could comfort her—the story of the God who loved her so much that he sent his only son for her.

That wasn't the only time the Charters buried one of their children or had to flee for their lives. When the Communists took over the country in 1949, they were based in a remote province. Realizing their presence could endanger the Chinese believers, they prepared for the arduous trek to a coastal port. In 1950 the CIM advised all their missionaries to leave, and in 1951 several missionaries, including the Charters with three children, headed for Hong Kong. But they left behind the body of one of their little girls.

"The trip took us more than a month!" says Vernon Charter, who later, with his wife, served on Prairie's staff. Although only three at the time, he still remembers images of the grueling ordeal. "We had to use whatever transportation we could find—including horse cart, river boat, or the top of an overloaded truck. We underwent sickness, many delays, and repeated questioning by authorities, along with searching through our personal effects.

"I know my parents looked upon those painful experiences in the light of the Cross. They knew the meaning of death to self and submission to God's will in all things—if necessary, even laying down their lives for the sake of Christ and the gospel!"

Back in Canada, Norman and Evelyn served at Prairie—Norman until his death in 1972, and Evelyn into the 1980s. She cared for her ailing husband and raised seven children. All seven attended Prairie and all took up full-time Christian ministry, serving in different parts of the world with C&MA, OMF, WEC, and Christian colleges.

"Maxwell could be both very severe and hilariously funny," Vern recollects. "When I was about 12, on learning of my fondness for fishing, he took me on a fishing trip—a very special memory for me. Later, his classes were the highlights of my Bible school years. LE's grasp of the Scriptures, his dynamic ability as a communicator, his love for God, and his Spirit-anointed ministry marked him as one of the spiritual 'giants' of the twentieth century."

In her book, *Into All the World*,[1] author Margaret Epp tells about Prairie grads she interviewed in North America and around the globe. Many were our classmates—others had graduated earlier or were yet to attend Prairie. Epp's book was a world travelogue about people who were making a difference in the lives of millions.

Priest of Spirit Worshipers

Thailand didn't happen to be on Epp's whirlwind itinerary, but Jim ('55) and Louise (Imbach '54) Morris, OMF, well remember LE's visit in the late 1950s. They were serving in a remote village in North Thailand.

---

[1] Epp, Margaret, *Into All the Workl.* Three Hills: Prairie Press, 1973.

To reach them, Maxwell had to bump along a dusty road in a rice truck for 80 kilometers. It was his birthday, so the Morrises celebrated with a rice casserole, a cake, and a precious can of pears. The only problem was that their house helper had never seen canned pears. When she put the casserole on the table, it contained some strange looking white lumps.

"I love potatoes!" enthused LE, diving in. The lumps turned out to be the pears!

"There were no Christians yet in our area," the Morrises relate. "We were trying to make friends with the tribal people, who worshipped demons. One of their most powerful priests was Old Monday. Since his family had proved friendly, we took Mr. Maxwell to meet him. We'll never forget the contrast. The two men were about the same age, both had large families; both were influential leaders and highly respected by their own people.

"But what a contrast: Mr. Maxwell, who had lived for Christ, and Old Monday who had lived under the power of evil spirits. We longed that Old Monday would believe. He later professed to follow Jesus, but eventually returned to worship the spirits.

"Shortly before I left for Thailand," recalls Louise, at that time single and not knowing what the future might hold; "I asked Mr. Maxwell to autograph *Abandoned to Christ*. He signed his book along with the words, 'Without reservation!' In the next years, that challenged me more than the book itself because it was his personal word to me. I had given my life to the Lord, but was I holding anything back, reserving just a little corner for myself?"

The gospel didn't seem to be making much headway at the time, but LE encouraged Jim and Louise to hang on to God's promises. For centuries Satan had gripped these people with fear. Only years later did spiritual fruit come. Many Pwo Karen people came to know Christ, and today little tribal churches dot those Thai hills.

Warring Tribes Make Peace

Back in the West, when "Peace Child" hit the screens in cinemas and churches, Don and Carol Richardson (both grads of '57) probably became the best known missionaries from Prairie. They hadn't planned on being "movie stars"—in 1962 they'd simply gone with Regions Beyond Missionary Union (now World Team) to Irian Jaya, the western half of a massive southwest Pacific island of New Guinea, just north of Australia.

Learning the language of the "stone-age" Sawi people, they nearly despaired of penetrating the culture with the gospel. Don and Carol knew that only the Lord could open this door. To these headhunters, deception and treachery were among the highest values in life. Judas would have been their hero! How to declare faith and peace among people whose traditions included "fattening up" a victim with kindness, in order later to kill and eat him?

Unexpectedly, warring Sawi elders provided the Richardsons with an incredibly poignant communication key. One day the missionary couple watched amazed as two warring tribes gave each other a child as a pledge of peace. When Don and Carol later told them the story of God's gift of his Son even though we were his enemies, the elders' eyes glistened with understanding. Jesus was the eternal Peace Child! The missionaries had stumbled on a "redemptive analogy"—a tradition they believed God had placed deep in Sawi culture to prepare the tribe to understand and accept the gospel.

Acceptance by the Sawi was not instantaneous. It took much patience and teaching. Fear of spirits held back the people. But a breakthrough came one day, then another—until hundreds were turning to Christ. At the time, the Sawi tribe numbered about 2,700 people. Now they have probably increased to more than 5,000, because they no longer kill each other and they have better hygiene and access to medicine. Church elders also report healings in response to the prayer of faith. That too helps population growth! Up to 70% of the current population profess faith in Christ.

Today thatch-roofed churches pepper the Sawi swamps and dot mountain slopes where other tribes of Irian Jaya have welcomed salvation. Even while surrounding tribes were continuing to kill, Sawi believers turned in their barbed arrows and spears for the sword of the Word of God. They've helped carry the gospel into other remote areas.

Later Don described the remarkable saga in *Peace Child*.[1] The best-seller became the basis for a movie of the same name. It authentically recreated the tumult of warring tribes with swarms of fierce-looking but willing warriors. They weren't just acting their parts—before conversion many had taken part in tribal battles. But now they wanted to show the rest of the world what Jesus, the Peace Child, had done for them and their society! Next to The Jesus Film in number of showings, *Peace Child* has been shown in 26 languages in over 50 countries since it was released in 1974, resulting in an estimated one million professions of faith.

Don eventually found time to develop studies in "redemptive analogies" in other cultures.[2] His research and writing have advanced the communication of the gospel and the study of missiology.

"Drastic Purging"

"God even uses the stresses of missionary work to deepen our lives," Maxwell reminded us. Even in veteran missionaries? Clifton and Alma (Jesperson) McElheran ('35) testify to the truth of that. Related to the original farmhouse family in Three Hills, they spent 30 years with SIM in Nigeria developing what became the largest indigenous mission society. Then misunderstandings arose that caused deep hurts and disruption in their personal lives.

"We now see that God had a deeper purpose in mind. True, we had seen much blessing and growth in the churches and the Evangelical Missionary Society, but God wanted more fruit in our lives. That

[1] Richardson, Don, *Peace Child*. Glendale: Regal, 1974.
[2] ---, *Eternity in Their Hearts*. Ventura: Regal Books, 1981.

required drastic purging. We believe it was similar to Peter's life when Jesus said, 'Satan has desired to sift you but I have prayed for you that your faith fail not.'

"As we allowed the crucifixion of self in deeper areas of our lives we came out as conquerors, renewed in spirit by the Holy Spirit and with a fresh outreach to others. We have never been happier or more contented!"

Prairie and Missions—it's been the outgrowth of the Cross in the lives of students. As to the number of graduates serving in churches, home missions, and overseas missions, various figures in the thousands have been used, but the school hasn't attempted to keep statistics. The Alumni Association does state: "Alumni are working in 114 countries around the globe" (2002). Although Maxwell's main ministry was centered on the school in Three Hills, he could have said with John Wesley, "The world is my parish!"

"I have met graduates from this school all over the world," states Stephen F. Olford, who himself was born of missionary parents in Angola. "They are usually known for two distinctive Christian qualities—spirituality and stickability—the result of Maxwell's unique ministry through his example, preaching, teaching, and writing."

"The man with his zest for life and strong victorious message challenged young people to serve well the missionary enterprise," states Ian M. Hay, General Director Emeritus of SIM. "The remarkable expansion of the Church around the world in those years is a tribute to God's blessing on a life and ministry."

No Turf Protectors

"Prairie has been used by God not only by sending missionaries around the world but also in home missions by establishing churches," stated Ted S. Rendall at a recent chapel service. "As well, Prairie graduates have helped develop home ministries such as the Northern Canada

Evangelical Mission, the Canadian Sunday School Mission (especially in Alberta), and Village Missions.

"Historian Robert Burkinshaw says Prairie was probably the most important agent in the formation of the Evangelical Free Church in Canada. I think we could say the same about Christian and Missionary Alliance in western Canada. Here is what Burkinshaw states:

> The interdenominational Prairie Bible Institute is perhaps known for its enormous impact on world missions through its training of several thousand missionaries. Less well known is PBI's impact on numerous evangelical denominations. Many PBI graduates who did not go into foreign missions saw vast, often isolated, regions of western Canada as an important home missions field and became engaged in the planting of large numbers of churches. Many of which eventually entered evangelical denominations. For example, PBI was probably the single most formative influence upon the Canadian Evangelical Free Church.[1]

Maxwell's large heart reached out to many a pastor as well as other Christian leaders. He never thought in terms of protecting his "turf" but encouraged other Bible schools on the Prairies. A Prairie graduate and the remarkable missions-minded Balisky family founded the Peace River Bible Institute.

Henry and Inger Hildebrand recall Maxwell's personal encouragement. As Founder and President of the Briercrest Family of Schools, Caronport, Sask., Hildebrand remembers being guest speaker at a youth camp, during which a memorial service was held for a staffer who had died saving the life of a camper. Because the staffer was a Prairie graduate, the family asked L. E. Maxwell to come and preach at the service. To comfort and challenge the relatives, he stressed God's plan for the

---

[1] Robert K. Burkinshaw, "Evangelical Bible Colleges in Twentieth-Century Canada," published in Rawlyk, G.A., Ed., *Aspects of the Canadian Evangelical Experience.* Montreal: Queen's University Press, 1977.

believer's life—an immediate plan and an ultimate plan in glory, all with the purpose of showing "the exceeding riches of his grace."[2]

"When I returned home, I shared these thoughts with my wife, Inger," remembers Hildebrand; "because our doctor had just diagnosed our 12-year-old David as having Hodgkin's Disease. In view of David's shortened life expectancy, we prayed God would help us prepare our son for his 'ultimate ministry.' But God gave our boy another 39 years with us, during which time he and his wife blessed many others.

"Then when David and Jeannie died suddenly in a car collision, what comfort we had in knowing they were called to a greater ministry in glory!"

Secular or Religious—Both Spiritual

Prairie's missionary emphasis was such that some people gained the impression a secular vocation was "second best." Maxwell knew differently. Prairie could not have existed without friends in secular professions and occupations. That included agriculture, health, thermo-dynamics, construction, mechanics, and numerous other skills. Business people prayed and gave financially to the Institute. Others donated their expertise during visits to the school. LE viewed both secular and "sacred" as equally spiritual if committed to God.

"PC means Preach Christ or Plough Corn—whichever God calls you to do," he explained. "Remember the Moravian motto: Ready for Either." The Herrnhut (Moravian) community in Germany produced some of the earliest missionaries in the "modern" (18th C. on) era.[2] The motto appeared above an ox standing between a plough (symbol of service) and an altar (symbol of sacrifice). Maxwell's challenge was for "complete abandonment" to God's will—whatever he wanted to use us to do.

---

[1] Maxwell based his message on an exposition of Ephesians 1.1-10.
[2] A tiny community, Moravians nevertheless provided over half the Protestant missionaries of the 18th Century.

Problem Solved—"Out of the Blue!"

An aeronautics engineer, Avery Hall, provided a rather dramatic illustration of God's using secular skills to advance his work. In the late 1950s the school drew up plans for a spacious student dining hall to replace the outgrown facilities. Space free of pillars would be ideal, especially for multi-purpose use—but how to erect a roof span of some 23,000 square feet (not including entry porticoes), with over half of it minimally supported? A roof able to hold up under winter snowfalls and howling winds that at times swept the plains! The engineering logistics were beyond Prairie's resources.

Then unannounced, American businessman Avery Hall landed his small plane at the campus airstrip in the summer of 1959. When he asked for the business manager, he found himself talking with a quiet little man named Henry Muddle.

"I don't know why I'm here," Hall started, "but I felt God wanted me to come!" He explained to the astonished Muddle that he'd flown over from Philadelphia—only some two thousand air miles and two time zones away! "What can I do for you?"

"Well, what's your profession?" inquired Muddle, now puzzled.

"I'm an aeronautics engineer," explained Hall. "I work mostly on stress design."

Once the engineer discovered the school's desire to build a dining hall with a minimal number of support pillars, Hall volunteered to work out the stress factors. In fact, he moved his family to Three Hills and stayed on the job until the Sanford Hanson Dining Room was complete. Only six pillars support 13,000 square feet of the roof, providing lots of free space. Another 10,000 square feet provide kitchen and small-group facilities. The roof hasn't sagged once!

So Prairie has taken shape through the years, stage by stage, by prayer and sacrifice and hard work—and all without debt. We knew that the campus buildings and other facilities—still very utilitarian in appearance—were only mere scaffolding for the spiritual construction that was taking place in our lives through the teaching of the Word.

Chapter 7: Master Mentor

"Faith and life always go together. Believe and behave!"—LEM

GOLD NUGGETS AND HOT COALS

EXAMPLES OF CLASSIC MAXWELL enlivened my first two years, as he spoke in student chapel on special occasions or on Sunday mornings in the Tab. These nibbles only increased my hunger for the man's whole message. That came in my Junior and Senior years.

Day after day we students sat spellbound in Bible III and Bible IV. The class hour passed too quickly as this skillful teacher explicated the Scriptures—Romans, Galatians, Ephesians, and on—chapter by chapter, verse by verse, layer by layer, like an archaeologist uncovering priceless treasure. In studying Law and Grace, Maxwell panned each phrase for gold, and we had to be quick to grasp the nuggets. He dug out truths we had never understood, much less applied.

Sometimes in place of nuggets he would throw us a hot coal that would purify our lips (as Isaiah 6.1) or burn into our hearts with conviction, if we allowed it to. This disciple-cum-discipler obviously had been with Jesus. His method was not simply to lecture but to mentor— to make us disciples of the one who said, "If anyone would come after me, he must deny himself and take up his cross daily and follow me."[1]

While our Prof. zeroed in on his topic, he seemed aware of everything going on in the crowded classroom. The rustic campus was overflowing with the post-war influx, but LE saw us as individuals. "There are a couple of seats over here!" he'd interrupt his discourse as he spotted a married couple arriving late. He knew they'd had to check on their baby between classes. "I want everyone to be comfortable!"

---

[1] Luke 9.23

"We Made It!"

Tough war veteran though he was, jabbing the air to drive home his piercing aphorisms, he had a warm heart just a hand-span below his angular jaw. Lily Graber came to appreciate that. She struggled through four years of studies while caring for three children. At the graduation ceremony, she was obviously expecting her fourth. As the principal placed her graduation certificate in her hand, he leaned closer and whispered with that infectious chuckle, "We made it!"

LE's classes were the outstanding feature of our years at Prairie. They made the spartan rules and conditions irrelevant to the warmth in our hearts. As we trudged through snow and piled our winter togs on back benches, our teacher strode past us, slung his beaver hat and duffel coat over the platform rail, joked about "The Alberta Hammer" (as a frigid front was called), and opened his well-thumbed Bible.

Without delay, Maxwell launched into the text just where he had closed the previous session. "Now, then—how is the Law a schoolmaster? What . . . ." And we forgot the weather, the hard benches, the segregated seating, and even ourselves. We sat at the feet of a master teacher who knew the Master.

As we came out of class, our faces glowed either with delight or with conviction—depending on what the Holy Spirit was applying to our individual needs. We couldn't leave unaffected. LE didn't simply lecture, nor did he preach. His style was a forceful combination of exposition, illustration, declaration, counsel, and entreaty—punctuated with pithy aphorisms and homespun wit. He realized we represented a wide range of life experience and spiritual growth. Some of us were hurting, needing an encouraging arm around our shoulders. Others of us needed a punch from the shoulder to wake us up to our spiritual need.

"Notice how the Apostle Paul wrote to these carnal Christians in Corinth!" he said, opening his floppy Bible. "They were so spiritually weak he couldn't give them strong meat. He had to feed them milk—

74

look at 1 Corinthians 3.2. But before leveling with them, he found something to commend—note 1 Corinthians 1.4-9. With one arm he embraced them; with the other he delivered a convicting jab!"

LE did both. When he did deliver the punch, we received it in the spirit of love in which he gave it. "Beloved!" he would begin his punch line, and we knew he did love us even as we reeled from the impact of biblical truth.

Maestro, Artist, or Prophet?

So this was the man who, as a student in Kansas City, was terrified of speaking in public and didn't think he could teach? He'd grown into a skilled professor, able to bring together Scripture, history, quotations, and powerful poetry along with contemporary realities. Or was he a maestro conductor, creatively calling on the strings, the woodwinds, the brass, and the percussion section—each as needed to interpret the full intent of the Divine Composer?

Perhaps at heart he was an artist—in each class his palette knife splashing victorious life over the somber darkness of sinful nature and God's judgment. Or a drama producer—changing the backdrops and props as needed by the biblical characters he brought to life on the classroom stage.

He certainly was a prophet—a proclaimer of truth, giving a clarion call to us as students and to the Church at large.

Whatever the topic from the Word, LE's enthusiasm seemed irrepressible. He was bursting with vigor, bubbling over with Scripture. Yet we never sensed any showmanship or flippancy. This was genuine Maxwell, balancing satire with sincerity, humor with holiness, insight with integrity. Most of all, we knew he lived what he taught and preached. He was a servant of God filled with the Holy Spirit. We were blessed. We wished we could forever sit under his teaching. But what was that he was saying . . . ?

"The word is nigh you!" thunders our mentor in a Romans class

The last complete family photo,
taken at parents' Fiftieth Wedding Anniversary (1975)
(L-R) Ernest, Anna, Lois, Miriam, Eleanor, Ruth, Paul,

"Now don't you go home with a 'holier-than-thou' attitude!" our mentor warned us at the end of Spring Conference. "That's one of the curses of conferences. The speakers you've been hearing at Prairie this week have had ten, twenty years—some a lifetime—of experience. So don't expect your pastor at home to come up with the same. Don't criticize him. Pray for him, encourage him!"

Digging for Gold

"Scripture is its own best commentary!" LE often paraphrased renowned expositor R. A. Torrey, who wrote: "There is no other commentary on the Bible so helpful as the Bible itself. There is not a difficult passage in the Bible that is not explained and made clear by other passages of the Bible."[1]

Examining Scripture rather than passively absorbing lectures really was the main educational approach of Prairie, using the Search-Question system of study. It was adapted from the system[2] so effectively used by the Bible school in Kansas at which both Leslie and Pearl had studied. The questions prepared us for class input and discussion by sending us searching through passages and cross-references to develop our own exegesis.

This inductive method put into our hands a valuable tool we'd use long after graduation. Regardless of how many commentaries and treatises we eventually would study, we developed an initial reliance on Scripture itself as its own best expositor.

"The Search-Question method of Bible study was the highlight of our time at Prairie," said Ralph Jacobson. "That involved finding out what Scripture actually said, understanding the context, and relating the passage to our need today. The Bible became central to our thinking and our teaching. This method forced us to become students of the Word."

---

[1] *The Treasury of Scripture Knowledge,* Introduction by R.A. Torrey, n.d.
[2] Apparently developed by scholarly William Stevens even before he founded Midland Bible Institute.

The system attracted a wide range of students. For instance, in my last year a young engineering graduate, Ralph D. Winter, a brilliant but quiet-spoken academic type, interrupted post-graduate studies in Anthropology and Linguistics at Cornell University to spend a couple of semesters at Prairie.

"I'd heard of the school's inductive system and wanted to see first hand how it worked," Ralph told me when I caught up with him years later. He went on to serve in missions in Central America and eventually helped initiate Theological Education by Extension (TEE) and Programmed Instruction—both of which became valuable systems in Bible teaching programs worldwide. He employed the Question-and-Answer method in his widely used Missions Perspectives Courses. As Ralph developed the US Center for World Missions and William Carey University we continued our friendship.

The Histrionic Speaker

"The first time I heard Mr. Maxwell speak was in 1946 at InterVarsity's first missions conference held at the University of Toronto." Ralph told me. At the time he'd been doing post-graduate studies at Princeton and hitchhiked to Toronto. "I'd never heard such an histrionic speaker! But when I later went to Prairie and sat in his classes, I enjoyed his style and teaching. I felt comfortable at Prairie—maybe my change in attitude reflected my own spiritual growth!"

"Histrionic" was not a word I'd heard to describe LE—"dramatic," yes, but "histrionic" sounded sensational. Anyway, that's how the speaker came across to my friend Ralph, a stoical slide-rule type.

To those who didn't know LE, in his earlier years he might have seemed histrionic. People told me about his jumping over a platform railing or—horrors!—standing on the pulpit, in his desire to get through to his listeners. On one occasion at a summer camp, he woke up sleepy listeners by splashing water from the speaker's glass over their heads![1]

---

[1] Dramatic preaching was common in some circles in North America. Leslie's conversion was influenced by the vivid preaching of a Methodist evangelist, who fell flat on the platform to illustrate the lost condition of sinners! Both D. L. Moody and his successor, Billy Sunday preached dramatically to vast crowds.

Histrionic or not, his imaginative preaching made a lasting impression on his audience. Brad and Ruth Hartt (LE's daughter) met a Californian who years before had heard the lively preacher from Three Hills speak in her staid Presbyterian church.

"His text was Proverbs 18.10, 'The name of the Lord is a strong tower; the righteous run to it and are safe,'" the woman recalled. "After speaking on the first part, he began quoting the second, but before getting to "safe" he ran from the platform, out a side door, and around the building. We sat there wondering what was happening! Bursting through a door on the opposite side and back up to the platform, he shouted, 'SAFE!' I'll never forget that message! It still reassures me of my position in Christ."

We who regularly sat under his teaching knew he wasn't putting on an act. It was genuine exuberance, not showmanship. He seemed to fulfil all that the Apostle Paul implied in the word "constrains" when Paul wrote: "The love of Christ constrains me!" This man believed the message he saw in Scripture. He was consumed by it. His heart burned with it, and he wanted our hearts to likewise burn. If the Word of God was a sword, to LE it was a flaming sword.

While his lively illustrations caught our attention, what left a lasting impression was his solemn sense of God's presence. When leading us in prayer, sometimes he would stand at the lectern, head bowed in silence after sighing, "Oh-h Lord!" It was as if Aaron were leading us into the very presence of the Holy One. A hush would spread across the gathering, and we'd instinctively begin communing with God in our own hearts before our mentor would lead us in corporate prayer.

After Ralph Winter became somewhat of a guru to evangelical missionaries, he was surprised at the name-recognition people accorded the rustic school on the Prairies. "When I addressed the Latin American Association of Schools, the members were polite but not warm—until I happened to mention I'd looked into the inductive method at Prairie. Immediately they became responsive—most of the missionaries were Prairie grads!"

Valued Mentoring

Self-help methods plus mentoring by LE was why men and women from across the continent and across the oceans came to Prairie. Some, after having earned a secular degree, sensed their need for spiritual under-girding and arrived specifically for immersion in the Word.

That's what brought Elisabeth Elliot. I remembered her, for she was the daughter of my father's close editor friend, Phillip Howard Sr. She came for a year of intensive Bible study. "Mr. Maxwell was the most significant teacher I ever had!" she stated years later. By then she'd become known as the widow of Jim Elliot, martyred by the Aucas, and as an author and conference speaker. It was her father who had asked LE to write a series of articles on the theme, "The Cross in the Life of the Believer," for his widely read *Sunday School Times*.[1] Fittingly, Elliot later wrote the biography of Amy Carmichael—who for LE was one of the greatest living examples of the "crucified and resurrected life."[2]

A University of Toronto engineering graduate, Howard Dowdell, wanted some kind of Bible course in preparation for missionary service and gathered information from several institutes and seminaries. When he discovered that the principal of Prairie Bible Institute was speaking nearby, he went to hear him. Howard was impressed by Maxwell's vision and message, but had reservations about his demonstrative style. However, the next day Howard pulled up on his BSA motorcycle outside SIM headquarters, where the speaker was staying. After Howard explained his desire to take an "immersion" Bible course, the principal thought that could be worked out. As the interview ended, LE hopped on the back of the BSA for a spin around the block.

This was not some "stuffed shirt" conference speaker, Howard concluded, but a down-to-earth man of vision and action. That Fall, Howard rode his BSA out west—2,600 road miles of sun, rain, and wind

---

[1] That series became the basis for Maxwell's first book, *Born Crucified*, published by Moody Press, 1945.
[2] Elisabeth Elliot, *A Chance to Die*. Old Tappan: Revell, 1987. See Chapter 4 re. Amy Carmichael.

across the flat plains. As the gaunt Three Hills elevators and stark school buildings rose up ahead, this graduate of Toronto's ivy-clad engineering college paused by the side of the gravel road. Somewhat as I'd done upon my earlier arrival, Howard wondered, "What am I getting into?" Hearing that Howard was coming, I was glad to show him the ropes— or how to stay off the ropes!

"I found knowledge and blessing from the Word under LE," Howard commented later.

"Taking into consideration some of the university courses and night school Bible courses I'd had in Toronto, the school tailored a two-year course that fulfilled diploma requirements. I wrote papers during school breaks and graduated along with the largest class in Prairie's history."

Later in Africa Dowdell, never one to let problems hold him back, broke through organizational red tape to develop Nigeria's top-rated secondary school. He also ushered in a new concept of using short-term missionary teachers to help raise up a generation of national Christian educators. The message of the Cross didn't destroy Howard's driving personality (any more than it had the Apostle Peter's), but it changed his focus from self-ambition to glorifying the Christ of the Cross.

Chapter 8: Classroom Sanctuary

It's the small, simple things that show
which way the wind is blowing.—LEM

UNCLE ABE LIVES AGAIN

ANY STRANGER PASSING the wooden frame classroom might rightly wonder what theater drama was performing inside. But it was LE's class on the Book of Job—hardly entertainment and certainly not high on any list of seminary treatises. We sat spellbound as LE introduced us to Job in Chapter 1 and expounded through to Chapter 42—all in one class hour!

With shouts, groans, and laughter, Maxwell the Master Story Teller dramatized the characters and conversations of God, Satan, Job, his wife, and his "comforters." Yet Maxwell the Instructor left no theological stone unturned. He set the book in historical context ("Remember, Job had no Book of Job to refer to") and also applied it to contemporary conditions ("Job lost everything—and we know how quickly entire cities and fortunes can disappear today").

[Ah, here were lessons we could use in future ministry to a consumer-mad world, we told ourselves.]

Our teacher poked fun at his alliterated outline: Job's Perfection, Poverty, Persecution, Pessimism, Problem, Purpose ("We teachers love 'sweet peas'"). [Class laughter.] He derided Job's self-important comforters. "They sound like pastors comparing notes—you know, 'I got rather thrilled over my own exegesis!'"

[Knowing glances between students, thinking of people we knew. The "comforters" provided lessons in counseling.]

Yet in describing Job's woes, LE rejected flippant attitudes to

82

problems. "Can you imagine Job saying, 'It could be worse!' Some Christians never face the sad reality of life's tragedies. As Jonah was drowning with seaweed tangled around his neck, do you think he said, 'It could be worse!' [Pained laughter.] Job was in serious trouble from every quarter. The Mystery of Tribulation is revealed in this book."

[Now we knew the theme and congratulated ourselves for understanding the book.]

But the "sweet peas" and shards of piercing humor were only to help us absorb heavier truths. Verbally LE painted a graphic backdrop of the titanic contest swirling around forlorn Job on the ash heap: God in the heavens, Satan prowling the earth, and angels peering from the balconies.

"Remember," LE pointed out, "no place is too sacred for Satan to intrude!"

The teacher's mood grew serious. "Let's understand the Great Drama we are observing in the Theater of Earth and Heaven. In Ephesians 3.10 Paul describes it. Think of the eternal stakes! If Job's profession is hollow, all faith is hollow. Grace fails; God fails. It's impossible to live righteously in this world. The Devil wins!"

[By then we'd been lifted up into the amphitheater of spiritual warfare. Although we'd already slogged through the preparatory Search Questions, here at last our teacher had revealed Job's theme and grand purpose. Now we glowed in the new insights we had acquired. That's it—the "yin and yang" of the universe; God versus Satan. This was almost heady!]

But our mentor wasn't finished.

An "I" Specialist

"By Chapter 31," he continued, "everyone knew that Job was righteous and faithful. His friends knew it, his wife knew it, the Devil knew it, God knew it, and Job knew it. In his defense before his friends (Chapters 29-31), he uses the personal pronoun 189 times. He had become an "I" specialist! That was Job's problem. God had to start in on him. The real purpose was to bring him to a new spiritual experience—the believer's repentance.

"In Chapter 40 Job is muzzled, silenced, stunned! But he's not there yet. He still can't pray for his friends. Finally in Chapter 42, Job cries out to God in a believer's repentance, 'I abhor-r-r myself!!'" LE bellowed the word in agony, dragging it out as if crucifying it on Golgotha.

[We began to understand. Job had come to see self, the flesh, as God saw it. That's what Christ nailed to his cross, in his own body. That must become our position in Christ before we could effectively live for others.]

"At last Job could pray for his friends!"

[You mean that's also the lesson?]

We sat as stunned as Job. Then this master of English slipped into homey vernacular, so we wouldn't misunderstand his punch line:

"What a miserable bunch of unsanctified junk we are!"

From the macro big picture he'd zoomed the lens of God's Word right down to the micro recesses of our hearts. Euphoria over our new academic insight into the earliest book of the Bible dissipated into soul-searching.

"I want to be charitable here," LE concluded, his voice becoming tender; "but God couldn't send some of you to pray for your friends. You'd feel a little superior. You'd be thinking, 'That's why God's chosen me to pray for them!'

"Let's pray." And the class was over.

Had we just received a scholarly exposition of Job? For an hour had the Mystery of Tribulation spellbound us? Yes—but more. An hour earlier we'd entered a rustic classroom on the second floor; now we silently filed out of a hallowed Upper Room. We'd learned the Purpose of the Book of Job—to lead us into a new spiritual experience in our walk with God. LE had transmuted cold pages of type onto the flesh-and-blood tablets of our hearts. The Word could change us if we let it.

*   *   *   *

If the Book of Job hadn't been written long ago, Prairie graduates in Africa could well have illustrated it from the contemporary record of trials Ethiopian believers passed through.

Ethiopian "Bible Characters"

"We often thought of LE's Bible characters when we lived in Ethiopia," Ralph and Doris Jacobson told me. "For one thing, their culture and dress were right out of the Old Testament. But their faith! Many suffered persecution stirred up by Orthodox priests. There was Wandaro, who still carried the marks of cruel beatings. His persecutors also tore his beard out of his face. But instead of cursing God, he turned out to be the sweetest person and greatest soul winner in the countryside.[1]

"We learned much from their faith and commitment under trial," Ralph and Doris said. "Those believers looked upon the persecution as a privilege to bear for Christ. They told us, 'The more we suffered, the more we loved our Savior—and the faster the Church grew!'"

In the 1960s the Jacobsons returned from Africa to represent SIM in western Canada. Their hearts were torn when Communism took over Ethiopia in the 1970s. They knew their Ethiopian friends were suffering even more intensely.

The "Revolutionaries" arrested Christians, torturing and imprison-

---

[1] Later I met Wandaro and wrote his story in *Run While the Sun Is Hot* (Toronto: SIM, 1967).

ing numbers of them. Talk about the trials of Job! Many believers lost all they possessed—house, property, farm, livestock, even children, and wives. Yet in these harsh trials, like Job they refused to curse God. They remained faithful, some unto death. Officials closed hundreds of churches, forcing believers to meet secretly.[1]

Returning to Ethiopia during the Communist regime, the Jacobsons experienced something of the stress their colleagues were going through. Marxist ideologues from outside stirred up the villagers against "the foreigners." Screaming, stone-throwing mobs hounded several missionaries out of town. It was hard to bear, because formerly friendly villagers, whom the missionaries had lovingly helped, were caught up in the brain-washing propaganda.

One day agitators dragged Ralph off to the local police post, accusing him of being a CIA spy. They trumped up the charge that his documents were not "in order."

From the midst of the rabble, Ralph recognized a church elder in the distance coming toward him. Ralph didn't want to endanger this man's life and motioned to him not to come further. But the elder pushed his way through. There was nothing he could do to free Ralph, but he risked his own freedom by identifying with "the foreigner."

"We're praying for you, brother!" he whispered furtively as he gave Ralph the customary greeting on each cheek. "And we've sent a runner to SIM HQ in Addis with the news." Then he slipped away into the crowd.

"We'll get rid of these!"

"I could hear a couple of revolutionaries talking about what the Communists had done to the Christians in China," Ralph remembers. "They said, 'We're going to get these people too!'"

---

[1] The suffering of believers under Ethiopia's Communist regime is vividly documented by John Cumbers in *Count It All Joy.* Kearney: Morris. 1995. See also Kay Bascom, *Hidden Triumphs in Ethiopia.* Pasadena: Wm. Carey Library, 2001. (Both available through SIM offices.)

Ralph, under escort, finally arrived back in the capital, Addis Ababa, where the Chief of Police sent the supposed "CIA spy" to the Interior Ministry. There a trusted Ethiopian friend of SIM, Ato Lako, met Ralph. Eventually a senior police official declared that Ralph's travel papers were indeed valid—and then he reprimanded the revolutionary zealots for harassing this visitor. Ralph was free!

Cleaning up at SIM's headquarters, Ralph heard a knock at the door. "A policeman says he needs to see you urgently!" a staff member reported. It was the policeman who had escorted him to the capital.

"He said he came to check whether I was all right," says Ralph, "but I realized he was stranded in the city because of a traffic curfew imposed that morning. This was 'revolutionary Ethiopia' and being from the lowlands, he wouldn't be allowed to stay in the local police barracks. He had no money to lodge elsewhere or to travel back to his village when the curfew lifted. I pressed a few Ethiopian birr into his hand, and he broke into a big smile. Thanking me profusely, my erstwhile captor gave me a typical Ethiopian embrace before he left."

Another case in which "the Lord turned the captivity of Job"![1]

Uncle Abe and Nephew Lot

"But remember, God deals with people in different ways," Maxwell reminded us. "We are to profit from their experiences."

Job was only one book and one character. Taking his cue from the Apostle Paul, Maxwell effectively used the lives of Bible characters "for our admonition" (1 Cor. 10.11). The whole parade of God's dealing with men and women in Scripture led us onward through spiritual cities of a Promised Land we could either possess or lose in defeat.

Among his many Bible character studies, LE took us on pilgrim-

---

[1] Job 41.10

age with Abraham and Lot.[1] But first he gave us a humorous wakeup call: "You need to use your ears—both of them. Keep one open and plug the other—lest things go right through, you understand!" He chuckled, and we were "all ears" for the rest of the class. We knew we were in for a fast-paced but deeply meaningful study.

"As commentary on these two Bible characters, look at 1 Corinthians 3.10-15," LE began. It was a passage I hadn't connected with the story, but that's the kind of thought-provoking treatment our mentor often exposed us to:

> According to the grace of God which was given to me, as a wise master builder I laid a foundation, and another is building upon it. . . . If any man's work which he has built upon it remains, he shall receive a reward. If any man's work is burned up, he shall suffer loss; but he himself shall be saved, yet so as through fire [NASB].

"As if by fire!" LE repeated. "Sometimes a conquering general set captives free if they'd run through a corridor of flames. That's what happened to Lot—he chose the fertile plains of Goshen and became prosperous, even mayor of Sodom. We might even wonder if Lot were a believer, but Peter tells us that Sodom vexed the soul of 'righteous Lot' (2 Peter 2.7, 8). Sodomites were happy there but not Lot. He built his castle of wood, hay, and stubble, and at the end he escaped as if through a corridor of fire—everything else burned!"

Fork in the Road

LE then compared the two men—uncle and nephew, both righteous, both rejecting Chaldean idolatry. They parted amicably, generous Abraham giving Lot first choice.

"But that was the fork in the road!" LE pointed out. "From there on, their motives were different. Abraham walked in the Spirit; Lot

---

[1] Genesis 13-19

walked in the flesh. The two walks are antagonistic to each other, Paul tells us. That fork in the road, legitimate as the choice was, became decisive for their destinies. Abraham looked for a spiritual city to come. Lot had no thought of seeking God's will—only immediate material advantage. So he pitched his tent toward Sodom, unaware that beneath this 'paradise' were volcanic fires ready to spew out fire and brimstone.

"Jesus said to remember Lot's wife.[1] Once in a while I let my imagination work—I trust it's sanctified a bit, or it would be dangerous. [Class laughter.] I can hear Mrs. Lot saying, 'What's the use pitching our tent toward the city, hubby? How're we going to help these people unless we live right among them? It would be good for our children—for their culture and education. We don't want a lot of squares and oddballs in our family.'"

[We might have felt like asking our Prof., "Aren't you being a little extreme?" But we'd often heard him state that in God's will, PC could mean either "Plough Corn" or Preach Christ." We knew Prairie graduates who served in professional and government circles—bearing witness in "the market place." In fact, a Prairie grad later became mayor of Three Hills. LE wasn't against that. He was making a different point.]

"There's no problem going to a city to glorify God—in whatever profession. The problem was that Lot went to Sodom not as a missionary but as a mercenary. He went for immediate advantage. You can build your house on the doorstep of Hell if God sends you there!"

A Red Light Testimony

Lot ended up as a frightful red light—a warning to others not to walk that way, our teacher pointed out. "No reputation, no genealogy, no complete family, no record, no souls influenced for God. Nothing except a scorched smell! He had compromised his testimony, and Genesis 19 tells us that when he at last warned his family and neighbors of judgment, he

---

[1] Luke 17.32

89

seemed like a joke to them. When you and I live for the same material things as the world lives for, they'll take us for a joke!

"I know God wants us to be assured, positive, trustful," LE continued. "But we must never be presumptuous. We need warnings. It was the good Calvinist Bishop Ryle who said, 'The most miserable deathbeds I've attended have been backsliders who can only lie there in despair.' The warning to us as believers is that if we build with wood, hay, and stubble, we shall be saved—yet as if through a corridor of fire.

"And Uncle Abe? Out there on the hills, he turned out to be the only one who could help Sodom—he interceded for the city, for his nephew and family. He came to the end of his life with only a tent, a well, and an altar—not even so much real estate as to put his foot on. But he died with the promise of more offspring than the stars in the sky. And the spiritual returns on his inheritance are still coming in as the gospel spreads around the world![1]

"Remember, our tent is pitched not in a paradise, but on the battle-field!"

Maxwell taught with excellence but never merely on an academic level. He was essentially a discipler for Christ. Whatever the lesson, he pressed for inner response in us. If we were walking with God, he wanted us to walk more closely. If we were living for self, he taught and preached for conviction, repentance, and victory in Christ. That is how the Holy Spirit had worked in his own life.

"Reminds me of my visit, after many years, to my uncle's home in Kansas City," LE told us. "His son (my cousin) and I had been childhood neighbors. We played ball and mostly played the fool together with others. We were a profligate bunch, and but for the mercy of God I'd still be one of them.

"The night before my visit, my uncle's wife had died, and the

---

[1] Hebrews 11.8-12; Galatians 6.6-14.

family sat mourning. I read a Psalm and prayed, and then I said, 'You'd no idea what was going through my mind when we young fellows used to dance the night away. But later I trusted in Jesus as Savior and he changed my life. I want you to know I'm completely satisfied with the years I've had serving him.'

"My cousin, sitting in the corner, could only hang his head and shake it sadly. When we were young, we came to a fork in the road. I took one way; he took the other. And now he was miserable, an outcast. Oh, the tragedy of making the wrong decision, as Lot did, at the fork in the road!"

Character under Trial

But LE wasn't through. He had one more lesson for us from the story of Abraham and Lot. Often he'd emphasize the value of building character through self-discipline—the daily Cross in our lives. He had a thesis about character under trial. He once heard a pastor defend the moral lapse of an assistant by saying, "Never judge a man when he's under fire!"

"Nonsense!" exploded Maxwell, the military veteran. "The reactions of a person under pressure reveal his true character. Untried innocence may hide sleeping sin. The Devil insinuated that in his accusation of Job."

Now LE gave us the other half of that thesis: The decisions we make in life are governed by our true character. "Times, places, choices, decisions—these reveal character and determine the destiny of our lives," he stated. The fork in the road revealed both Abraham's and Lot's character.

"Remember," LE concluded; "we all come to a fork in the road daily—whether to walk in the Spirit or walk in the flesh that day. How often did our Lord say we should take up his Cross?"

"*Daily*," we replied in subdued chorus. That's what I hadn't realized when I wrote my father that first semester at Prairie: "Harold Fuller is a pile of ashes!" I needed to die to self daily, constantly. That's what I saw in the life of our Mentor.

Chapter 9: Personal Growth

"A holy life is made up of little things."—LEM

WHAT MADE MAXWELL TICK?

"ALAS, I TRIED, but who can describe that wonderful man?" author Elisabeth Elliot replied when I asked for her comments. "I will never forget him—a man of deep compassion, side-splitting humor, and an unswerving determination to follow his God!"

"He was a riveting speaker who held us students spellbound, at times pounding the pulpit as he portrayed the love of God. He reminded us that 'the hardest thing in the world was'—and we students finished the sentence, '*to keep balanced!*'"

So what made Maxwell tick? Had he always been the prophet we knew in mid-century? Or had he grown into that role? Or perhaps, like the Apostle Paul, did he have some heavenly revelation and divine commissioning? In 1922 had he arrived in Three Hills like this, or had he grown in grace as we also could grow? As we got to know him, we found several surprising answers. But it was all God's grace, he told us.

The Making of Maxwell

"It's a miracle to me that I ever got delivered!" he commented in recalling his feckless life before he met Christ as Savior. "As far as I know, none of those I hobnobbed with ever came to Christ."

It was God's grace that "hounded him to heaven"[1] to find salvation, and God's grace that "crowded him to Christ" to experience the Cross in his life. And he pointed to his Aunt Christina as the one who not

---

[1] Leslie's Grandpa Anderson set a godly example of Bible reading, and God used the fiery "old-time" preaching of Methodist "revivalists" to bring him to the point of conviction and repentance.

only prayed him into the Kingdom but also hung on to him in prayer as he grew spiritually.

"How else do you explain how she found me a job to keep me out of mischief, and how God saved me from a dissolute life, kept me physically and spiritually in the army, and provided a Bible school right nearby, where I learned to walk with the Lord?" he asked.

Godly grandparents had drilled into his memory a verse he'd never forget: "Thou God seest me!" But Leslie lived carelessly—although the death of his nine-year-old brother, Ernest, made 11-year-old Leslie think of eternity. Even that sobering moment seemed to fade during his teens, until at 20 he came under deep conviction and turned to the Savior one night. He began reading the Scriptures avidly.

During World War I he served with the US Army in France. Above his bunk he hung a motto Aunt Christina sent him: "The Blood of Jesus Christ, God's Son, Cleanseth Us from All Sin."

When his father died shortly after Leslie was discharged, the young war veteran shouldered the care of his widowed mother and her seven remaining younger children. Although he felt the need for Bible study, that seemed out of the question. He had no money to go away for studies—and anyway, he needed to stick close to home to handle family responsibilities.

Then in God's providence, Midland Bible Institute opened in nearby Kansas City. He could take classes and still work part-time to send monthly help to his mother. The principal was William C. Stevens,[1] who had previously been principal of the Missionary Training Institute, which became Nyack College of the C&MA, NY. A deeply spiritual man, Stevens instructed his students in the way of the Cross, but it took a humiliating experience to bring the bombastic Leslie Maxwell to embrace the Cross in his life.

---

[1] A scholarly linguist, theologian, and author of seven books, Stevens earned degrees at Union Seminary, did post-graduate studies in Germany, and became a Presbyterian minister before joining the C&MA.

Zealous Leslie had been quick to set himself up as judge of another student's actions. When Stevens showed him how presumptuous he'd been, the Holy Spirit convicted him. He confessed with tears in front of the other students.

Struggle through the Night

That night Leslie spent in prayer and Bible reading, longing to know more intimately "Christ and the power of his resurrection."[1] True, he'd already found salvation, he'd even witnessed to others, and he'd zealously studied the Scriptures—but self had never been placed on the Cross. The Holy Spirit searched his heart.

Why had he sought to judge his fellow student without talking face to face. Why had he informed other students instead? Had he done it in the spirit of love or for self-glory? Leslie was learning about personal identification with the death and resurrection of Jesus Christ.

At Midland Bible Institute he'd been nervous about public speaking—something it was difficult for us to imagine! Obviously, the rookie Bible teacher of 1922 had grown through the years—"in the school of hard knocks," he called it.

Midland stayed open just long enough for him to graduate before it closed a year later.[2]

During his last year that letter from far-away Canada arrived. Before setting off for Three Hills, Leslie told his mother he'd somehow continue sending her $40.00 a month.

So the young Bible school graduate had arrived in Three Hills with something of the message of the Cross in the life of the believer. The same Holy Spirit who had worked in Leslie Maxwell back in Kansas was working in the life of the farmer who invited him to Canada, Fergus

---

[1] Philippians 3.10.
[2] Midland opened in 1918, closing in 1923, a year after Leslie's graduation.

Kirk. Fergus had struggled with his personal goals and had committed himself to obey his Lord. God had prepared the team. But both of them continued learning about the Cross life as the trials in the work forced them to take up the Cross daily in discipleship.

During our time at school, listening to this ebullient ("ebullient"— that was the word exactly!¹) teacher expound with such confidence, none of us could imagine he'd ever been assailed by anxiety and fear. But Maxwell's peace and confidence had come through experiences that forced him to "take up his Cross."

Maxwell—*Worried to Death?*

"I remember a time in the early years, when I'd wake at 4 in the morning, worried to death over a threat!" LE confessed. "An elder and a minister in Three Hills threatened to put me in jail for three years. In our school paper I'd expressed my sadness that the elder's son—a young man who'd earlier professed to follow Christ—had returned from seminary with his faith ruined. The young man clearly showed that in his 'modernist' preaching. But the father shook with rage, charging me with 'libeling' his son.

"Did I suffer! I worried and fretted. The principal of Prairie in prison! What would happen to the school? Worrying affected my study and preaching. I'd try to get peace in my head, but my heart would be filled with anxiety. God didn't seem to chasten me but simply reminded me, 'Be still!' In Isaiah 26.3 I read: 'Thou wilt keep him in perfect peace, whose mind is stayed on thee, because he trusteth in thee' [AV]. I was trying to trust, but I had to learn that trusting begins in the heart, not the mind."

About a month later, after Maxwell had preached against "modernism" on his radio broadcast, Dorothy Miller, his one-time Bible

---

¹ *Ebullient*—bubbling over with fervor, enthusiasm, excitement.

teacher and now vice-principal, commented, "Well, you said all you dare say, didn't you!"

"Did she mean I was too outspoken—too rash?" LE wondered. "Fear took hold of me all over again. There goes my radio time, I thought—and the school's reputation! I could only offer a panicky prayer: 'Lord, if something terrible doesn't come out of that broadcast, I'll miss my guess!'"

In his anxiety, Maxwell thought of the disciples' reaction when they were imprisoned and beaten for their faith: "Rejoicing that they were counted worthy to suffer shame for his name."[1]

"I had to confess to God that I didn't count it a privilege, much less enjoy, suffering for his name!" LE recalled. "It was a real heart confession. This was something I'd never faced—an issue that would continue to haunt me unless I settled it. All at once the burden of the past month, all my worry and struggle to trust and find peace—they were gone. That day I found victory and experienced perfect peace.

"No one sued us. The time came when that elder's wife died. She'd requested that I take the funeral. So the man and his son had to sit through the funeral message I gave!"

Our mentor had had to learn by embracing the Cross in his own life. That's why he could lead us.

Hungry for More

Maxwell also grew in understanding as he devoured the works of men and women who, like Enoch, had walked with God—people like Horatius Bonar, Amy Carmichael, Oswald Chambers, Charles G. Finney, A. J. Gordon, Madame Guyon, Frances Ridley Havergal, Roy Hession, F. J. Huegel, William Law, Robert Murray McCheyne,

---

[1] Acts 5.41 (AV)

H. C. G. Moule, Andrew Murray, Jessie Penn-Lewis, Hannah Whitall Smith, Charles Spurgeon, Gerhard Ter Steegen, and others. Each one had found the truth of identification with Christ in his death and resurrection.

We could list a library of books that helped to shape Maxwell's message. In the foregoing pages we've mentioned several key volumes. One that LE's son-in-law, Bob Spaulding, would add is a book he inherited from LE's personal library.

"I'm convinced that David Gracey's scholarly book, *Sin and the Unfolding of Salvation*,[1] greatly influenced LE's message—especially his teaching on Law and Grace," Spaulding states. "It is well underlined, with comments and cross-references in LE's hand in the margins.

"If nothing else, it's a commentary on LE's continuing self-education. Professor Gracey was principal of Pastor's College, London, founded by the noted preacher C. H. Spurgeon. The introduction to the book is by Spurgeon's son Thomas."

LE also valued early church fathers and missionaries (such as Augustine, Clement of Rome, Polycarp of Smyrna, Boniface, and Francis of Assisi) as well as contemporary evangelical theologians who applied God's Word to the issues of modern and post-modern society. He respected their scholarship and fidelity to Scripture.

The result of this pilgrimage was Maxwell the Proclaimer, Prophet on the Prairies. Soaked in the Scriptures, he read, absorbed, and distilled insights from these, and then allowed the Holy Spirit to focus the message through teaching in Maxwell's own inimitable way.

"This book is written," Maxwell stated in the preface to *Born Crucified*,[2] "to show the believer that, from the moment he is saved, he

---

[1] Gracey, David, *Sin and the Unfolding of Salvation*. London: Passmore and Alabaster, 1894.
Paul Maxwell and Ted Rendall concur with the importance of this volume to LE.

[2] L.E. Maxwell, *op.cit.*

is so related to the Cross that, if he henceforth fails to live by the Cross, he is an utter contradiction to himself and to his position in Christ.

"The Cross is the key to all situations as well as to all Scripture. If I lose that key, I miss the road not only in the Bible but also in the whole of my life."

"I lost 15 pounds praying for victory."

To anyone who implied he was some angelic messenger who dropped out of the heavens into Three Hills, Maxwell would have responded with an incredulous laugh (right from the diaphragm, voice teacher Aunt Katherine would have noted approvingly). He sometimes recounted experiences of human frailty that contributed to his spiritual growth— and to the message that grew with him.

"As a young Christian I yearned to find spiritual victory in my life," he recalled. "I could see that my Aunt Christina had victory in her life, so I read all kinds of tracts she gave me on 'victorious living' and overcoming the Old Nature. I tried praying the Old Man out and the New Man in. I struggled over this so much that I lost 15 pounds—excess weight I'd picked up in the Army. But to no avail. I seemed to get victory and then lose it. I was miserable."

"Later in Bible school I had that humiliating experience. God used it to show me I no longer needed to struggle to get rid of the Old Man and let the New Man in. For the first time I really believed what Paul wrote in Galatians 2.20: 'I have been crucified with Christ; yet no longer I but Christ liveth in me' [AV]. I didn't have to struggle in prayer but rather accept that when I was saved, I was 'crucified with Christ.' That was the beginning of stepping into victory!"

This teacher who became a giant of faith (though he'd never label himself such) readily acknowledged men and women who had helped his spiritual growth, including Aunt Christina and W. C. Stevens. Later in life he credited his sweetheart, Pearl, for her part in his personal growth throughout their marriage.

Prayer was a major part of Maxwell's life. Before the other members of his family stirred, he'd be kneeling at his bedside, offering himself afresh to the Lord for the day and covering its events in prayer. While on his daily exercise walk, he brought requests before God. He covered every interview, every lesson, every business session in prayer.

"Once at Lake Sammamish Bible camp, I was sitting on a bench with friends as Mr. Maxwell passed without noticing us," remembers Jeannette Chugg ('50). "As he walked along the path he was praying. Every now and then he'd clap his hands and laugh. He was rejoicing in the Lord as he walked and prayed, not conscious that anyone else could hear him!"

Objective Self-Assessment

Academically, Maxwell never wanted to imply he was "man-made"— that is, the product of some institutional system. While he acknowledged his indebtedness to many others, he considered any achievement to be all of grace.

Maxwell had come to the place where he looked upon himself as unworthy to be a disciple of Christ, and yet in Christ able to "do all things."[1] He'd learned to think of himself objectively, "not more highly than [he] ought to, but with sober judgment, in accordance with the measure of faith God has given...."[2] Did he have spiritual gifts? Yes. Was he proud about them? No. Did he disparage them? No. He simply gave thanks for what God had given and returned all to the service of God.

"The Apostle Paul was a scholar, trained under the great teacher Gamaliel," Maxwell pointed out. "Yet that did not make him a man of God. Quite the opposite! It was only when he himself met with the Lord and gave himself completely to the one whom he had been persecuting, that Saul became Paul—an anointed messenger of God."

---

1 Philippians 4.13.

2 Romans 12.3. Greek scholar Kenneth Wuest renders "sober" as "sensible appraisal."

"Daddy Maxwell had a unique anointing from the Holy Spirit that made him what he was," his son-in-law, Allen, later commented. "This was God's unique gift to him that made him fit for the calling he had. There's no other way to explain him fully."

Iddings was right. His father-in-law emphasized the need for the Holy Spirit to anoint each of us for the task to which he would call us. At the same time, Maxwell would never have wanted us to think he was some anointed icon beyond the realm of our own potential experience with God. He taught the importance of denying self and also obeying God's will—"abandoned to Christ," he described it. Then the Holy Spirit would anoint the gifts he had given as we offered them back to him. That potential was available to each one of us.

The Making of the Message

But how to describe his message? Was it the Keswick Message? The Deeper Life? The Abundant Life? The Victorious Life? Sanctification? The Second Blessing? People tended to use different labels.

While many of LE's pungent sayings arose from his own creative mind, he also borrowed quotes and illustrations from different sources. Yet his message was very much his own, for it resulted from his walk with God and his saturation in the Scriptures. He sought to avoid the spiritual pride that can arise from terms such as the Deeper Life and the impression of belonging to an inner circle of super saints. "Walking in the Spirit" was neither a cult nor a generalization. Maxwell had a specific biblical concept with a practical application. "A lot of things don't need praying about; they need obeying about!" he told us.

Sanctification he did teach, but not as a *fait accompli*—a completed experience that banished "the Old Nature" and replaced it with "the New Nature." In writing to my father after the 1946 student revival, I had verged on that concept—"Harold Fuller is a pile of ashes." I even wrote the date in my Bible flyleaf, as if that was that! I had to learn what the Apostle Paul meant by the constant struggle between the flesh and the Spirit. I had to learn to "die daily"—no, more than just daily: constantly.

Sanctification was a continuing work of the Holy Spirit, not a "Second Blessing" that accompanied a "Baptism in the Spirit." When we were "born again" of the Spirit, we were baptized into Christ, LE taught. That meant the Holy Spirit was living within us, helping us grow into the image of God's Son.[1] We could remain spiritual babes because of sin, disobedience, or by not allowing Christ's Spirit to have his way. If so, we needed to repent and accept Christ's Lordship—completely.

For many, this was a crisis experience following conversion (hence the term "Second Blessing" used by some), but being "conformed to the likeness of [God's] Son" should be a continuing process, LE taught.

Call it what one might, the message was that victorious spiritual living came through experiencing the Cross of Christ in our lives.

---

[1] Romans 8.29.

Chapter 10: Defining the Crux

"The Cross contradicts human nature at every point."—LEM

SO WHAT IS THIS CROSS?

"WHAT DOES THE CROSS MEAN TO YOU?" we students asked a railroad vendor en route to Three Hills. Vendors boarded the train at one station on the prairies, selling refreshments and trinkets to passengers until a stop further along (where they'd get off and wait for a passenger train going the opposite way). Discovering that our railroad car was filled with Bible school students, this vendor offered ornamental crosses on necklaces and tiepins. (Obvious contextualization!)

"A dollar fifty!" he shot back. He'd seen Bible school students before and wasn't about to get involved in a theological discussion.

We students arrived at Prairie with different concepts of the Cross. We all agreed it represented our salvation. Some came from denominations that treated the Cross as an icon. Someone irreverently joked about the child who asked for his favorite hymn about the cross-eyed bear. (He meant the hymn with the line, "Gladly the Cross I'd bear . . .")

"I guess my roommate is the cross I've been given to bear!" sighed one frustrated student. "What a cross to bear through life!" someone exclaimed about a spastic child. Human nature tended to see an affliction or burden as some kind of fate we must manfully bear for Christ's sake. Seeing the Cross that way could lead to morbid gratification through suffering—like monks who wore hair shirts or whipped themselves to enter into Christ's sufferings!

Just what, then, was the "Cross" at the center of the message of Prairie's founder? He referred to "the Cross in the life of the believer." We understood (we thought) the illustration of a grain of wheat needing to die before it could bring forth fruit. So we needed to die to self, place

103

our lives on the altar, so to speak, and God would resurrect our talents and use them to his glory? (Now *that's* a mix of metaphors!)

Not quite. We were getting close to the meaning, but there was more than that. The grain of wheat was an apt illustration—and of course scriptural. But we could wrongly interpret it as a time of hibernation for the self life. Identifying ourselves with the death and resurrection of Christ implied a deeper meaning—one we could easily miss, as I did in my first-semester act of self-immolation—"a pile of ashes."

Not an Add-On

Was it an add-on concept to the Cross of salvation? Maxwell often warned against the Galatian heresy of needing "Christ-plus": faith was all well and good, but to really achieve acceptance with God, believers (Jew and Gentile) needed also to keep the rituals of the Law.

Then there was the Corinthian heresy: believers also had to have a charismatic experience before they were really sanctified.

Or the Colossian heresy pressed by Gnostic elements in the early church: "Christ plus knowledge through special revelation," the "Word of Wisdom."

To Eastern Orthodox Christians, the Cross was a holy icon; to Roman Catholics, a sacred means of grace; to the superstitious poor, a good luck charm. Communists hated it, Jews resented it.

More contemporary distortions of the Cross were on the way. By mid-century, Liberation Theology—a Marxist hermeneutic of society— was infiltrating Latin American Christianity. In its view, the Cross sanctioned violent overthrow of oppression; therefore elements in the church "embraced" it for political purposes. On the other hand, radical feminists opposed the Cross because they viewed it as condoning violence by (male) oppressors!

The Cross of Christ was none of the above, LE told us. Instead of adding something to the salvation experience, he reduced it to the basic truth. We listened carefully so as not to miss the point. Many of us carried on silent dialogues with our mentor as he taught, line upon line, truth on truth, text after text:[1]

"Salvation became possible only through the death of Christ as our sacrifice for sin. He paid the price; only he, the sinless Son of God, could satisfy the holiness of God by fulfilling the Law. God's holiness decreed the death penalty for sin—and Christ paid that penalty for us."

[Yes, yes! We understand that!]

"But that's not some Universalist truism that we're meant to affirm intellectually and be on our way—our own way. When Christ died on the Cross, we with our sins were nailed there in his body. Salvation became ours potentially, because he died that 'whosoever' believes should not perish but have everlasting life. But none of us personally experienced salvation until we admitted that we were there on that Cross with Christ in his death."

[But we were saved when we accepted Christ as our Savior. We simply knew he loved us; we repented of our sin and trusted in him. We know that didn't just give us a free ticket to Heaven—a pardon from going to Hell, so we could live for ourselves. But you mean more was involved?]

The Cross Involves More?

"The Holy Spirit brought you to the place of accepting eternal life through Jesus Christ," LE continued. "You may not have understood at the time what took place. But when you admitted you were a sinner for whom Christ died, in reality you were saying, 'That's right—he died for me, in my place. I was there hanging on the Cross in the person of my

---

[1] The following paragraphs are a collation of L. E. Maxwell's teaching, not verbatim quotations.

Savior. That's what my sinful self deserved. That's the punishment I received—except that Christ took it for me. It's the only way I can enter into eternal life.

"The Holy Father now sees me 'accepted in the Beloved,' in the death and resurrection of his Son. Don't you see—you and I were spiritually 'born crucified'!"

[We're beginning to see. That's what you mean by being "Born Crucified." But what's the application to us now?]

"Beloved, although that's our position, many of us deny it by our lives. We live for self. We follow the ways of the flesh. We try to benefit by the crucifixion while trying to escape crucifixion! An external cross demands an internal cross. We're just like the carnal Corinthian Christians Paul wrote to!"

Then LE quoted what was probably his life Scripture, Galatians 2.20 (AV): "I am crucified with Christ; nevertheless I live, yet not I, but Christ liveth in me; and the life which I now live in the flesh I live by the faith of the Son of God, who loved me and gave himself for me."

[OK. We received eternal life through being crucified with Christ. When we accepted him as Savior, that became our position. And we live now only by his life. We agree. But . . . but, we know we aren't experiencing his life as we want to. How do we get there?]

"The Apostle Paul experienced the tension between his potential position in Christ and his daily experience," LE was telling us. "We read his dialogue with himself in the book of Romans. At last he cried out, 'O wretched man that I am, who shall deliver me from this body of death?' (Rom. 7.24). And of course the answer was Christ himself. But Paul also took us through the process."

[That took us back to the book of Romans, where Paul wrote of the need to "reckon yourselves to be dead unto sin and alive unto Christ." This was rich stuff. So the Cross in the life of the believer was basically

embracing the Cross of Christ in our daily living. That meant not only dying to self daily but also in the little things as well as the big things that crossed our paths. Wow! Could we do it?]

"Yet not I—it is Christ that lives in me."

[Oh! But this Cross in our lives—what was it really? We know it's not an icon or an ornament, and you say it's not the aches and pains and trials that we so often talk about as "the cross God has given me to bear." And what's it got to do with the Law?]

What's the Law's Purpose?

Romans held the answer once more. Many students had heard the prevalent teaching that the Law was the way to righteousness given by God to Moses, and that Jesus ushered in a new era called the Age of Grace. Maxwell had a different viewpoint. Grace, he maintained, had always been available—from Adam on through Abraham and Moses. Through the Ark of the Covenant, repentant sinners could present their offerings at the Mercy Seat and, by faith, receive forgiveness. The sacrifice for sin symbolized Christ's eternal sacrifice—the lamb slain since the creation of the world (Rev. 13.8).

So what purpose the Law? It, LE taught, was a "schoolmaster" (Galatians 3.24) to drive sinners to the eternal sacrifice for sin. In his book, *Crowded to Christ*, he explained his point. For the Jews, the Law became an end in itself. Apart from those who were called "children of Abraham" because of their faith, most Jews trusted in observation of the jots and tittles of the Law as the means of their salvation. They failed to see the Law as God's instrument to make us plead "guilty" and in repentance and faith accept the gift of salvation. And Gentiles, in essence, do exactly the same in seeking salvation by works.

Followers of other religions do likewise.

We realized afresh that's what makes the Gospel of Christ such

Good News—Jesus took upon himself the curse of the Law for us; he died for our sins. And we receive eternal life by accepting that fact. Potentially we ourselves died in Christ's death and became alive eternally in his resurrection life.

"Today," LE continued, "God will use anything to drive us to himself, to that position of denying self, of dying to self and living to righteousness. It may be some difficult relationship, it may be physical suffering, it may be some crisis or shortage. We can embrace it as the means of shutting us up to God, or we can fret under it and continue in self-will. That's not our 'cross'; it's simply the instrument God is trying to use to make us take up Christ's cross and follow him in that particular situation."

[So all those distressing things we'd tended to call "our cross" were really opportunities to embrace the real Cross in our lives? To die to self and become alive to righteousness? Yes—to identify ourselves with Christ on the Cross!]

The Cross in the life of the believer. This was not some cult, some optional "add-on." It was a significant aspect of God's super-instrument of salvation, sanctification, and service: the Cross. We were beginning to see why the death-resurrection experience (some would call it "sanctification"—but that word has its own "baggage") was the vital link between salvation and service—the key to Maxwell's message, the secret of the power in his own life.

A Coin with Two Sides

"If I'm dead and buried, you can come to the cemetery, stand on my gravestone, and call me the worst scoundrel in town," said LE, graphically illustrating his core message: "We were therefore buried with [Christ] through baptism into his death, that just as Christ was raised from the dead through the glory of the Father, we too may live a new life."[1]

Defining the Crux

"Whatever you call me, I won't respond. The next person can come and praise me to the sky. I still won't respond. You see, I'm dead. Hallelujah—in Christ I'm dead to sin. Sin has no claim on me."

Maxwell's favorite illustration was about George Wyatt, who was called to bear arms during the American Civil War. Since Wyatt had a wife and six children, a single young man named Richard Pratt volunteered to take his place—which meant taking his identity also. Pratt unfortunately died in action. As the war continued, conscriptors came across Wyatt and sought to draft him again. Wyatt successfully proved to the authorities that, according to their own records, he had died in the person of Pratt. That placed him beyond the claim of the draft law.

"There we have the truth of identification in a nutshell," Maxwell wrote in his book *Born Crucified.*[2] "Wyatt died in the person of his representative!"

But his was a two-fold truth. LE didn't stop at dying to self. While he knew that we'd never give up the self life unless the Holy Spirit brought us to that Cross experience, he also knew that by itself, dying to self could be a truncated objective. It was not an end in itself. It was only a passage to victorious living—the true objective God has in mind for each believer.

So our mentor went on to the second half of the verse— the resurrected life. "We are spiritually born crucified—identified with Christ in his death—so that we can live the resurrected life, the victorious life," he explained. "That's how God wants us to live! Praise the Lord!"

I'll never forget being overwhelmed by the truth of that one day as LE opened up Galatians 2.20 (AV): "*I am crucified with Christ; nevertheless I live, yet not I, but Christ liveth in me; and the life which I now live in the flesh I live by the faith of the Son of God, who loved me and gave himself for me.*"

---

[1] Romans 6.4. In using these illustrations, Maxwell was not intending to imply that sin could no longer appeal to us. See page 210.
[2] *Op. cit.*

A New Perspective

Christ's sacrifice I'd accepted since childhood. It was something personal but also a logical transaction I made with God: I accepted Christ's sacrifice for my sin, and he gave me eternal life.

I was typical of most Christians—recognizing the Cross, Christ's vicarious death for our salvation. To many Christians, the cross was only a symbol of their faith. Like me, they were missing the deep meaning of the Cross of Christ. It was almost as if Christendom had lost that meaning; it remained hidden from many believers.

That deeper meaning gripped me as I realized I had no life apart from Christ, and the only way I could receive his life was through "counting" myself dead with him on that cross. True—he died vicariously for me. But here was an amazing deeper, complementary truth: by accepting his death for me, I had died in him.

Talk about "virtual reality"! If he took my place, that meant I deserved to die. Yet as long as I continued living the self-life, I was virtually denying that fact—I was denying that I had died in Christ. If Christ died and rose for me, my only chance of having life was to die to self and rise to newness of life in him. Without Christ I simply had no life; in him I had abundant life—and I'd better start letting Christ (my life) live abundantly through me.

In that moment my Christian life took on a new perspective. As a child I had trusted Jesus as Savior. As a first-year Bible student I had surrendered to him my will. Later I'd learned that rather than becoming (once-for-all) "ashes on God's altar," I was on a pilgrimage. I needed to learn more of the Master; I needed to become Christ-like.

Then a fact burst upon me, like a spiritual dawn: it was not I but Christ! Hadn't I known that since childhood? Yes, but as a Scripture motto, a memorized cliché. Now it took on personal meaning. I was a big zero! "With the rim knocked off," as LE often put it!

"Without me you can do nothing," Jesus had said. Not even become Christ-like? Exactly! I began to understand that conceit and other elements of the old nature would always be ready to revive within me, but that his life was really my only source of spiritual existence. The secret was to "reckon myself dead to sin"—dying, dying, dying to every impulse of the old nature—but "alive to God"—living, living, living through Christ indwelling me. Walking moment by moment in the Spirit.

Chapter 11: The Paradox

"Christ's dying for me makes inevitable my death with him."—LEM

A DOUBLE-EDGED SWORD

M AXWELL SPOKE at Gull Lake Conference with all his usual zest, shaking up the good folk in Michigan about their materialism—particularly their cars!" remembers Ian M. Hay, who became General Director Emeritus of SIM. "During my graduate work at Columbia International University in '50-'51, I read *Born Crucified* and later learned of Maxwell's close friendship with Robert C. McQuilkin."

> Prairie Bible Institute in western Canada and Columbia Bible College and Seminary (as it was earlier known) in the southeast of the United States were thousands of miles apart, each in a different social milieu, yet they shared the same basic message of the victorious life.

McQuilkin's son Robertson, who served as a missionary in Japan before following his father as president of Columbia, remembers the relationship: "My father and L. E. Maxwell had much in common— a firm confidence in the glorious possibility of triumphant Christian living, an unflagging commitment to world evangelism, a powerful pulpit ministry, and a fondness for one another. They weren't alike in much else!

"Of course, R. C. McQuilkin would not have endorsed L. E. Maxwell so heartily if he didn't believe and preach 'born crucified,'" Robertson added. "Nor would Maxwell have sent students to Columbia if he didn't believe and proclaim the life of resurrection power. The emphasis may have differed, but the core message was the same."

Life Follows Death

LE knew the subtlety of the self-life—how it could thrive in heroic commitment, sacrificial volunteerism, and dedicated service to the poor and suffering, even in the most difficult corners of the earth. After all, if it was possible to give one's body to be burned and yet not have love[1], it was just as possible to minister without really identifying with the Cross in one's personal life. He also knew that students could struggle through his classes as an academic exercise to complete the course, yet never experience the "release" of dying to self.

"Years ago I was visiting a couple of Prairie grads taking further studies elsewhere," recalls Bob Spaulding, son-in-law of the Maxwells. "They commented how they had had to 'work their way through Maxwell's message,' but I got the feeling they'd missed 'dying' in the process!"

Our mentor had a specific focus. In spite of its motto at the time, "Training Disciplined Soldiers for Christ," Prairie was not a mill to turn out "Christian workers." Its prime objective was to see Christ formed in us—to help us become disciples who would daily take up our Savior's Cross. Ministry would follow.

> *"Paradox: contrary to commonly accepted opinion."*
> *—Random House Dictionary.*

So the death-to-life paradox described the Christian life. I realized it shouldn't surprise us. The earthly life of Jesus was a paradox—and so was his death. Principal Maxwell grasped the Paradox of the Cross and applied it to us who want to be disciples of Jesus. It is a simple yet profound paradox. Self-evident yet self-contradictory. Logical in an awesome sense, yet beyond earthly reason. Liberating truth that offends

---

[1] 1 Corinthians 13.1-3

human nature. Maxwell opened up mysteries of the spiritual life—"hidden" secrets because largely undiscovered, nevertheless open secrets.

Missing Link of the Christian Life

In fact, Maxwell saw a missing link in the experience of a Christian who skipped from accepting Christ as Savior (justification) right into service (consecration). The personal death-and-resurrection experience was a vital part of our pilgrimage. Without that link, there was a spiritual hiatus in our walk with God. This sequence was one of LE's most important truths. It helped explain the moral casualties littering the spiritual battlefield.

Thinking back to the campus revival of 1946, I realized how quick many of us were to rush into frenetic witnessing. "Personal evangelism," as we called it, was right—a responsibility to the world around. But did the objects of our witness see only dedicated self, or did they see the love of Jesus Christ? We knew the Cross of salvation, and we presented the redeeming Cross to sinners, but we had much to learn about the power of the Cross in our own lives.

"In some of our best churches," wrote Maxwell, "[Christians] have been taken from the justification of Romans 5.1 to the truth of consecration as set forth in Romans 12.1, 2. . . . [But] the blessed truths clustering around our death-resurrection union with Christ, as set forth in Romans 6-8, lay the basis for a successful consecration—so clearly set forth in Romans 12.1, 2."[1]

"The flesh seeks to glory in God's very presence," Maxwell reminded us. "Martin Luther wrote, 'It is the continual purpose of the flesh to come to the throne without being crucified!'"[2]

It was scary to realize we could go out as preachers, missionaries,

---

[1] L.E. Maxwell, *Born Crucified,* op.cit., pp43,44. Romans 12.1,22 begins "Therefore . . . in view of God's mercies, offer your bodies as living sacrifices."
[2] Stephen Spaulding, *op. cit.* p. 233.

musicians, "worship" leaders, teachers—zealously "serving" without having experienced the vital step between salvation and consecration. We began to see the importance of this "missing step" in a disciple's pilgrimage. Many in Christian service were hyper-active for God, but so often in self-promotion. Then there were other disciples whose ministries showed forth Christ, not self. LE was fond of quoting the poem,[1]

> *To learn—to learn, and yet to learn while life goes by,*
> *So pass the student days,*
> *And thus be great and do great things and die*
> *And lie, embalmed with praise.*
>
> *My work is but to lose and to forget,*
> *Thus small, despised to be,*
> *All to unlearn, this task before me set:*
> *Unlearn all else but Thee.* (Anon.)

Stammering into Liberty

Maxwell's classes on Romans helped students experience this sequence. Norman D. Carlson was one. In childhood he'd been afraid to talk because of a stammering problem. When his sister often had to interpret for him, that was further humiliation. Later studying Romans at Prairie, he found a sense of grace—freedom, liberty in Christ!

It might seem unbelievable that Norm found self-assurance from the book of Romans, where Paul wrote, "There is none that does good, no not one!" Where Paul cried out, "O wretched man that I am!" Didn't he state, "All have sinned and come short of the glory of God"? And "I am carnal, sold under sin"?

But that's how Norm found liberty. The classes on Romans helped Norm see beyond the penalty of the Law, right to the Cross; beyond the

---

[1] Cited by Stephen Spaulding, *op. cit.* p. 240.

wages of sin, death, to victorious life in the risen Savior. He read Paul's affirming words, "There is now no condemnation to them who are in Christ Jesus." He realized that in Christ he indeed was "special" as he read, "You did not receive a spirit that makes you a slave again to fear, but you received the Spirit of sonship."[1]

When Norm had to give a sermon in Homiletics class, he opened his mouth and amazed himself—he didn't stammer! It was a deliverance, yet one he never boasted of—it was just part of his pilgrimage as a disciple of Christ.

And how much self-confidence did he gain? One day he asked the principal for his daughter Miriam's hand in marriage. (See Family Reminiscences, Chapter 24.)

Looking into Blinding Light—and Seeing!

Gradually the pieces of Maxwell's message were clicking into place. I'd read or heard many messages on "the Deeper Spiritual Life" or "Victorious Living." My father had taught about the grain of wheat needing to die before bringing forth life, but I hadn't really understood the message. Nowhere else had I heard such stress on dying to self. Was LE hung up on death or was he being morbid? I came to realize that neither was true. His emphasis stemmed from an awareness (a personal revelation?) of two things:
> The holiness of God.
> The awfulness of sin.

At first I had little understanding of God's holiness. Oh, since childhood I'd sung "Holy! holy! holy! Lord God almighty!" on Sunday mornings. But Isaiah's exclamation, "I am a man of unclean lips!" made us all sit up and think.

Was this noted prophet of Israel making such a statement? Wasn't

---

[1] Scriptures in these paragraphs: Romans 3.12; 7.24; 3.23; 7.14; 8.1; 8.15.

this Isaiah who would be entrusted with the amazing announcement of the Messiah's impending birth and his vicarious sacrifice for us all?[1] Yet this man we'd call "a holy prophet" was overcome with his own unworthiness when he caught a glimpse of the holiness of God! Where did that leave the rest of us, who thoughtlessly almost wallowed in the muck of the world's sin—"the lust of the flesh, the lust of the eyes, and the pride of life"?[2]

"Even If It Makes Me Throw Up!"

"I'm asking God to help me understand how holy he is," confided Jim Birkitt after one class. Like me, he'd served in World War II. "I want to see sin as God sees it, even if it makes me throw up!" A little melodramatic, I thought—yet John quotes the Spirit as saying lukewarm Christians cause God to "spew them out of his mouth." I began to realize I knew very little about God's holiness and therefore less about the awfulness of sin. Sin could not survive in the holy presence of "our God who is a consuming fire."[3]

I thought back to my Navy days. After growing up in a very protected Christian environment, enlistment for me was like being plucked from a blossoming garden and tossed into a cesspool, morally speaking. Although God did keep me, the sin all around me seemed so, well . . . natural. The world ran on the principles of "lust of the flesh, lust of the eyes, and the pride of life—all that is in the world." My shipmates were good guys serving a good cause. Their immoral lives were just part of the culture, weren't they?

Then at Prairie we students began to realize how much "all that is in the world" (and therefore "not of the Father") had permeated our own hearts, our worldview, even our churches. Increasingly, there was very little difference between the average Christian's morality and that of the average non-believer.[3]

---

[1] Isaiah 9.1-7; 53.1-12.

[2] 1 John 2.16.

[3] Hebrews 12.29.

[4] For instance, a recent poll indicates that spousal abuse and divorce are as common among evangelical church members as among non-church members in North America.

As we thought of churches across our nations, we realized many were failing to fill the niche of holy living that the world, "without hope and without God,"[1] could not fill. Did we have the mistaken belief that we could somehow communicate the gospel more effectively by becoming more like the world? Scripture warned against that.[2]

Now I was beginning to see myself and my world in a new light. I had to understand that as fallen creatures, we have no consciousness of sin apart from conscience (too often weak or dead or corrupted), the Word of God, and the work of the Holy Spirit.[3]

What Does a Holy God Think of Sin?

But LE knew from his own youth, from his experience in the world, and from his study of Scripture, that the old nature was completely fallen, beyond repair. Only the new nature of Christ could lead us into victorious living.

In the light of God's pure holiness, Maxwell understood the truth of God's description of mankind. I think he'd looked into the human heart and seen something worse than mere death. He'd seen the hideous nature of sin, which had brought God's sentence of death.

LE took us through the Scripture's description of total human depravity: In Noah's day, "God saw that every intent of the thoughts of [man's] heart was only evil continually." Some two thousand years later, Isaiah declared, "All our righteousnesses are as filthy rags." Jeremiah added God's description: "The heart is deceitful above all things, and desperately wicked; who can know it?" Centuries passed, the Messiah came, and the Rabbi *cum* Apostle Paul still stated categorically, "There is none that does good—no not one." In his letter to Rome he even described our fallen nature—true of all humanity, without exception.[4]

---

[1] Ephesians 2.12.
[2] Romans 12.2.
[3] Who, Jesus said, will "reprove the world of sin and of righteousness" (John 16.8).
[4] Scriptures in this paragraph: Genesis 6.5; Isaiah 64.6; Jeremiah 17.9; Romans 1.18-32; 3.23.

Maxwell pointed out that the judgments of the Old Testament and the Crucifixion of the New Testament are incomprehensible to human nature unless seen in the light of God's holiness. Without that understanding, people could even resent God's demands—making him out to be a bully, despot, tyrant, or vengeful monster. That might be if God were not the Divine Being and man were a god, we realized.

Did Jim Birkitt and many others of us want to understand how God viewed sin? LE pointed to Christ on the cross. The sinless Son of God gave his life for us because our sin was so offensive, so abhorrent, to the holiness of God. He became sin for us? Unthinkable! Because of the awfulness of sin, the Father could not look upon his Son? No wonder Jesus cried out, "Father, why have you forsaken me!" It was because of us, our sin. We had our answer, Jim.[1]

Now It Makes Sense

Against this background (the heinousness of sin against a holy God), Maxwell's emphasis on dying to the old nature in order to experience Christ's new life made sense.

Without that dual consciousness, our mentor's message could sound macabre, negative. But LE knew that the old nature could never be made presentable to win righteousness. "You shall surely die," the Creator had warned innocent Adam and Eve if they sinned. And they did die: "As by one man sin entered into the world, and so death through sin spread to all men ...."[2] Since the old nature became the incarnation of death, the only escape was to "reckon it" to be crucified on Christ's cross.

"Were we not declared righteous in Christ that we might be holy in life?" LE asked. "Most people want happiness without holiness!"

Like Isaiah, Maxwell had glimpsed God's holiness, and it changed the way he saw himself and sin and the path to life. We had discovered a vital key to understanding Maxwell's message.

---

[1] Jim Burkitt later founded Christian Enterprises, which included a radio station in the Carolinas.
[2] Romans 5.12.

Strength out of Weakness

We'd come to the school that promised to prepare disciplined soldiers for Christ. LE taught that before we could go out to do battle with the enemy of souls, we first needed to surrender ourselves to Christ. But we war veterans hadn't fought against Hitler and other tyrants by being weak. It seemed like another paradox. It certainly wasn't the world's way of winning battles. It wasn't human nature. In chapel we'd sing, "Onward Christian soldiers, marching as to war," but then our mentor also quoted from George Matheson's poem:[1]

> *Make me a captive, Lord,*
> *And then I shall be free;*
> *Force me to render up my sword,*
> *And I shall conqueror be.*
> *My will is not my own*
> *Till Thou has made it Thine;*
> *If it would reach a monarch's throne,*
> *It must its crown resign.*

This was the paradox that the German philosopher Friedrich Nietzsche misunderstood and caricaturized. Nietzsche despised Christianity above all religions for what he saw as its appeal to weakness. His ideal was "Aryan manhood"—"everything that heightens the feeling of power in man, the will to power, power itself."

"What is more harmful than any vice?" he asked. "Active pity for all the failures and the weak: Christianity." Misunderstanding the paradox of biblical Christianity (strength out of weakness, life out of death), Nietzsche set the stage for the rise of Adolph Hitler and Nazism—and the world war a number of us had just been helping to fight.

We were two centuries removed from The Enlightenment—which

---

[1] Matheson (1842-1906) was a Church of Scotland minister, orator, and author. His best known hymn is "O Love that will not let me go"—penned out of spiritual victory over deep discouragement and affliction.

was supposed to usher in a new rationalistic era of steadily improving humanity, evolving into superman. Two devastating world wars had disillusioned the idealists. But society, even Christians, seemed to act as if the fallen nature could evolve into goodness—a Buddhist philosophy. At Prairie we learned that only through death could we achieve life.

Opening up the paradox, LE quoted the medieval mystic, Francis of Assisi:

"God is a tower without a stair, and his perfection loves despair."

Ah, yes! We recalled the Apostle Paul's despairing cry: "Oh wretched man that I am!" It was all part of the paradox of the life and death of Jesus. The long-anticipated Messiah who fed the multitudes bread refused to become their Bread King. Instead he announced the way into the Kingdom was by "eating his flesh and drinking his blood"—forecasting his crucifixion instead of his coronation. No wonder even some of his own disciples found this too difficult to hear—and left him.[1]

A Two-Fold Truth

Many who heard the first part of Maxwell's paradox took offense because they didn't wait to hear him out: "The glorious truth of the Cross is that the blood of Jesus Christ frees us from all sin! Satan no longer has a claim on us. We are not under bondage to the Law, for Christ has fulfilled it. In him we are free from the curse of the law of sin! We are meant to be victorious!"

Although LE knew his strong emphasis on the sinfulness of the flesh (the Adamic nature) was needed to bring us to the foot of the Cross, he also realized that Satan (who quoted Scripture even to Jesus) could use that very teaching to place some believers in bondage and keep them from victorious living.

---

[1] John 6.62-66.

"It's true we are *unimprovable* in our old natures," he reminded us; "but the wonderful truth is we are *unreprovable* in Christ Jesus. Colossians 1.21-22 [AV] tells us, 'You that were sometime alienated and enemies in your mind by wicked works, yet now hath he reconciled in the body of his flesh through death, to present you holy and unblameable and unreproveable in his sight.'"

"After you've come to the Cross and received forgiveness, the Devil may perch on your shoulder like a mocking bird and laugh, 'Aha, aha! See, you've failed again. Just quote this Scripture to him: 'In Christ I am unreprovable.'"

No Condemnation

"'Who shall separate us from the love of God?'" he quoted from the book of Romans, seeking to encourage sincere students who seemed to dwell on their failings instead of crossing their spiritual Jordan into the land of victory. "The thought is that Christ doesn't condemn us, because he's the one who gave himself to remove the condemnation. Note Paul goes on to say, 'Therefore, there is now no condemnation for those who are in Christ Jesus, because through Christ Jesus the law of the Spirit of life set me free from the law of sin and death.'"[1]

The paradox of the Christian life was that we were indeed "worms" and yet "kings and priests." We could reconcile the paradox through becoming dead to self and alive to God. That's what we saw in our mentor on campus. He modeled the victorious life. He didn't go around despondent, defeated, but seemed to exude the "abundant life"—love, joy, peace. Today we might call it "successful living" in spiritual terms.

Most staff and faculty reflected the principal's positive outlook, but there were one or two who did not seem to model love, joy, and peace. Perhaps they bore scars from their own background; perhaps they had stopped at the emphasis on death and not entered into the joyous life

---

[1] Romans 8.1,2.

of liberty. True, they had sacrificed to serve us with professional excellence. They were concerned that we become "disciplined soldiers for Christ." But for whatever reasons, they displayed the scars of death without the healing fragrance of vibrant life.

"God has shown me that his joy was missing from my life," one teacher wrote me years later. She'd taught her classes well, but I don't remember ever hearing her laugh. "I thank the Holy Spirit for freeing me from that kind of bondage." And I gave thanks that she who had helped teach me in class had also grown in her spirit. The Christian walk, after all, is a pilgrimage. We are all learning to walk.

The medieval mystic, Bernard of Clairvaux, expressed this paradox:

We taste of Thee, Thou Living Bread,
And long to feast upon Thee still;
We drink of Thee, the Fountain Head,
And thirst our souls from Thee to fill.

Combined choirs and orchestra annually presented Handle's "Messiah."

Chapter 12: Maturity

"The hardest thing in the world is to keep balanced."—LEM

MAXWELL 1.1—KEEPING BALANCED

SOME PEOPLE CLAIM Prairie is too Calvinistic—once saved, always saved," LE told us. "Others tell us we are too Arminian—you know, saved today, lost tomorrow. Hyper Calvinists say we're tainted. Hyper Arminians say 't'aint enough! The fact both extremes criticize our position should tell us something. They both would like us to teach a polarized position; they want to put us in one camp or another. But, as James M. Gray says, 'Any truth pressed to extremes becomes error.' Or as others have expressed it, 'A text used out of context can become pre-text.' Scripture contains correctives when you are turning from the truth.

"'If we regard the doctrine of sinless perfection as a heresy, we regard contentment with sinful imperfection as a greater heresy.'" LE quoted the noted Bible expositor, A. J. Gordon.[1]

"Remember, the hardest thing in the world is to keep balanced." We called that statement Maxwell 1.1. It was the aphorism he most often repeated:*"The hardest thing in the world is to keep balanced."*

Is it OK to call a doctor?

LE himself was a lesson in balance, for early in his Christian life he believed that divine healing of the body was part of the believer's inheritance assured by Christ's Atonement. Divine physical healing was therefore as guaranteed as was salvation of the soul—a doctrine sometimes called "Healing in the Atonement" (although there are various definitions of this). Therefore, seeking medical help would indicate a lack of faith.

---

[1] Maxwell's views had both a theological and historical base. The moderating influence of Arminianism on Calvanism an dvice versa is documented by Klaus Fiedler in *The Sotry of Faith Missions*. Oxford: Regnum Books, 1994.

At Midland Leslie had run into this emphasis. "My wife and I tried to practice this after we came to Three Hills," LE later recalled. "She almost died—when we should have called a doctor!"

In God's providence, a neighbor called the doctor, and Pearl recovered. It was an experience that helped Leslie and Pearl, early in their marriage, to find the balance of trusting for God's blessing on the use of medical "means." Beyond that, the Maxwells had faith in the Lord's ability to heal when "means" were not available. And throughout, they experienced peaceful trust in God's will to be done.

They again faced spiritual trials when Pearl was hospitalized with double pneumonia some dozen years later.

"Daddy was afraid she was going to die and he'd be left with motherless children," recalls his daughter Ruth. Eleanor remembers her own alarm. "Daddy decided that, besides praying, God wanted him to call the doctor. He did and Mother finally recovered. It was a confirming experience."

At Prairie, while LE did not continue to espouse the doctrine of Healing in the Atonement, his highly respected vice-principal, Dorothy Ruth Miller did. In spite of that difference of view, it was never an issue between them. They were close colleagues.[1]

As an example of the believer's scriptural focus, Maxwell often quoted from C&MA founder A. B. Simpson's hymn:

> *Once it was the blessing; now it is the Lord.*
> *Once it was the feeling; now it is his Word.*
> *Once his gifts I wanted; now the Giver own.*
> *Once I sought for healing; now himself alone.*

"The Holy Spirit applies Scripture to meet you in the direction you are headed," LE explained as he dealt with controversial passages on

---

[1] Miss Miller died in 1944.

other topics, such as Eternal Security. "If you are cocksure of yourself in the flesh, God can give you a warning that will make you tremble. If the Devil is assailing you with doubts, the Word has passages of strong reassurance."

Like a Drunken Peasant

Early in his ministry, young Maxwell had read a booklet that bridged the two poles of Calvinism and Arminianism regarding the believer's security: *The Twofoldness of Divine Truth*. Years later Hector Kirk, brother of Prairie's co-founder Fergus, wrote a booklet on the same theme: *Balanced Security*.[1] Both authors avowed that "there is no contradiction in Scripture," but that on a number of positions the Bible seems to state two different positions in order to present the full truth and correct a one-sided interpretation.

"Man," both quoted Martin Luther as saying, "is like a drunken peasant; you help him up on one side of his horse, and he falls over on the other."

While some observers charged that "Prairie grads don't know where they stand," that was because critics expected them to polarize Scripture. As students we had strong affirmation of our eternal destiny in Christ and of his ability to keep us in time and eternity. But we also took seriously scriptural warnings against spiritual complacency and chronic living in sin. Only the Holy Spirit knew the genuineness of one's conversion and where the dividing line was in a person's life. It was up to us to live as far as possible from that dividing line, assured by the Word and the Spirit of our eternal security in Christ.

Final word—Scripture

And it was always the Word that had "the last word." Maxwell so zealously wanted us to search the Scriptures to find answers to puzzling

---

[1] The two booklets: R. Govett, *The Twofoldness of Divine Truth*. Harrisburg: Christian Publications c.1900; Hector A. Kirk, *Balanced Security*. Maple: Beacon Press, c. 1940.

passages, that he was almost enigmatic on some questions. We knew he knew what he believed. He didn't want us simply to swallow what the lecturer told us, but to become convinced from our own study. Finally before our graduation he opened his treasure chest of personal beliefs and let us peek in.

We discovered that he was indeed a Calvinist, but one who had been saved in a Methodist "camp meeting." While convinced of God's sovereignty, he also respected the positive aspects of the Holiness Movement that included the will of man in accepting God's grace. Maxwell saw biblical balance as "Keeping Truth in Tension."

Whereas some observers felt Prairie "represented the 'sectish' form of Canadian evangelicals"[1], ironically the Institute actually represented a biblical, evangelical ecumenism ("all one in Christ") by its refusal to bear sectarian labels. A non-denominational Bible school like Prairie had to cope with all kinds of church backgrounds and viewpoints.

Boisterous Believer

"How y'all?" waved one new student as he hauled an army fatigue bag from the trunk of the vintage car he and three others had driven all the way from the southern USA. Mutt (his improbable nickname) still wore his camouflage uniform from the US Marine Corps. His people had emigrated from Moravia.

Before arrival in Three Hills, Mutt had received the gospel. He was wonderfully transformed from a foul-mouthed serviceman into such a boisterous believer that some people thought he'd lost his mind. Once when my father appeared on campus, Mutt bounced up to meet him. "Heh y'all!" he bubbled. "You know what? Harold loves *Jesus*!" A reserved Englishman, Dad smiled benignly at the exuberant Mutt.

Now Mutt wanted the full spiritual experience—whatever it was. He sought to speak in tongues and to wrestle with demons. A new

---

[1] Stackhouse, John G. Jr., *Canadian Evangelicalism in the 20th Century.* Toronto: University of Toronto Press, 1993, p. 75.

believer full of questions, he posed such theological but earthy questions as this: "Is it possible to kiss my wife without lusting?" His attitude was a far cry from Mortimer's, the student who had felt guilty for looking at an attractive girl across the balcony. But Mutt needed to learn, among other things, the difference between lust and legitimate passion. The unique Mutt was at least refreshing!

New students arrived with their denominational backgrounds, and some expected everyone to take the same position. LE felt they should be free to keep their particular interpretations after searching the Word for themselves, but that they should not impose a polarized viewpoint on others. On basic doctrines such as the uniqueness of Christ and the way of salvation there could be no compromise.

Differing views on secondary matters enriched campus life. We learned that noted Bible teachers held opposing positions on eschatology, for instance—yet were devout believers and humble servants of God. They sincerely used Scripture to support their different positions on secondary topics.

For instance, Mark Maxwell, at Prairie in the 1970s, was impressed that while his grandfather taught a "pre-trib" rapture, Ted Rendall (who became Vice-Principal in 1960 and Principal in 1967) held a "post-trib" position. "That convinced me—opposing views on secondary matters could be supported from Scripture, and Christians could accept disagreement!"

"The Devil May Run with You"

Prairie taught the reality of spiritual warfare, and the need for the believer to understand that "we wrestle not against flesh and blood but against . . . spiritual wickedness in high places."[1] LE quoted the writings of mystics such as Jessie Penn-Lewis.

But when some Christians taught that believers could be possessed

---

1 Ephesians 6.12.

by the Devil, he drew the line. "When Satan finds he can't overcome you by opposing you, he'll run with you until he slowly pushes you out of God's will," he warned. "Remember, the hardest thing in the world is to keep balanced! May the Lord deliver us from being more occupied with the Devil than we are with Christ!"

When exorcism became popular in some religious circles (and secular movies), a student claimed she was possessed of multiple evil spirits. Fellow students and staff prayed to no avail. "She'd lie writhing on the floor while people prayed over her," LE told me on one of my furloughs. "We finally realized she was enjoying all this attention and pretending to be possessed!"

LE had shown great wisdom during the campus revival that had touched so many of us. After one lengthy session of confession, he took time to instruct us all. "Some of you are making confessions that should be only to the Lord, or between you and the person you have offended. If so, don't come up here to put on a public display!"

The hardest thing in the world is to keep balanced!

The revival emphasized the work of the Holy Spirit, first in convicting of sin and then empowering the believer. There were students who thought of the Spirit's infilling as "the Second Blessing"—a "baptism" by the Spirit distinct from salvation. But LE used the illustration of our lives as a house, into which we have invited Christ as Savior but have reserved certain rooms—whether ambitions or habits or relationships—for ourselves.

In his booklet, *The Pentecostal Baptism,*[1] Maxwell regretted the lack of the Holy Spirit's power in the lives of many a Christian worker, and he rejected the view of some that miracles had been restricted to the first generation of Christians. But he also warned against "wild fire" and seeking feelings or signs of the Spirit's indwelling.

"When I left Three Hills to get married, I forgot to take the wedding ring," he wrote by way of illustration. "But that lack did not keep

[1] Maxwell, L.E., *The Pentecostal Baptism*. Three Hills: Prairie Press, 1971.

us from being happily married....The ring was a sign, but my wife could say, 'What need have I of a ring? I have him!' Concerning some external token of the Spirit's infilling, every believer should be able to say, 'What need have I of a sign? I have him!'"

Keeping balanced!

Gender: No Debate

"Wherever the gospel goes, it betters the lot of women," stated LE. His balanced, courageous thinking was never more evident than in his attitude to the role of women in ministry. At the same time, it highlighted his prior commitment to Scripture—not the wisdom of the day or the traditions of men. In fact, we learned a lot about our mentor because of his attitude to the Gender Debate.

His openness to women in ministry began naturally enough, not as an ideology or crusade. In the first place, he greatly respected his mother, whose care he pledged when his somewhat wastrel of a father died. It was a woman, Aunt Christina, who prayed him into the Kingdom and helped him grow spiritually. Writings of the mystic and missionary Amy Carmichael helped form his sense of spiritual self-discipline. At Midland Bible Institute, his most capable teacher, apart from the principal, was Dorothy Ruth Miller. She had a degree in English from Columbia University and in History from New York University, but most of all she had deep spiritual insights.

"Miss Miller" not only taught the Word but also on occasion preached with great conviction. In the man's world of that era, she won respect and a hearing by her Spirit-filled life and giftedness. Far from being a feminist, she turned down an offer from the President of Wheaton College, Charles A. Blanchard,[1] to take the chair of Bible because she felt that position was a man's place.

"As a girl I never took kindly to the idea of women preachers or

---

[1] Son of Wheaton founder Jonathan Blanchard, an anti-slavery clergyman who declared, "The first alteration which Christianity made in the polity of Judaism was to abrogate the oppressive distinction of sexes [in which] woman had almost no rights."

doctors," she wrote. "So far as I can remember, this arose from a rather poor opinion of women's intellects! Rather funny, is it not?"[1]

"She was a great teacher and speaker—so well organized," remembers Ralph Jacobson. "Some students thought of her as a kind of Moses—a bit untouchable! But we enjoyed her. One Christmas we drove her around Calgary to enjoy the festive decorations.

"'Isn't it wonderful to be able to enjoy this beauty without having the heartache of living in some of those dwellings!' she remarked. I'm sure she, as a lecturer, could have had much of the owner's wealth, but she gave it all up to teach us the Word of God."

As a young believer, she had attended an adult Baptist Sunday School class. The other members—both men and women—asked her to teach *them*! The pastor (although—according to her—"strongly tinged" with male bias) recognized she had "a gift from the Lord" and urged her to develop it theologically. Reluctantly she enrolled at the C&MA school in Nyack, and ended up as faculty there. Eventually she taught at Midland, and then from 1928 to 1943 taught at Prairie.

"All through my Christian service," she later recalled, "I have had the clear, definite witness of the Spirit that I was in his will as to my service." At the same time, she taught her students the family relationships she saw in Scripture. Commenting on the phrase, "be in obedience," Miller stated, "I fear that this is not always observed by those women who are strong on silence in the churches. They do not learn [from] their husbands at home but lay down the law to them!"[2]

With this kind of colleague, Principal Maxwell thought nothing of asking his VP to preach in the school chapel. She was his first choice for replacing him when he ministered elsewhere. In early years, he asked her to preach on Sunday mornings, while he gave the evening message. But when he heard murmuring from certain male worshippers, he reversed the order. That seemed slightly more acceptable to some.

---

[2] Dorothy Ruth Miller, "On Women Speaking," *The Prairie Pastor,* Three Hills, December 1939.
[2] L.E. Maxwell (Ed. Ruth C. Dearing), *op. cit.*

"Daddy believed a woman has a scriptural right to any position of authority for which she is qualified," Lois (Maxwell) Friesen told me. "Miss Miller's messages on Sunday morning blessed us before we realized people weren't supposed to get blessed by a woman preacher! But various factors helped him modify his practices. The fact he yielded to the advice and opinion of fellow workers on disputable issues gave us respect for his sense of judgment."

Respect Yes; Compromise No

At the time, Three Hills was a typical macho "western frontiers" kind of town. Hard working, frugal, and honest, farmers also shared the male worldview of many an immigrant from Europe. Wisely, LE was sensitive to their culture and also that of many students from male-oriented denominational backgrounds. In the words of Scripture, he wouldn't "eat meat" if it "offended his brother."[1]

But while Maxwell avoided any unnecessary offense to the school's community, he wouldn't compromise on truth. The dominant male interpretation of certain Scriptures sent him examining the whole Word. What about women's "keeping silence" in the church and not "having authority over man"? He felt that most commentaries on those few "proof texts" just didn't line up with overall biblical teaching.

Our principal was practicing what he preached: "Scripture is its own best commentary." He was doing exactly what he told us to do: "Search the Scriptures to see if these things are so."[2] This was a distinctive of the man. Soaked first in the Scriptures, he worked from them outwards to their practical application, even if it conflicted with tradition. He didn't look for "proof texts" to support worldviews, but examined popular views to see if they were confirmed by Scripture. Once convinced, he was unafraid to state a biblical view even though it was contrary to commonly accepted opinion.

---

[1] Romans 14.15-20.
[2] As the Berean believers did: Acts 17.11.

Women in Ministry was the result.[1] Studying his Hebrew and Greek lexicons, perusing church history, and reading many sources, both pro and con, he became convinced that the translated renderings of some words and the commentaries on them didn't line up with the tenor of Scripture. When passages appeared to conflict, he looked for the reason until he reconciled the seeming conflict—all within Scripture.

Setting Women Free

"His desire was that women might be set free from what he felt were unscriptural restrictions placed on them by many churches and Christian leaders," wrote Dean of Women and faculty member Ruth C. Dearing in her Introduction to his book. "His only fear was that he might appear to endorse the 'women's lib' movement, which was then coming to the fore.

"Mr. Maxwell's broad view of women's ministry has made possible for me a far wider field of service than I had dreamed possible!" she commented. Once when a male student wanted to drop out of a Bible class taught by Ruth Dearing, LE told him, "You will take her class or you won't graduate!"

As Ted Rendall pointed out in his Foreword to the book, LE did not have access to more recent scholarship on the subject[2] (his failing eyesight hindering further reading). Yet the arguments he put forth from his exhaustive knowledge of Scripture make a clear case for the public ministry of women—although Rendall mentions that he did stop short of endorsing the vexed topic of the ordination of women.

"Inasmuch as we claim to make the Bible our sole rule of faith and practice," Maxwell began his treatise, "we must discuss our subject from the standpoint of God's eternal Word." He proceeded to list from Scripture examples of women leading in community, nation, and reli-

---

[3] *Op cit..* Quotes in this section regarding women in ministry are from the same source.

[1] For instance, he did not seem familiar with evidence that the Apostle Paul was really dealing with Gnostic teaching that Eve was the mother goddess, and that the word translated "authority" in 1 Timothy 2.12 may well be a mis-translation influenced by the dominant worldview of the translators. See Kroeger, Richard Clark, and Catherine Clark Kroeger, *I Suffer Not a Woman: Rethinking 1 Timothy 2.11-15 in the Light of Ancient Evidence.* Grand Rapids: Baker Book House, 1992.

gious life. He pointed out similar instances from church history. "Such anointing [of women] does not controvert the Scriptures but is and always will be in harmony with God's *inerrant* Word" [italics mine—WHF].

Maxwell failed to find Old Testament prohibition of women leading. Instead he faulted rabbinical teaching, male worldview, and medieval tradition as causes of continued bias against women in ministry. He quoted respected evangelical exegetes of earlier decades (such as A. J. Gordon and A. T. Pierson) who rejected such attitudes.

"Fancy Turnings and Twisting"

"Man's attempt to circumvent the clear teaching of Scripture may be likened to a sign over the door of a skillful cabinetmaker's shop: 'Here we do all kinds of fancy turnings and twisting," Maxwell commented with typical pithiness. However, he realized the topic was highly emotional. "Perhaps on no subject more than the present one has there been greater bondage to 'the letter that killeth,'" he wrote.

Some groups sincerely felt he was disobedient to Scripture. After a great response to his messages on the Cross at a Brethren Assembly, a nearby fundamentalist church strongly rebuked the Assembly. "At Prairie Bible Institute women as well as men are allowed to speak in public assemblies!" they charged. But the Assembly astutely reminded the fundamentalist group that even they allowed furloughing women missionaries to address their assemblies.

One shy Prairie graduate, Ingrid Stippa, faced the gender objection after she had conducted a much-appreciated Sunday service for passengers on her Borneo-bound ship. Afterwards, a male missionary pointedly handed her a tract with the heading, "It is a sin for women to preach!"

Another graduate, Leatha Humes, answered wisely when confronted by male seminary students after she'd taught them Religious Instruction. "How can you teach men in view of what Paul said?" they demanded.

"Do you think," she asked, "I should have refused to do what my boss asked me to do, when I was the only one available with the training needed to do that job? Would that not have been a lack of submission?" Debate over!

Although the topic was important, LE didn't allow it to sidetrack him from his central theme: "The Cross in the life of the believer." But the myopia of many men upset some of us. Why couldn't evangelicals investigate the Word as LE had done? Why did they leave it up to radical secularists and liberal theologians to argue for the full emancipation of women in our churches? Unbelievers based their arguments on philosophy and stereotyped us as bigots; whereas we were the ones who should be teaching that the Scriptures truly liberate women. We should be leading their emancipation within our own churches.

"How sad that the prevailing prejudice against women's participation in public ministry deters some from heeding God's call to service," wrote Maxwell. "Go to . . . places where Christianity is not known, and you will see women enslaved, oppressed, and degraded. But where the gospel is preached, where the love of Jesus is magnified, and where the victory of Calvary is proclaimed—there woman is given her proper place as revealed in the Word of God."

Sometimes after a woman speaker described some ordeal in her missionary service, Maxwell exclaimed, "Never man spake like that woman!" He used the moment to challenge men to volunteer to serve in the world's rugged areas.

"Shortly after Grandpa died, and before I left for Liberia," relates granddaughter Ruth L. Maxwell; "a researcher interviewed me about women in ministry. I explained that Grandpa didn't just talk about women in ministry; he enabled them and gave them legitimate roles."

"Your grandfather was a couple of generations ahead of his time!" exclaimed the visitor.

Chapter 13: Lordship

"The Holy Spirit cannot guide where he does not govern."—LEM

"LORD OF ALL OR NOT AT ALL"

C HRIST IS LORD OF ALL or not at all!" Maxwell reminded us. It was a contradiction, an anomaly to call Jesus "Lord" when we hadn't allowed his Spirit to fill us—every room—with his presence. This helped us understand how we could be committed, dedicated, and conse-crated in so many ways, and yet have areas of our lives unyielded to Christ. There could be rooms to which we'd kept the keys for self to use. And that, we learned, turned us into hypocrites—we called Jesus, "Lord," but didn't allow him to have every room: "Lord of all or not at all."

I remember how pumped up we were after experiencing the campus revival. We'd heard testimonies of Christians who were power-less in their witness until they'd given their lives completely to Christ. Mutt and several of us would head into town and start talking with anyone we could find on the streets, in an attempt to win them to the Lord. Our "button-hole" techniques may have made us feel like "soul winners," but we didn't endear the Institute to the townspeople, who had become wearied by successive waves of students practicing their evangelism.

We "Young Turks" were duly impressed by a visiting evangelist who described his hitchhiking tactics for witnessing. He selected a wardrobe for the day with an eye on the area he hoped to witness in—a cowboy outfit for the western plains, a suit coat for urban towers, jeans for the inner city, or knapsack and red bandana for hippie communes. His outfit also influenced what kind of person picked him up. Once on board, he'd pitch his witness accordingly. All very impressive method-ology, we thought, but then we began to wonder how much the jaunty evangelist relied on manipulation and how much on the Spirit's leading.

The hardest thing in the world is to keep balanced—the reminder rang in our heads as we came to realize that evangelism was first of all glorifying God, not the evangelist; and evangelization wasn't just proclamation but involved friendships and relationships. The Apostle Paul wrote about people who had "zeal without knowledge."[1]

Scared to Death of Prairie!

C. Wesley Davidson ('49), whose grandparents had homesteaded near Three Hills, was born before the school opened. He remembered Prairie's earlier years. "Mr. Maxwell had a great concern for spiritually lost people. He held gospel meetings in the old 'sawdust trail' style, with students walking the aisles to help repentant sinners to the front during the 'altar call.' Mr. Maxwell was often blunt but had a kindly way about him, so he knew when to hold back, and when to press for decisions. We felt the Holy Spirit was guiding him. But some zealous students tried to copy his boldness without having his grace.

"As a result, people for one hundred miles around were scared to death of the school!" remembers Wes. "Students would hand out tracts to everyone and confront them with their need of salvation. I came to realize that people needed friendship before they'd listen to the gospel.

"So I promised one farmer, Bill, I wouldn't let anyone bother him, as long as he came to a gospel service to see for himself. To my surprise, Bill came that night and was the first to respond to the altar call!

"Right after the service, students came to ask for 'the fellow that got saved tonight.' They'd rounded up several people and wanted Bill to tell them how he'd come to Christ. But I'd made a promise to Bill and didn't tell the students who he was. Today Bill is a strong, radiant Christian whose life is a witness in itself. And he's telling others!"

Even the Coyotes Knew

As the gospel changed people and their communities, even the coyotes

---

[1] Romans 10.2.

seemed to know when it was Sunday, Wes told me. "They boldly roamed the plains on 'the Lord's Day,' as if they knew the hunters wouldn't be out. But the rest of the week you could scarce find one!"

Christian farmers had a conviction Sunday should be a day of rest. They used to say that people who disregarded the Lord's Day by harvesting would lose a couple of days during the week due to rain or equipment breakdown—and it often turned out that way!

"I knew a church elder at Delburne who finally gave in to a neighbor's request and agreed to help him thresh on Sunday," Wes recounted. "But the neighbor fell sick Saturday night and was rushed to hospital. So the elder agreed to work the following Sunday. But on Saturday the farmer's axe slipped and gashed his leg as he worked on his corral, and he spent Sunday in bed!"

Back in Three Hills, relations with the town did improve as the school became a participant in civic matters, instead of treating Three Hills as target practice. Eventually the town even elected a Prairie grad as mayor.

Many of the students came from churches known for their compromising spirit—watering down the truth of the gospel in order to accommodate rational philosophy. They came to value Prairie's clearcut stand on "what the Bible says." LE spoke about Pilate's cynical rhetorical question, "What is truth?" contrasting it with Paul's assurance, "I know whom I have believed!" That of course was based on Jesus' affirmation, "I am the way, the truth, and the life."[1]

But even in emphasizing truth, Maxwell wisely pointed out danger: taking truth out of context, becoming legalistic, or "riding a hobby horse" of one truth without preaching the whole truth. He told us of a man who was "true as steel, and twice as hard." In handling truth, we needed to "speak the truth in love."[2]

1 John 14.6.
2 Ephesians 4.15.

The hardest thing in the world—yes, we'd remember that the rest of our lives as we saw good people, servants of God, go off on tangents that crippled them and their ministries.

Struggles during the Radio Hour

Balance—I had to learn it in my own life as I struggled with conceit and personal pride. I remember sitting at LE's elbow early on Sunday mornings in the radio studio. After taking part in the musical presentations of the radio choir, I stepped down to the table where LE sat. I gave the children's story, but LE's voice was ringing in my memory's ear: "I've never heard of such consummate conceit!" He'd forgotten that little episode, but I hadn't. I knew it was true.

Now I was the Prairie Radio Hour children's story author and narrator. To be humble, I used a pseudonym—but I found that anonymity didn't rule out pride. I knew that some authors (spiritual giants) used to use only their initials, to avoid self-glory. But a cloistered monk could still be, as some students joked, "proud of my humility!"

Even if no one else knew who wrote and narrated those stories, I knew—and my ego even enjoyed the secret! Wasn't anonymity a kind of piety? Why was it so difficult to be humble? Ah, that was the problem—I was striving in the flesh to be spiritual! I wasn't simply reckoning myself dead to sin and alive to God.

The man I was sharing the mike with didn't seem conscious of self—even in the midst of prominence. Radio preacher, school president, conference speaker, and author—yet completely unaffected. He understood the value of having a true estimate of oneself (as the Apostle Paul put it)[1] without arrogating to himself pride for what he knew God had given him. He was very much himself, "free from all men,"[2] not comparing himself with others.[3] During four years of observing him, I

---

[1] Romans 12.3-8.
[2] 1 Corinthians 9.19.
[3] 2 Corinthians 10.12.

never once felt he was posturing. He was a true Nathaniel, "an Israelite without guile,"[1] transparent, genuine. He had found the secret of abundant life: Christ at the center. Christ could be preeminent because self no longer occupied the center. LE had reckoned himself crucified with Christ and so was alive in Christ.

As I worked alongside this mentor, I learned simply to acknowledge, "Lord, you know I am nothing. Anything you allow me to do is the result of grace. Any gift I may have is because you gave it to me. The man beside me knows that. So what do I have to be proud about or humble about? Instead, I thank you that you gave me this gift and that you are allowing me to use it. Now please bless it to someone's good."

The Monument Crumbles

What was happening in me, as in many other students, was the rebuilding of a personality built on self. Since earliest childhood I'd built up an artificial personality. I'd been a sickly youngster, forbidden by our family doctor to play sports or even run upstairs. To compensate I'd tried to prove myself. As I later gained physical strength, I also developed conceits—including my attitude to some Christians I looked down on as wimps. Little things became self important—my "little prides," as Michael Griffiths of OMF termed such.

The message of *Born Crucified* was my undoing. The personality monument to self I'd built up had feet of clay and crumbled when struck by Christ the Rock. I'd so depended on the *persona*, the conceited personality I'd built up, that when my self-image collapsed, I became uncharacteristically unsure of myself. A psychologist might have concluded that for me "religion" was self-destructive.

But it was a cathartic experience. The "former things" had to be replaced by "the new life," Ephesians 4.22-24 told me. I had to learn, line upon line, the truth of Romans 8.29: God had predestined me as his child "to be conformed to the likeness of his Son."

---

[1] John 1.47.

I'd started, but it soon became evident this was a continuing process that wouldn't happen overnight! The message that was my "downfall" was also the source of my rebuilding—allowing "him who began a good work in [me], to continue it to the day of Jesus Christ" (Philippians 1.6). I was on a pilgrimage without end—right through Heaven's Gate.

Meanwhile, I was learning not to be in bondage to guilt. After all, my old nature really was sinful, and I really was a zero—but in Christ "there is no condemnation." So I learned to relax at that microphone table beside LE, giving thanks that Christ was my life, and Christ was my all. What I needed was time for God to bring forth the fruit of his Spirit instead of the works of the flesh in my life.[1]

We were to see a public example of humble acceptance of prominence. In 1949 LE encouraged us to pray for a little-known young evangelist who was preaching in Los Angeles to huge crowds—unheard of for a gospel campaign in the post-war world. His name was Billy Graham.[2] Several dramatic conversions—including Hollywood celebrities, sports stars, a Mafia electronics wizard, and swelling crowds had drawn the attention of the media—including the Hearst chain of newspapers, *Time* magazine, and radio talk shows.

"Lord," our principal led in prayer, "keep your hand upon this young man. Help him to stay at the foot of the Cross!" We later learned that after his first meeting in L.A., Billy Graham had told everyone on the team bus, "Before we drive off, we're going to bow in prayer and give God the glory. It doesn't belong to us!" After 72 meetings during eight weeks, an exhausted Graham, his wife Ruth, and team did the same thing while their train pulled out of L.A. They had learned how to link the Cross of salvation with the Cross of service through the Cross in their own lives—rejecting glory for themselves.

At the time Billy Graham had no idea how widely God was going

---

[1] As Galatians 5.16-26 spelled out.
[2] Armin Gesswein, the revivalist God had used to stir us at Prairie in 1946, had helped prepare the way for Graham's remarkable meetings by forming prayer groups all over the area.

to use him and his team, but his experience in Los Angeles assured us that it was possible to walk humbly in the Spirit even as God prominently used the spiritual gifts he had given. It was a lesson we'd already seen in our principal's life.

Chapter 14: The Call?

"This gospel is indeed good news,
but good only to the man who gets it."—LEM

MORE THAN A SLIDE SHOW

CLUTCHING HIS BROW, the furloughing missionary showing slides of Africa suddenly stopped speaking and staggered from the lectern. The Africa Prayer Group leader jumped up to steady him from falling. "I have to sit down!" Cecil Kirk, nephew of Prairie's president, gasped. He'd been telling us about the lovable, needy people in Nigeria to whom he and his wife, Myrtle,[1] had given their hearts for Christ's sake.

The packed gathering assumed the speaker had felt faint but would soon be able to continue his slide presentation. Someone began to sing a chorus. But sitting among the hundred or so students, I noticed his nephew, Herb Jacobson, helping the stricken speaker out a side door. Obviously, he wouldn't be able to continue showing the slides.

"Keep showing the pictures!" I whispered to the projector operator as the group leader led in prayer for the speaker. "I viewed them at the Kirks' home last week. I'll try to carry on the narration." I remembered enough to be able to describe the scenes—although details such as "Pastor Dauda" had to become simply "a pastor." As the group spent the rest of the hour in prayer for the Kirks' work and other ministries on the continent, I wondered what the Lord was trying to say to me.

As a child I'd been impressed by Africa's need. "Maybe I'll be a missionary there one day," I'd thought. Now the Kirks were asking God for someone to work with them. Was I supposed to be that person? But

---

[1] Myrtle was the daughter of the Jacobsons who enrolled at Prairie in 1926 (see Chapter 2).

writing seemed to be my gift. How could I use it in that part of Nigeria, at the time largely illiterate? After the prayer meeting, my confusion increased when I learned that a massive stroke had felled Cecil. He died within the hour. I'd had to step in to complete his slide presentation. Was I to step in to follow up his work in Africa? His widow and young daughter returned to Nigeria alone.

"Forget it young man!"

Maybe I should talk with LE about my burden to write for missions. I always enjoyed discussing writing with LE. We thought along similar lines. "An article has to grab the reader's attention right away!" he'd tell me, as we talked about the dullness of many Christian publications at the time.

"Even within the first five words, newspaper editors say," I added. While at Prairie, I concurrently took a correspondence course from the Newspaper Institute of America. Prairie's English classes improved my foundation in grammar. During my Junior year, my assigned "gratis" in the English Department helped develop editing skills. One of my assignments was to critique and mark Senior class essays (incognito, of course—for personal protection!).

But when I asked LE what he thought about my seeking a writing career in missions, I was surprised he didn't see me as God's gift to the world.

"Forget it, young man!" he volleyed. "Wait till you've got something to write about."

Years later LE told me he'd never before or since given such a dismissive reply to a student asking advice about vocation. I don't know if he knew at the time, or whether the Holy Spirit put into his mouth the advice I needed. I mean, books on developing spiritual gifts wouldn't recommend that kind of write-off!

Since childhood I'd wanted to write, having watched my father at his editor's desk. I'd write while sitting on a bus or in church. Any scrap of paper—the back of an envelope or a pew welcome card—would do for parchment. I was happiest in a corner with my pencil or (later) portable typewriter (in pre-computer days). I'd heard that literacy in Africa was increasing, particularly in coastal cities. Communism and commerce were pouring their literature into the readership vacuum. I had visions of using my gifts to "save Africa" through Christian writing.

The thought of giving up that vision and working in another language became a kind of crucifixion of my ambitions. What if I lost my writing skills, working in another language among illiterates? In fact, what if my English itself suffered through non-use? But I knew what LE meant—I needed to know Christ and to learn of him in the crucible of life in order to write effectively. And without the Holy Spirit's empowering, my missionary effort would simply be professionalism.

Then my father appeared on campus one day, on one of his evangelistic treks across Canada. Mr. Maxwell had asked his long-time friend to speak at morning chapel. What was Dad's message? "Unless a kernel of wheat falls to the ground and dies, it remains only a single seed. But if it dies it produces many seeds" (John 12.24).

His illustration was from life. Dad had ridden horseback across the rolling plains of Southern Alberta, taking the gospel to struggling settlers. As arctic air froze the black clay, streamers of snow whistled over the furrows sown with winter wheat—dead, to all appearances. Dad always marveled when those buried seeds sprang to life in Spring and the weather-beaten plains turned to soft green, producing Alberta's prized "winter wheat." Dad didn't have to press home his point.

Not again! I struggled once more with Christ's call to discipleship: "Whosoever does not carry his own cross and come after me cannot be my disciple."

You mean Christ wanted not only me but also my ambitions—even the spiritual gift I felt he'd given me, and my concept of Christian service? Finally I surrendered those too. In my Senior year, I applied to SIM (then Sudan Interior Mission) for general mission work, not a "writing career." I left the type of assignment up to the mission—wherever they felt I could meet a need. I'd come to realize that a writer could be especially prone to pride, conscious that people were reading *his* work. I told God I'd place my writing future at the Cross—leaving it up to him to resurrect it if and when he wanted to.

"This young man doesn't lack conceit!"

But my commitment was to face a further test. I'd read about the onslaught of Communist ideology in Africa. Colorful magazines extolled Lenin and Marx. Flowing along with this political literature was a stream of lurid magazines from overseas. In my covering letter to SIM, I'd mentioned my concern for Bible teaching in Africa to counteract "the junk that was flowing into the continent."

In Nigeria, SIM was publishing *The West Africa Christian*, a rather nondescript digest of Christian articles—few written in Africa. Apparently the SIM Secretary misunderstood my reference to "junk" and somehow thought I was criticizing the Mission's publishing efforts. Besides, he noted I didn't have a high school diploma. The Secretary wrote to tell me I'd need to complete that basic mission requirement before applying.

I fired back a list of reasons I didn't think I should wait to complete high school. True, I'd dropped out after the ninth grade (first year high school) for family financial reasons, trying to catch up through night school classes, courses in the Navy, ongoing reading, and now courses at Prairie. Besides, I argued, I was already 25—taking another three years to complete high school would make me "an old man" before I arrived in Africa!

Reading my letter, Helen Bingham, wife of SIM's founder, commented, "This young man doesn't lack conceit!" (Discerning woman!)

Unknown to me at the time, SIM wrote to ask the principal for his opinion on the suitability of this "upstart."

"We'd considered asking Mr. Fuller to stay and teach here," replied LE, coming to my rescue. "But he felt God was calling him to overseas mission work."

Personally, I'd prefer more education. But while I was thankful that God enabled me to continue informal studies as well as attend Prairie, SIM's questioning caused me to search my motives. I wrote the mission to apologize for the way I'd come across. They finally accepted me—maybe in a "high risk" category.

Prepared For War

Earlier in 1949, our class had chosen "Prepared for War" as our theme.[1] It was a fitting motto (taken from Joshua 4.13) for a class with a number of ex-service people in it. At Prairie we'd been making the transition from World War II warfare to preparation for the spiritual warfare ahead. The motto tied in with the school's slogan at the time, "Preparing Disciplined Soldiers for Christ." Our class wall display depicted a fist grasping a sword, while a serpent rose menacingly over a world map in the background.

In spite of my dismal first-year doggerel, "Ode to a Sock on the Head," my classmates were a forgiving bunch and asked me to write the class poem and class song. I tried to capture the theme of spiritual warfare in the first stanza of the poem:

> *O God, of sin the Victor, we follow at thy call;*
> *For service in fierce conflict we give to thee our all.*
> *'Mid fire we will not waver, for thou has gone before;*
> *Thy soldiers now are ready, by thee PREPARED FOR WAR!*

---

[1] Each Junior class chose a motto that was illustrated in a large wall-hanging or display and mounted on a campus indoor wall. At a graduation banquet in honor of the Seniors, the Junior class president gave a "charge" to the Seniors, and the class choir sang the class song.

Another year, and my time at Prairie came to a close. I said good-bye to L. E. Maxwell and the many faculty and staff I'd come to respect and love. Their self-denial and faithfulness modeled the message of the Cross. Their calling was as sacrificial as that of any missionary. After all they had poured into our lives, I felt for them, having to face the next wave of freshmen to arrive—surprises, conceits, problems, everything they had endured during our time at the school.

Four years earlier, I'd arrived in Three Hills with my seaman's duffel bag and a lot of "personality baggage." As I left, what did I take away with me? Above all else, I'd come to understand the role of the Cross in my life as a disciple, and my need to take up that Cross daily, moment by moment. As to my studies, there were lots of gaps in my preparation for missions—gaps that I'd need to fill as I continued learning, whether by experience, reading, or formal courses. But the main tool I now had in my bag was personal study of the Word. That tool I'd use in every situation wherever I traveled, throughout life.

That which LE had poured into us students would be tested in many different circumstances and lands. Little did I know the way of the Cross that lay ahead in Africa.

The day I was leaving Three Hills, a swarthy student stood in my doorway. I recognized Kassa Wolde Mariam, an Ethiopian on scholarship provided by Alberta Member of Parliament and benefactor Robert N. Thompson.[1]

"I'm sorry to interrupt you!" he began apologetically, "but I hear you are going to my continent."

"That's right, Kassa." I expected he wanted me to take verbal greetings or a letter to somebody.

"Well, would you mind if I prayed for you?" the handsome

---

[1] Thompson served in Ethiopia with SIM and later was instrumental in Trinity Western University's receiving BC provincial degree-granting status (a first for a Christian university in Canada).

Ethiopian continued. "I'd like to be your prayer partner when you're in Africa."

I was smitten. Asking me if I minded his praying for me! That was the beginning of a precious friendship with an African brother. From Prairie, Kassa went on to study at university. Returning to Ethiopia, he married one of Emperor Haile Selassie's granddaughters and received the royal title of Lij Kassa. He became a provincial govenor. The Emperor, titular head of the ancient Ethiopian Orthodox Church (at the time a largely ritualistic body), personally professed faith in Jesus Christ as his Savior. Several of his grandchildren experienced "the new birth" through personal faith in Christ while studying in Britain.

At the Center of Empire

Ten years later I again met Lij Kassa in Ethiopia—no longer a student but President of the University of Ethiopia. We prayed together in his teak-paneled office and shared what God was doing in both of our lives. President Kassa was living for Christ in the heart of the ancient Kingdom of Ethiopia. There were few officials like him, who personally knew the power of the resurrected Christ in their lives. The ornate Ethiopian Orthodox cross was prominent among the ruling Amhars, but chiefly as an icon, a symbol of ecclesiastical pomp and state power.

Then Marxist-Leninist rebels took over the country, assassinating Emperor Haile Selassie. The rebels imprisoned Kassa and other males connected with the royal family. Although that must have been an ordeal more dreadful than I could imagine, I knew Kassa's prison cell could not shut out the comforting presence of the crucified One to whom he had dedicated his life back in the little Prairie town of Three Hills. The Cross of Christ had liberated him from the law of death. Shackles could not bind his spirit.

Now it was my turn to pray for Kassa. Nine years later I heard that the Communist regime had just hanged Kassa and the other royal princes. I was saddened, but I also gave thanks for this outstanding

Ethiopian who had learned the truth of Galatians 2:20. "I have been crucified with Christ, and I no longer live, but Christ lives in me."

The Cross in Kassa's life conveyed a revolutionary message the Marxists couldn't eradicate. Kassa lived that message at the heart of academia, within the royal family, and finally in rat-infested dungeons. I could almost hear my prayer partner Kassa singing the closing line of Martin Luther's great hymn, *"The body they may kill: God's truth abideth still; His Kingdom is forever!"*

The Communist regime closed the university and most churches. Many Christians worshipped in secret. Prairie grads were among the missionaries who responded to the pleas of "the underground church" to stay in the country. They discreetly encouraged believers in the Word, helping courageous Ethiopians set up a covert system of study and leadership training. When in the late 1980s the country overthrew the Communists, the church resurfaced, stronger than ever.[1]

In Ethiopia, one of the earliest Christian kingdoms, the power of the Cross was displayed—not as an icon, but through humble believers who endured unbelievable privation and torture. They were overcomers!

But before all that, I had headed out to Nigeria—on the opposite side of the continent from Ethiopia.

People of Another Tongue

Camels and turbaned riders, blowing traditional long trumpets, welcomed our British Airways flight at Kano in Northern Nigeria. The Saharan heat swallowed me, but this ancient walled city was the gateway to my first assignment—studying the Hausa language in preparation for general mission work.

The SIM language school was located further south in one of the

---

[1] Cumbers, John; Bascom, Kay, *op.cit.*

most neglected parts of Nigeria's heartland. I'd been told that the local people there greeted only in a lengthy series of grunts, continuing until they were out of earshot of one another. My worst linguistic fears seemed confirmed! I'd soon lose my ability in the English language along with my writing skills, I thought.

Then I remembered the corn of wheat. Perhaps the Council would later post me to teach Bible in some inland village, as Ernest Maxwell, who preceded me by a year (1950), was preparing to do.

Ernest had come into Kano for SIM's annual missionary conference. His father had traveled to Africa to be the Bible speaker. Field Secretary Hector Kirk (brother of Prairie's co-founder), allowed me to attend before I headed south. Of course he'd received my candidate papers from Toronto, and no doubt—like Prairie's Dean—he felt "the conference would do me good"!

L. E. Maxwell's message was "Born Crucified." I couldn't escape it! The Word touched the hearts of us newcomers as well as missionary veterans. The latter were dedicated men and women, daily toiling under tropical conditions to share Christ's love. Yet the message of dying to self and living to God convicted many afresh.

One veteran who'd given most of his years to translating the Scriptures, wept openly as he confessed impatience and anger. "I struck my son!" he sobbed. The rest of us could not be judgmental. We knew that his mentally handicapped son was a test of anyone's patience, and only Calvary love could provide enough.

"I recall," Maxwell later wrote, "that one of the most untiring and hard-working missionaries stood up during a visitation of God's Spirit and confessed: 'I have driven three missionaries off my station!' Her sharp tongue and evil temper had well-nigh ruined her own career as well as that of several others."[1]

---

[1] L.E. Maxwell in *Prairie Harvesters* Alumni Bulletin, July-December 1954.

Obviously, God had to work among us missionaries as well as among those we'd come to serve.

The following week I found myself among the Gbagyi,[1] the people who greeted with grunts. (I later discovered how rich and complex their vernacular really was.) The Hausa, for the most part Muslim, looked down on the tribe as "pagan." For one thing, Gbagyi worshipped spirits and ate dog meat at feasts. Also their women, at the time, wore only a bustle of leaves around their waists and carried massive loads of fire-wood on the nape of their necks. Other tribes considered them inferior, superstitious beasts of burden. But missionaries and local evangelists saw them as people God "so loved."

Thirty of us in language school studied Hausa (*lingua franca* for the whole Region) with the aid of pure-bred Hausa speakers brought in from the Muslim North. I soon forgot my linguistic fears and fell in love with a language that Hector Kirk and his pioneer linguist/medical friend Andrew Stirrett called, "The language of Heaven." It certainly was a language as developed as English—and more complex because of a tonal system that could give one word several meanings.

Secret Romance

"You're a Prairie graduate, aren't you?" asked Freeda Jones, a language student from America's mid-west. She confided that she and Ernest Maxwell were corresponding. Right then he was stationed in a remote Hausa village, without telephone or electricity. They were separated by a long day's drive on rough roads.

At the time, Nigerian rural culture frowned upon any social contact between unmarried men and women. Parents arranged marriages. To avoid appearance of impropriety, SIM rules forbade casual dating, and if engagement were intended, administration had first to give permis-sion. The engaged couple could not reside on the same station (even

---

[1] Also known as Gbari or Gwari—the way Hausa and foreigners mispronounced their name.

with other missionaries resident), and could meet only once a month—under supervision. (No, this was not Prairie Bible Institute!)

A further factor in SIM romances was that there were some 300 single women missionaries—most of whom had put aside, for Christ's sake, prospects of marriage, considering there were only 30 single male members. Any hint of interest between Miss A and Mr. B would spread across the SIM grapevine faster than the Nigerian telegraph service (in those days, the only reliable and fast way of long-distance communication). In that context, we all knew it was important to prevent dashed hopes and broken hearts. Hence Freeda's whispered announcement to me that day.

Before coming to language school, Freeda had met Ernest at the mission rest home in another part of the country. She'd found his exuberance "loud" and wondered what he was really like. Several years earlier, while Freeda was a student at Moody Bible Institute,[1] she worked in the editorial department and proof-read L. E. Maxwell's book, *Born Crucified*, for publication.

"Wouldn't it be wonderful to have a dad like him!" she found herself musing, at the time not knowing he had a son headed for Africa. She was also impressed with the grace and kindness that came through in Maxwell's messages at a Moody missions conference.

When she'd earlier accepted the lordship of Christ in her life, her commitment included willingness to prepare for missionary service. This was a radical change from her teen years. Some friends wondered if she'd be able to stand up to the pressures around her, let alone succeed as a missionary. But along with the Cross of salvation and the Cross of consecration, she'd recognized the Cross of self denial—the reality of what LE's book called being "born crucified."

Now as we sat under a flame-of-the-forest tree on the mission compound in Nigeria, Freeda had lots of questions. Quiet and introspective,

---

[1] MBI was founded by Dwight L. Moody, a contemporary of A. B. Simpson and the missionary-evangelist H. Grattan Guinness in 1889—six years after Simpson's MTI opened.

she needed a husband whom she could trust with her deepest emotions. Ernest was intelligent; would he also be understanding? He was perceptive, but he also seemed brusque. He was usually right in sizing up a problem, whether with the churches or his fellow missionaries. But sometimes they found his terse dictums difficult to take.

Ernest was "the vest-pocket edition" of his father in many ways, but had he absorbed the graciousness God had woven into LE's life through years in the "school of hard knocks"? What were relationships like among his family? What kind of in-laws would they make?

I assured Freeda that the Maxwell family were caring, down-to-earth, and approachable. She'd love Ernest's parents, sisters, and brother. In many respects, Freeda reminded me of Ernest's mother.[1]

Love Letters

Soon I began receiving letters from Ernest, with sealed enclosures to pass on to Freeda. So Freeda and I often sat together at meals or chatted on the swing seat under the scarlet-blossomed tree out front.[2] Of course the other missionaries assumed Freeda and I were romantically interested in each other—and we both enjoyed misleading them. ("Serves them right!" LE would have chuckled.)

One Sunday we walked to church together so we could talk out of earshot. Up behind us pulled the pickup truck of a couple who were studying language. The driver leaned out the window and asked with a wink and chuckle, "You two wouldn't want a ride to church, would you?" We shocked the couple by accepting their offer, climbing into the back of the truck.

A week later handsome young Ernest Maxwell (very much like his father had looked in his twenties) drove on to the language school compound, stepped out of his LandRover, and took the hand of starry-eyed Freeda—to everyone's surprise. The secret was out! SIM had approved

[1] See Family Album, Chapter 23, and Family Reminiscences, Chapter 24.
[2] In the context of the language school, national staff understood this as morally acceptable within our Western culture, and so it was not a stumbling block.

the engagement, and after the obligatory six-month wait (half the required period of earlier years), Ernest Edwin Maxwell and Freeda LaVon Jones became Mr. and Mrs. Maxwell on April 12, 1952.

The young couple transferred to the Eastern Gbagyi area and immersed themselves in a Bible school project in the heart of Nigeria. Both became proficient in Hausa, which the Gbagyi students would need as a *lingua franca* for ministry and further study. Ernest used his theological insights in teaching and preaching, as well as his practical skills in running a Bible school. Freeda used her editing experience to develop training programs for church leaders.

Although the Gbagyi area had been bypassed by governments in the past, it later was included in the new federal capital territory—and there is now a strong evangelical presence witnessing from the heart of the nation, despite pressures of Muslims to Islamize the newly incorporated capital.

Another Prairie graduate and his wife, George and Ruth Foxall, worked with the Maxwells in adapting Theological Education by Extension (TEE) curricula and Programmed Instruction (PI) materials.[1] TEE made Bible study available to village pastors and lay people throughout Africa. Foxall became Coordinator of the Accrediting Council for Theological Education in Africa (ACTEA), and a member of the global International Council of Evangelical Theological Education (ICETE).

With this involvement in Ernest and Freeda's romance, I took a special interest in their onward pilgrimage as they raised three children in Nigeria's hinterland. Through the years, God's grace and the Cross in their lives enabled Ernest and Freeda to accept the differences in each other. However, I could not have imagined the family tragedy that we'd one day face.

But that's getting ahead of my story.

---

[1] TEE and PI, tools used worldwide, were based on systems developed by educators Ted Ward, Samuel F. Rowen, and Ralph D. Winter, the latter having studied the Search Question method used by Prairie. Full circle!

Chapter 15: Penetrating Culture

"In your weariest and weakest and most bewildered moment, simply say, 'Now, Lord, here is my chance—and thine: my chance to die, thy chance to manifest the life of Jesus.'"—quoted by LEM

CHALLENGE-ING ASSIGNMENT

I'm burying writing as a career until you resurrect it—if you ever want to," I'd told the Lord when I applied for Nigeria. As far as I knew, I'd be assigned to the kind of work that Cecil and Myrtle Kirk had been doing, discipling believers in some isolated village. I didn't realize that a New Zealand journalist had joined SIM the year before and had just launched a newspaper-style Christian magazine in Nigeria, called *African Challenge.*

Published in Lagos down on the coast, its first issue hit the streets of the port city the month I arrived in the country. Response was amazing. Written for readers whose first language was not English, it combined educational and news features with gospel stories and Bible studies. New literates pouring into the cities snapped it up, and teachers pressured their pupils to buy it (at a subsidized two pennies), since they lacked textbooks and other reading material.

Problem: the project grew faster than its staff could handle. At SIM HQ in Jos, Hector Kirk and other administrators scoured candidate files to find anyone who knew anything about editorial work. No one was applying for that kind of ministry. Once more through the files they looked, when someone waved my application papers in the air.

"Here's someone who's studied Journalism!" she called out. "He applied for general mission work, but he listed Journalism among his studies. And he's here in Nigeria—in language school right now!"

SIM General Director Guy Playfair (an occasional Prairie conference speaker) ordered me south to the coast at once. By that time I was so enjoying Hausa studies that I begged to finish my six-month course and spend another six months using it in a village. I didn't want to lose what I'd learned. But HQ was adamant: "Get you down to Lagos!" So I found myself at the offices of *African Challenge* in Nigeria's most boisterous city, surrounded by people of different ethnic languages.

The Urban Jungle

"A City Like No Other" was the title of a documentary the British Broadcasting Corporation produced on Lagos—and I soon found out why. A one-time pirate city, from the air it looked fairly idyllic—a tropical island set in a blue lagoon fringed by green palms. But on land, my eyes, ears, and nose brought me "down to earth." Parts of the island were below sea level; so the city's open sewers had nowhere to run until, brimming with putrid green scum, they spilled raw sewage into the surrounding lagoon.

Here on the coast, it could rain any month, and the humidity was so high that anything leather (our shoes and even our Bibles) was soon covered with mould. But villagers continued to pour into the capital city[1], with great expectations of finding work. Instead, many had to steal and rob to feed themselves. Their numbers overflowed onto the mainland, forming one sprawling, overgrown village. But unlike peaceful inland villages, this metropolis "village" was filled with noise, the stench of rotting garbage, and violence.

At the time, there was only one bridge to the island, and all traffic funneled across it, creating a colossal traffic backup that took an hour to crawl one mile—through muddy craters in spots. Rusting vehicles spewed black exhaust while spindly youths ran alongside, trying to sell anything—including items they'd just stolen. Enterprising "market mammies" squatted beside the road wrapping bread in used plastic,

---

[1] A new national capital has since been built inland at Abuja, but Lagos remains the largest city.

so the loaves had some semblance of hygiene despite swarms of flies. Children sidled through the crowds, deftly balancing on their heads hand-basins of bananas and oranges or peanuts for sale. Impatient car horns competed with the angry shouts of sweating drivers and pedestrians.

Welcome to urban Africa!

"This is where I belong!" I thought as I dodged a weaving cyclist.[1] Perhaps my Navy life had prepared me for the city's raw challenge. Later I was glad it wasn't I who had chosen the Lagos assignment. All that I'd learned at Prairie was soon to be tested.

The Cross and the Editor's Desk

"Someone's stolen my bow and arrows!" our night watchman complained one morning. "I know!" I replied as I handed them back to him. "I took them from you while you were sleeping at 2 a.m."

The Challenge operated out of a rented building in a squalid suburb, where mangy dogs barked all night and most residents employed "watchmen." In place of a gun, our guard preferred a bow and a sheaf of arrows. He stoutly maintained he never slept on duty. So one night when I was trying to meet an editorial deadline, as I turned off my office light, I borrowed the evidence! It was all part of my cultural orientation for writing for African readers.

"Wait till you've got something to write about!" LE had advised. Ready or not, I was thrust into journalism in a strange culture. Housing was limited, so I boarded with the editor and his wife. We enjoyed working together, until a rift developed between the editor and SIM administration. The editor threatened to resign unless he could be manager as well as editor. When management didn't prove to be his skill, the staff

---

[1] Nigeria was the British Commonwealth's biggest importer of bicycles—they could make better time than cars through the traffic-clogged streets.

appealed to SIM's Director to solve the problem. In short, SIM accepted the editor's resignation, asking me to take over his responsibilities.

"In short," I say, but the months of that ordeal seemed endless. Although I was the newcomer and a somewhat "innocent bystander," day by day I had to work alongside a very angry couple. Meal after meal I battled indigestion as I ate across the table from the glowering editor and his wife. I had to practice the way of the Cross each moment, asking for grace to show love while handling my responsibilities within a tense situation.

These were two dedicated, talented Christians who loved the Lord and were seeking to win others to him—yet somehow, in this crisis, they couldn't embrace the Cross that would have meant death to self in their personal and professional ambitions. They'd even read Roy and Revel Hession's book, *The Calvary Road*, and recommended it to others. They were an object lesson to me: it was possible to sacrifice for Christ and to preach his Cross, without "reckoning ourselves dead . . . and alive."[1]

Even though the editor's quarrel was with Mission administration, I became the impostor, because if he and his wife did leave, I'd be the one to take over. If I really had put my grain of wheat into the earth, it was being thoroughly stomped on. ("And manure was dumped on it!" someone later commented.) I wasn't sure if the "wheat" would ever be able to spring up! I kept remembering an illustration from Prairie days: was I willing to be a doormat, to be walked over? My Lagos "baptism" experience sounded almost like the teaching of Prairie to which I'd objected years before: "Those who go out weeping, carrying seed to sow, will return with songs of joy…!"

"*The Challenge* will collapse within a month!" the editor

---

[1] This experience taught me a sober paradox: while preaching the Cross, we missionaries could miss applying the Cross in some aspect of our own lives. In my subsequent contacts with missionaries worldwide, I would come across all the foibles that showed up in quarreling Paul and Barnabas, pig-headed Peter, hot-eyed James and John Zebedee. I learned afresh that regardless of our commitment, each of us needs to "die daily" to self in every compartment of life—and God uses different situations to bring us to the Cross.

generously prophesied as he left. And as far as I knew, it would—but for the Lord's help.[1] Close friends of the work, both in Africa and overseas, mysteriously heard what a bad lot we were at *The Challenge*. We could only commit the work and even its reputation to the Lord—and concentrate on the next issue.

Best-Seller

In God's mercy, *African Challenge* became better known than Coca-Cola. The name sometimes got me through awkward situations, such as riots. In circulation, it became the highest monthly in West Africa and second highest on the continent. (A gaudy secular South African magazine was highest.) The US-based Evangelical Literature Overseas later reported that a dozen gospel magazines were spawned by other organizations worldwide, using the *Challenge* mass-circulation formula of news, education, and gospel features.

But after the editor resigned, I was the only trained journalist on staff (although my colleagues formed a great team in business management, printing, and supportive editorial staff). All at once everything I had ever enjoyed in publishing—everything I'd been willing to give up—was dumped on my desk. Until we found more help, I had to write the news, editorial, educational feature, gospel fiction story, testimony, and the salvation message that each issue contained. I took the photos, drew the cartoons and story illustrations, and designed the pages.

Once I'd come to the end of my own ambition, it seemed God was saying, "You gave up writing until I'd give it back? Well, since you know you can't do this in your own strength—here it is. Now *I'll* enable you to handle it!"

---

[1] The conviction that God brought me to Lagos was a strength. Before leaving Canada, I'd had to delay departure because my father appeared to be dying, and spiritual friends told me I was the one to lead his mission. Was this God's timing? Was my overseas "call" only a test of commitment? Were "foreign missions" more glamorous than "home missions?" Once again I had to examine my motives and want only God's will—even if that meant staying home. After my father recovered and I found myself at *Challenge*, I rested in the fact I hadn't requested the assignment—the mission had decided. God had placed me there.

The difference was that while writing was still a joy, pride in any writing ability had gone. God was simply allowing me to use gifts he'd given. So what was the big deal? It mattered not that my name now appeared as editor—albeit in tiny print at the bottom of the last page (a government requirement). Elsewhere I used appropriate pennames (an acceptable practice in journalism) for various columns and features until we could train African writers, artist, and photographer.

Now my main concern was not to save the world by writing but to survive—to get the next issue out on the streets. As publication deadlines loomed, I'd work through the night, stretching out on top of my desk to snatch an hour's sleep and then continue working, to have pages ready for the printer by dawn. Survival was the name of the game.

Jostling through a Crazy Circus

During the day I'd roam the city taking photos and snooping out stories. To interview someone across the city or to check out details, *forget* the telephones (they rarely worked); it was better to venture through the urban jungle. Soon I was feeling at home in this crazy circus, jostling with the rollicking crowds. I was learning about local culture, and there was lots of material for writing. Besides, it was so easy to talk about Jesus, my Savior!

Unknown to me, back home Prairie heard of my burial-and-resurrection experience. I don't know how they learned of the ordeal, for I didn't write about it to anyone. Perhaps SIM General Director Guy Playfair, a close friend of L. E. Maxwell, shared the information. Playfair had been involved in the previous editor's exit and became a great promoter of *Challenge*.

Years later I met Prairie grads of that era who greeted me with a grin: "So you're the guy Mr. Maxwell mentions in his classes!" Sure, he probably used me as an example of student mischief or conceit, I thought, but apparently the *Challenge* episode became another illustration of "a grain of wheat" experience.

"Forget it, young man! First get something to write about!" LE's cryptic advice came back to me as I battled to write for new literates in a continent I was trying to understand. I wished I could wait ten years while I learned from my readers, before I had to write for them. We knew that not only students but also teachers and politicians regularly read the magazine.

At the time, secular agencies estimated that in Africa as many as 15 people would read a single copy of a magazine, because of the culture and economy. Based on that figure, at our peak, circulation represented an amazing readership of about 2.5 million.

However, as we "put one issue to bed" (to use printer's jargon) there was nothing else to do but wade into preparing the next issue. No time to take off to learn more. Besides, I reasoned, by the time I'd waited ten years, although my head might be wiser, my energy could be sapped. Issue by relentless issue, I had to "get something to write about" from life around me and from the Word.

African friends taught me much. Christian leaders around the continent enriched our lives—people like Evangelist Nicholas Bhengu of South Africa (whom I'd first heard speak at Prairie), Bishop Allison of Sudan, and Bishop Erica Sabithi of Uganda, as well as grass-root believers whose testimonies we published. Many had come through fiery trials of persecution. Stories from the East African Revival stirred our readers as we published excerpts from *The Calvary Road*.[1] It told about the Cross in the lives of Ugandan and Rwandan believers.[2]

Strategic Publication

The majority of Africa's literates were under age 30, many the product of denominational mission schools that had lost their gospel message.

---

[1] *Op. cit.* Revival broke out after an African pastor and English medical missionary gave themselves to prayer. It continued over thirty years.

[2] My editorial work also enabled me to see how believers could miss the Cross in aspects of their own lives while serving with the greatest dedication and sacrifice. I visited the area (up the Cross River, ironically) where Scottish pioneer Mary Slessor once served. Her courage working alone among the warring tribes had challenged us at Prairie. Yet when I mentioned this to her successors in Africa, they commented, "Dear Mary, she couldn't get along with her colleagues, so the mission sent her to work by herself!" God graciously uses us in spite of ourselves, but we can easily miss the victorious life.

For these, *The Challenge* was often the first confrontation they'd had with the need for saving faith in the Savior. Every month, hundreds of queries about salvation poured into our counseling office. Villages formed Challenge Reading Units, in which readers discussed articles and read to non-literates.

Because of the magazine's wide readership and our strategic location in West Africa's largest port, Lagos, we often had Christian leaders from overseas visit us. Kenneth Taylor, then Director of Moody Press and later paraphraser of *The Living Bible,* came to discuss distribution of "Moody Pocket Books."

Theologian Carl F. H. Henry, first Editor of *Christianity Today*, did research for an African issue of *CT.*

Evangelist Billy Graham dropped by for an interview concerning his Lagos evangelistic meetings. What a joy to meet crusade soloist George Beverly Shea (whose nephew became an SIM Director) and Cliff Barrows, whose sister had served with SIM.[1] My mind went back to our Prairie prayer meetings for Graham as he first came to the attention of the world press.

In Lagos I'd covered some other prominent evangelists of a different genre. I was shocked by the way they could invite crowds to the Cross for salvation, and yet not display the Cross in their own lives. They'd fly in to Lagos with planeloads of equipment and TV cameras rolling—to record African crowd scenes they'd use back home for fundraising. I wondered, were they promoting Christ or themselves and their organizations?

Where was their integrity? Where was the Cross in their lives to back up the Cross in their message? Resident Christian workers often had to clear up the havoc left behind: dashed hopes of healing, nominal "decisions for Christ," misconceptions of the gospel, impres-

---

[1] Cliff Barrow's father sent a house-trailer to Nigeria for Cliff's sister, Shirley, to live in. Since there was no way to transport it across the Niger River to Shirley's medical station, it remained at the *Challenge.* It provided initial housing for the girl I later married, Lorna Parrott.

sions of mercenary evangelists manipulating and exploiting the crowds.

It all reminded me of Maxwell's warning of the danger of leaping from the Cross of personal salvation into the Cross of active service, without experiencing the Cross within—the truth of being "crucified with Christ." To me the amazing thing was that God often used Christians in spite of themselves. As the Apostle Paul put it concerning others with less than worthy motives in his day, "yet the gospel was preached."

In steamy Lagos, the Race Course was the only open area in which to hold mass events. Once during the campaign of an American evangelist-healer, I experimented with photographing a promotional crowd scene. The night before, I'd watched a cameraman take photos as the speaker asked, "Who wants to be successful in life by following Jesus?" Of course everyone's hands shot up in the air. I could imagine the photo caption in the evangelist's promotion in America reading, "Ten Thousand Receive Christ in Lagos!"

The next evening I arrived before the speaker and his party, mounted the dais, and pointed my journalist's camera at the capacity crowd. As soon as the people saw my lens pointing at them, they put their hands up in the air, as they'd done for the camera the evening before. Later I used that photo to explain to puzzled folk back home the difference between the misleading hype of such evangelists and the plodding efforts of some of their own missionaries.

Shortly the charismatic evangelist arrived and spoke with great flourish, pleading with people to accept Christ and be healed. As people were leaving after the service, I stayed to watch the team produce the next "commercial" to show on American TV. As the evangelist was pleading for funds "on camera," the hapless cameraman stopped the action. "We'll have to run that again," he explained. "Wrong film!"

I was dumbfounded to hear the evangelist, who had just been preaching miraculous deliverance, explode in rage: "Do you think I'm here for you to waste my time?"

Different Kind of Evangelist

Billy Graham wasn't that kind of evangelist. Years earlier he faced the fact that he must decrease and Christ increase. Together he and his wife Ruth, whose parents had been Presbyterian missionaries in China, denied their personal ambitions and sought only God's glory. The Cross that "Billy" preached on a platform was the Cross he lived every moment of the day. They and the team determined that "integrity would be the hallmark of both our lives and our ministry."[1] Their work was enduring.

Now as Graham sat in my office discussing his evangelistic crusade in Nigeria's capital, it was a joy to provide editorial coverage. It was also a sobering experience, because it made me think of his erstwhile co-evangelist, who had taken a far different path. As a teenager in Toronto I had sat enthralled by Youth for Christ's "Chuck" Templeton.

Eloquent, handsome, and persuasive, he filled what was then Toronto's largest auditorium with teenagers on Saturday nights. After Graham founded his Evangelistic Association (1950), he invited Templeton to join him as an associate speaker. As Graham recounts in his biography,[2] he was greatly saddened when his good friend Chuck began to doubt the Word of God while studying theology at Princeton University. Chuck left the team and also departed from the faith, ending life as an agnostic.[3]

The contrast between Graham and Templeton left us wondering. Two gifted evangelists, but choosing two different paths. As we thought back to the charming evangelist we flocked to hear in our teens, we wondered if he'd been carried along by his charismatic personality—showmanship. His superficial belief in Jesus could not stand the fires of liberal theology. Graham, on the other hand, had struggled through a period of doubt by clinging to the only solid rock he knew—faith in Christ's

---

[1] Part of "The Modesto Manifesto" the team drafted even prior to the Los Angeles breakthrough.
[2] *Just As I Am.* New York: HarperCollins, 1997.
[3] Charles Templeton died May 2001 with Alzheimer's. His last book was *Farewell to God.*

work on the Cross. We gave thanks for his consistent, humble ministry.

"If we begin to take the credit, God's blessing will be withdrawn," Graham would often state.

For me it was a stark contrast, bringing back to mind our years at Prairie. There we'd learned that self must die so the Spirit could live through us. LE had taught us that the work of the flesh would end up as "wood, hay, and stubble," while the work of the Spirit would last for eternity.

*   *   *

What I'd heard before coming to Africa was true. Communism understood the power of literature. On the streets we could buy, for a few pennies, full-color magazines extolling the virtues of Leninism and Marxism. But now newsboys were selling a gospel magazine right alongside the Communist ones—and *Challenge* was outselling the competition!

In the midst of press deadlines, I marveled at the privilege God had given us. Through this tool we could give thousands of readers across the continent the news of salvation and material for spiritual growth. Books, tracts, and Bible studies poured out of our printing presses. Besides the *Challenge* in English, we initiated a counterpart in French (Africa's second largest *lingua franca*) and a series of cartoon papers in Nigeria's three major languages. Editing the Hausa edition for us from an inland base were two Prairie grads: Ernest Maxwell with his wife Freeda, and James Jacobson (from the Jacobson clan of PBI's early years) with his wife Ruth.

Back in Three Hills in the 1940s, when I was wondering about a writing ministry, I couldn't have imagined its potential. Nor had I then understood the process of the Cross in order to reach that potential. God's grace used the talents he had given, as we on the staff placed them at the foot of the Cross. Dying to self was not a morbid experience—it was the introduction to a joyous, fruitful life of Christ living in us. It certainly was a more effective way of dealing with crises than the way of the flesh—anger, manipulation, or other forms of selfishness.

From Funeral Parlor to Printing Press

Later the SIM's printing press, Niger Press[1], moved from the interior and merged with our editorial offices on the coast, to form Niger-Challenge Press. One of the printers was John ("Johnny") Grant—a graduate of Prairie. The first time I met him, he was using a hacksaw on a plumbing pipe, to shape a replacement for a broken press bearing. "Prairie resourcefulness!" I thought.

Johnny was full of stories of pioneer days in Three Hills. His half-brother, Will, owned the farm adjacent to the McElheran's farmhouse (where "Prairie" was born) and was a member of the first board. His father lived in Ontario but had helped build the first dormitories.

"Dad worked as a handyman for the owner of a funeral parlor in Ontario," Johnny recalled. "As the little Bible school expanded, Dad would go to Three Hills as a volunteer carpenter when business was slow back home."

"Carpenter?" I asked. "I thought you said he worked in a funeral parlor."

"Right, but he was a handyman," Johnny explained. "Funeral parlors also sold coffins. Dad would try his hand at anything."

Little Johnny[2] wasn't much interested in Bible school but went along with his Dad to summer conferences at Prairie. The trip across Canada in their Model A was an adventure. On one visit, in 1933, they

---

[1] Niger Press was founded by Canadian SIM pioneer A. W. Banfield, who with three colleagues forayed up the Niger River in 1901 with a small hand-operated press. One of that pioneer party died of malaria and the other two had to return home ill. After reinforcements arrived, Banfield initiated the work of his sponsors, the United Missionary Society, later representing the British and Foreign Bible Society in West Africa.
[2] Grant was so short even as an adult that he earned the Hausa nickname of "half a tall man"—to his amusement.

found construction on a sorely needed dormitory halted because of lack of funds, in keeping with Prairie's "no-debt" policy. It would take a miracle in those Depression years for the school to come up with the needed money. Will and the other farmers *cum* carpenters straightened rusty nails and pieced together broken boards.

The staff spent most of that night and the next day in prayer. If they had money even for a keg of nails, they could continue building for a while.

"Next morning, Mr. Maxwell burst into the meeting to announce that someone had given him a cheque that would pay for a whole floor to be built—not just a keg of nails." Johnny continued. "After seeing the staff's commitment and God's provision, I couldn't hold back anything from the Lord! That changed my whole concept of Christianity." He signed up for Bible school. Years later Will told Johnny it was their father who wrote that cheque.

As a student, Johnny did his gratis in *The Prairie Overcomer* publishing department, eventually taking the place of his brother Albert[1] operating the vintage printing press.[2] After graduating he went to Africa with SIM as a printer and also passed on his Prairie "Search Questions" to Nigerian youth in Bible studies.

---

[1] Albert served with China Inland Mission (now Overseas Missionary Fellowship).

[2] Rumor had it that a previous owner in the "cow-town" of Calgary had used the press for counterfeiting. It certainly sold cheap and at PBI it was soundly "converted" to another purpose.

Reflecting changing conditions, closely regulated "social rules" of earlier years gave way in the 1980s to more normal campus life in a Christian environment.

Three Presidents of Prairie (L-R) Ted S. Rendall, Rick Down, Paul T. Maxwell (The fourth President to serve since "LE," Paul S. Ferris, was unavailable for this photo.)

Chapter 16: Priorities

"Lord, save us from being so right that we are rough." —LEM

PASSING THE BATON

I'LL DO YOUR WORK while you look after my business," I'd told the Lord when I arrived in Africa. His work, I knew, was to spread the gospel and disciple believers—in my case, through literature. The "business" I'd turned over to God was to find the woman of God's choice for marriage.

I'd had no time for romance anyway. Also, as in the case of Ernest Maxwell and Freeda Jones, the social context of Africa and of the Mission meant I had to be very sure of the right one before proposing. How I came to know that belongs to another story. Suffice it to say that in a few years, as staff developed, I could keep a more normal schedule in place of round-the-clock work and began to think about romance.

About that time, the mission assigned Lorna Parrott to Lagos. A Canadian who'd once been a commercial secretary, she'd graduated from Prairie and had worked on the Prairie Overcomer staff. In the mission's eyes, that qualified her to fill an urgent secretarial need at Niger Challenge Press, publisher of *African Challenge*.[1] Of course the relevant point to me was that I fell in love with Lorna, we married, and raised our family, a son and daughter, in Nigeria.

Imagine my astonishment years later, when "Mother Maxwell" said to me, "I always thought that Lorna Parrott would make a good wife for Harold Fuller." The wife of Prairie's principal—match-making, no less? When Lorna heard that, she commented, "But Mrs. Maxwell didn't even know me!"

---

[1] The first dictated letter Lorna took from me was to fellow missionary Ernest Maxwell!

She probably did, through her husband. LE's special interest was *The Overcomer*, and he knew the staff there more than they realized. Lorna later remembered one evening when she was working overtime, and "Daddy Maxwell" dropped in to see how things were coming along. Later, when Lorna headed for Nigeria, I suspect he thought that this young lady might be just the one that an editor there was looking for! And Pearl understood something of the pressures of living with an editor and publishing a magazine. She had done the entire mailing of *The Prairie Overcomer* when it began publication the same year Ernest was born. (It was a task she handled from the family's single room in the dormitory, in spite of having two children!)

More surprised was I when, on my first furlough, I visited Prairie. LE took me for a tour of campus developments. As we stood at the pulpit of the rebuilt "Tabernacle,"[1] he took hold of my elbow and said he'd like me to become his assistant. I was shocked. Did he think I'd grown spiritually more than I had? Did he realize that Prairie was no longer the Bible school he had founded, and his successors would need special gifts? It was indicative of the transparency—of the simple sincerity—of the man that he should so casually share his thoughts. I didn't think I was the one he needed, so I replied that I felt my work in Africa was not completed. That was in late 1957. The man God was preparing for further responsibility was already teaching Bible at Prairie. That was graduate Ted S. Rendall ('56).

Scottish Thistles or Alberta Roses?

Ted Rendall's own pilgrimage is a remarkable story in itself. As a child in Scotland, he nearly died from complications of tuberculosis. In the absence of specific medications, doctors recommended fresh air as the remedy, and Ted virtually lived in the open air for a while. At age 11 he weighed only 44 lbs. but recovered and started preaching at the age of 15. Later he realized the need for more in-depth Bible study.

---

[1] After the co-founder's death, it was renamed Maxwell Memorial Tabernacle.

"I'd heard of Prairie through some of its graduates," recalls Rendall. "There were several fine Bible and theological schools in Scotland, but I was attracted by Prairie's emphasis on the crucified life. I know God led me here—otherwise why should I leave the beautiful city of Edinburgh, with its ancient castles, its university life, and its museums, and come to Three Hills!"

So Rendall found himself in Three Hills in 1953. With his brilliant mind, he whizzed through Prairie's courses and after his Junior year became part-time pastor at a rural church, continuing to minister there for 20 years.

During his student years, Rendall worked at the school for two summers in various jobs, including building steam tunnels and sidewalks, skidding logs at Prairie's bush camp, and making windows. Upon graduation in 1956, he applied to serve on staff for a year in gratitude for Prairie's training.

"I was willing to undertake any task that would be assigned me," Rendall recalls. "To my amazement and delight I was assigned as resource person for Mr. Maxwell! This involved reading newspapers, magazines, and books and suggesting material for Mr. Maxwell's preaching, teaching, and writing."

One day in the summer of 1956, noting the great pressure the Editor was under while trying to get away for summer preaching, Ted tried his hand at writing several items for the section LE thought was most important in *The Prairie Overcomer*: "The World of Today in the Light of the Word." These were brief comments on current events from a biblical perspective.

"He was delighted, and I felt accepted by him. From then on we often wrote the section together, and since we didn't sign each item, few people could tell that it was a combination of LEM and TSR."

When the year was over, LE heard of Ted's plan to resign and return to Scotland to care for his widowed mother.

"Well, I'll write to tell your mother you're needed here!" Maxwell challenged him—not that he was unconcerned for a widowed mother. Then he continued, "I think there's a place here for you!"

"I didn't pray very much about my decision!" Rendall says. "I thought, 'Here's a man of God, a man whom I respect, telling me there is a place here for me.' I took his invitation as God's call to me and served at Prairie until 1998."

Rendall joined the faculty to teach second-year Bible. In 1960 the Board appointed him as Vice-Principal of the Bible Institute. When someone objected that this 27-year-old Scot was too young for the post, Maxwell responded, "There's nothing that time won't take care of!"

The demonstrative American and reserved Scot had totally different personalities, but as LE poured himself into his adopted Timothy, Ted S. Rendall proved to be the combination of theologian, Bible teacher, and editor needed to take on many responsibilities. Alan Kirk (grandson of Fergus), a university professor of New Testament Studies and Early Christianity, later said of him, "He has an encyclopedic mind." (Rendall eventually became Principal, when Maxwell's other "Timothy," Paul Timothy Maxwell, became President of the school.)

There were many others whom God brought together in the team as teachers and administrators. I'd returned to Africa, but as I heard of these developments, I gave thanks that God was building up the team for the transitions everyone knew must lie ahead.

Catching up with Change

In *Future Shock* [1] Alvin Toffler forecast that the pace of change would escalate exponentially in the latter half of the nineteenth century. Change was already taking place fast enough, it seemed to us who arrived on the scene earlier in the century. During World War II there were no

---

[1] Alvin Toffler, *Future Shock*. New York: Random House, 1970.

computers as we now know them. In the Navy we used a "modern marvel" the size of a billiard table to clock the position of an enemy submarine. It was full of dials we operated manually to enter information of the sub's estimated speed, direction, depth, distance, and our own speed. An engineer's slide rule was the nearest thing to a personal computer.

By the 1970s, computers were standard equipment in any sizeable business, and by the 1990s they were almost an essential for university students. But more than technology was changing. Western society was becoming radical, and developing nations were struggling with the responsibilities and revolutions of new-found Independence.

For the sprawling Bible Institute at Three Hills, that meant change also. Students arrived with different expectations and, indeed, a different worldview from what we had before the 1950s. And the school from which so many Christian workers had spread across North America and Europe and around the globe discovered that its graduates were going back into a world that demanded different skills and had different expectations than the world their parents had known.

Revolutionary Nations

This was true in North America and Europe. I certainly found it to be true overseas. When I first went to Africa, much of it was still under colonial rule. The experience of the Cross in my own life, gained at Prairie, was key in my taking the message of the Cross of salvation and discipleship into another culture—stresses, misunderstandings, and all. Beyond that, the Lord used the skills I'd acquired from my parents, naval service, extra-curricular studies, and home-mission service. The fact I had no academic degree didn't matter at the time. We missionaries of that era learned and served while wading through the swirling currents of those revolutionary years as countries gained Independence.

The changing demands of nations forced us to acquire paper evidence (certificates, diplomas, and degrees) that persuaded immigration to grant us visas, to help these nations physically as well as spiritually. Those demands arose not only from national governments trying to find employment for high school and university graduates churning on to the employment market (which couldn't develop as fast as the supply), but also by sectors of the population that needed more than the rudiments of reading, 'riting, and 'rithmetic.

These factors—the attitudes of incoming students and the needs of outgoing graduates—made their own impact on the school. Analyzing that bit of history is not in the realm of this story of *Maxwell's Passion and Power*. But it did need great wisdom on the part of Prairie's leadership, faculty, and staff through the transition years. They didn't want to lose the school's invaluable "immersion" in the Scriptures and death-and-resurrection pilgrimage. These were foundational to all else in preparing for service. Whatever else changed, the Cross in the life of the believer was at the heart of Prairie's *raison d'être*.

Added to all the changes was the stark reality that descended upon all Bible schools: student demographics were changing. There were now more Bible institutes, or Bible courses in other types of school. Churches sometimes offered Bible courses. As some Bible schools turned to more general liberal arts courses, Bible retreat centers helped meet the need for concentrated study and meditation in the Scriptures: places such as L'Abri, Capernwray, and InterVarsity camps. All Bible schools and seminaries across the continent faced dwindling enrolment.

Painting Prairie Pretty

Administration recognized the need to meet the changing context. John Thompson was a businessman with sales experience. After graduating in 1954, Thompson became Secretary to the school. That included supervising department managers. With an office next to LE's, he soon found that the principal was a born promoter. LE readily agreed with Thompson's suggestion of a campaign to make the campus more attractive. "Paint Prairie Pretty!" he named it.

Some of his ideas were a shock to faithful old-timers for whom the gray buildings symbolized a spartan spirit. "What's wrong with gray?"

a maintenance manager asked Thompson as they met on a sidewalk during the summer.

"Just turn around!" Thompson asked the man.

When the puzzled manager turned around, he found himself looking at a colorful flowerbed.

"What color are the blossoms?" Thompson asked. Point made, the manager selected green or rose or blue or yellow for repainting jobs. When winter snow later blanketed the campus, students enjoyed the more colorful buildings.

However, another significant change involved removing pink and blue—that is, symbolically. Ted Rendall, when president, dramatized banishment of the rumored "pink and blue sidewalks" during "Homecoming Week" one summer.

"We painted a section blue and a section pink," he told later classes of freshmen. "Then we covered the sections with white sheets—over which men and women walked together!" It was a new era. Men and women could walk downtown on the same day! Other "social regulations" loosened up from 1986 onwards.

"Feeling His Passionate Love for Christ"

Leigh Robinson was one of several men and woman who served in administration during that era. His work on staff and his subsequent ministry give insight into how the Institute's anchor held firm while the ship tossed in surging seas as society changed.

Robinson was one of the "international students" (he hailed from South Africa) who arrived at Prairie in 1967. The school was developing its administrative team, but LE, who had nearly died the year before while recuperating from retina surgery, was still teaching upper level Bible classes.

"When I think of Mr. Maxwell as a teacher and preacher," recalls Robinson; "I remember

- feeling the heat of his passionate love for Christ;
- being moved by his commitment to Scripture;
- feeling like a peeled onion as layer upon layer of my 'self' was exposed by his incisive and convicting preaching;
- laughing with him as he exposed the weakness of human strength and the folly of human wisdom, only to realize with a start that I was actually laughing at myself;
- seeing his lips quiver and hearing his voice break as he shared some moving story of Christian commitment and heroism;
- seeing the glory of God upon his face in a Hebrews class as he spoke, tears streaming down his cheeks, of the One who was made "a little lower than the angels" now "crowned with glory and honor";
- watching him leap over the platform rail in "G" Classroom, point his finger in the face of a startled female student, and cry out, "The word is near you; it is in your mouth and in your heart . . ." (Romans 10:8). The rest of the class rocked with laughter;
- how he addressed the Lord during prayer with a perfect blend of reverence, familiarity, and passion—often beginning with, "Now, Lord . . !"
- hearing him pray with passion for the "hot spots" of the world and crying out: "These poor sheep, what have they done?"
- hearing him mock sinful self-pity and chide us for being "thorry (sorry) for yourthelf (yourself)."

Graduating in 1971, Leigh joined the staff, eventually becoming Dean of Students, and also taught Bible and Practical Theology.

"My office was almost directly across the hall from LE's in the Academic Center," explained Robinson. "This gave me opportunity to watch his comings and goings, his interaction with people, and his study habits.

"For years he taught Bible IV in the second period (around 9 a.m.)

each day. He always arrived at his office between 7.30 and 8.00. Even though he was the president and approaching his eighties, he frequently arrived before other faculty members, and if snow needed to be swept from the steps of the building, he'd pick up a broom and do it himself.

Mining New Gems

"When he entered his office, he immediately went about the sacred work of preparing for his Romans class. I would peep through the window in his door and watch him standing at his sloping desk, his little 'sunshade' cap on his head, getting ready for class. Even though he had taught Romans more than forty times by then, he always went to class freshly prepared, and he was always mining new gems from the text.

"While on the faculty, I would try to go to afternoon tea in the dining room at the same time as he did, in hope of sitting at the same table. I always came away enriched by his insights into Scripture, his grasp of world affairs, and his ability to connect the Word with the life situations others brought up. I also enjoyed his sense of humor. He would throw his head back and laugh heartily over some funny incident or anecdote. It was easy to locate the table he was sitting at! But he was never shady or suggestive."

Maxwell readily admitted he was not much of a counselor—at least not one who sat and listened endlessly to people's problems. Those who expected more, often left disappointed. After listening for a little while, he'd put his finger on the problem and suddenly stand up.

"Well, my brother, you just need to die to yourself in this area!" he'd say, ushering the student to the door. But on the way out, he'd break into prayer: "Now, Lord, help this dear brother to . . ."

Robinson was only 24 when he became a member of Prairie's Board of Directors. LE was also on the Board.

"Being young and inexperienced, I didn't say much, but I looked and listened carefully," Leigh says. "Because the Board held

Mr. Maxwell in such high esteem, he could have exerted enormous influence and had his way on almost any issue. But he always listened graciously to the opinions of others, was open to change, and didn't cling to power."

"Thanks for Not Talking!"

One summer Robinson drove Maxwell home from a conference at which he'd been preaching—very near an assignment Leigh was taking. "I'll never forget that trip! I had LE all to myself for eight or ten hours, and we talked about a wide range of things. But we also traveled in silence for long stretches. When we reached Three Hills, I was glad I'd kept quiet at times."

"My brother," the aging Maxwell said as he left the car; "thank you for not talking to me the whole time. When some people give me rides they exhaust me with all their chatter!"

Leigh and his wife, Esther, and two-year-old son Jonathan visited their homeland of South Africa the summer of 1976. Tragically, Esther died in a motor accident. Broken-hearted, Leigh returned to Prairie with Jonathan to begin the new school term.

"I'll never forget Mr. Maxwell's compassion," Leigh says. "When I shared at an evening service the lessons God was teaching me, I could hear him groaning in identification with my pain. He closed in prayer, lifting Jonathan and me to the Lord with a father's tenderness."

Later when Leigh considered re-marrying, he and Irene (whom he eventually married) went to talk with LE, hoping for some light on the confusion both faced at the time.

"Beloved of the Lord!" welcomed LE, holding out both hands to grasp theirs. He listened and assured them that what they were going through was perfectly normal. After praying for them, he sent them on their way with lighter hearts.

"Firmly Embedded Nails"

"I remember the discipline with which he exercised, walking every night regardless of the weather," Robinson reminisced after 25 years of his own pastoral ministry.

"I remember the kindly way he treated Mrs. Maxwell. He always spoke to her with such graciousness, appreciation, and respect.

"I also recall his love for ice cream. When a hostess would ask if he'd like a little ice cream, he'd shock her by replying: "No thanks, I'd like a lot!" Once when he and I stayed in a university dormitory during a conference, he discovered a soft ice cream machine with unlimited use. He was in heaven!"

In 1978 Robinson returned to South Africa as a pastor. He confesses in his own ministry there have been low periods when his faith was tested or he was tempted to revise his theology.

"At such times I've thought, if the beliefs I hold are the same that shaped a life like Mr. Maxwell's, there can't be much wrong with them," Robinson recalls. "So I'd better hold on to them!"

When Ruth Maxwell, while serving in Africa, dropped in on Robinson's large church, she did so incognito. "I just wanted to worship like anyone else, not to be known as the granddaughter of someone people considered famous. To my surprise, I found that everyone seemed to know my Grandpa already—their pastor quoted him so often in his sermons!"

"It's true," Robinson later confirmed, after returning to Canada as Senior Pastor of historic Central Baptist Church in Victoria, BC. "Examples from his life and teaching from his lips have pervaded my preaching ministry. I sat under his teaching and preaching for eleven years, and many of his sayings are 'like firmly embedded nails' (Eccl. 12:11) in the walls of my mind! He influenced my life more than anyone else."

Chapter 17: Trauma

"God doesn't comfort us to make us comfortable,
but to make us comforters." —LEM

FIRST TO REACH HEAVEN

THE TWO-LANE TRANS-CANADA HIGHWAY stretched towards the horizon as Ernest and Freeda drove to their next missionary conference. When the SIM office in 1980 had asked Ernest and Freeda to consider staying in Canada to represent the mission on the Prairies, the whole family had unexpected opportunity for quality time together—especially while David, Ruth, and Mark went through adjustments to their own country's culture. Living in Three Hills also gave them the joy of spending time with the senior Maxwells—Freeda's first quality time to spend with her in-laws.

SIM's Canada Director Jack Phillips and I had been with Ernest and Freeda at InterVarsity's Urbana missions conference in Illinois the end of 1981, as part of SIM's team interacting with eager college students. Now on their way from a conference at Briercrest Bible Institute in Caronport, Saskatchewan, they were headed to a church in Fort St. John in northern Alberta. Ernest's sister, Lois Friesen, on furlough from Japan, had been with them at Briercrest. From there she traveled with them as far as Calgary before they headed north.

"How I treasure those last hours we shared together!" Lois since comments. Driving north, Ernest and Freeda left the snow-covered flat wheat plains behind and were driving through scrub forest. Ernest turned up the car heater as the winter sun kissed the horizon.

Without warning the car skidded sideways. They had hit a stretch of black ice—the dreaded sudden freeze of water. It was impossible to see before they were on it, and their car went out of control. An oncoming vehicle was also sliding across the ice. A tremendous crash reverberated through the brush to distant farm houses. Then silence!

Silence like that of a graveyard.

Police found three dead bodies in the mangled wreckage of the two vehicles. One was the driver of the other car. The other two were Ernest and Freeda. It was January 30, 1982. Ernest was 55; Freeda was 58. Ironically, they had survived suicidal road conditions, tropical disease, civil war, and other dangers in Nigeria, only to have a fatal accident on a quiet icy road while home in Canada!

Back in Ontario, our phone was ringing. I was totally unprepared for this call.

"The Maxwell children want you to preach at their parent's funeral service!" the phone call from Three Hills informed me after explaining the tragedy. I was stunned, my heart aching for the three left without parents.

I knew that life in Nigeria had not been easy for them. As a teen, David had reacted to his father's earlier rigid discipline. Ruth, like many daughters, struggled in her relations with her mother but related well to her father and enjoyed the fun of working alongside him. By the time Mark was born, Ernest had greatly mellowed. There was new understanding mixed with his discipline. As the children left home for further education and career, Ernest sought to strengthen the family bonds that had been stretched thin at times while the parents had been meeting others' needs. God had helped Ernest and Freeda bring the family closer together. At the same time, the Lord seemed to be preparing them for what lay ahead.

"During the last months before the accident I saw a remarkable growth in Dad and Mom's relationship with each other," Ruth recalls. "It was lovely to see their interdependence. But at the same time, I wondered how Dad would survive without Mom. And how would Mom survive without Dad? The change in their relationship with each other was so marked, I knew they would find it difficult to live without having each other."

Freeda had recently said to Mark, "I wish we could go in front of you and take all those hard bumps you'll face in life." David remembers her saying much the same to him years earlier while she packed his bags as he left home and Nigeria. "It revealed the strength of her faith that God would keep that which she'd committed to him," David recalls. "She was able to leave me in God's hands, knowing I had to take responsibility for my own decisions."

Now the parents had "gone in front" of them together and had taken the bump of death, literally. They left a gaping hole. All children need their parents—but "missionary kids" (MKs) have a special need after years of serial separations. As the father of two MKs, I wept inwardly arriving in Three Hills. "Lord, fill the void in each life!" I prayed, hugging David, Ruth, and Mark.

As Grandpa Maxwell sought to comfort them, he gave them a well-known verse but with a different, very relevant application: "When my father and mother forsake me, then will the Lord pick me up" (Psalm 27:10). To his own family he confessed, "This is the hardest thing I've experienced in my life!"

The Alabaster Box

"The Tab" was filled with students, faculty, staff, and friends from across Canada and USA, hushed in the presence of the Lord of Life and the reality of death. They were there to support the mourning family seated in the front rows. Yet "Mother Maxwell's" sorrow must have been mixed with the joy she remembered feeling when her eldest son had dedicated his life to serve in Africa—a calling she'd felt in her youth but could not realize for medical reasons. Similarly, "Daddy Maxwell" had looked upon Ernest as fulfilling the missionary burden for Africa he'd had as a young man.

Before my message, Ernest's father, shaky from Parkinson's disease, slowly rose to his feet to lead us in prayer. "There has to be something worse than having a firstborn son in Heaven!" he commented in a husky voice. "This dear lad and I have been very close for many years."

A sob spread through the congregation. But only the family knew that Ernest had been named after LE's young brother, killed in a farm accident. What childhood scenes were going through the father's mind?

Did he recall the tragedy when his younger brother, Ernest, had taken Leslie's place on the hay wagon because Leslie was not well? In a sense, when young Ernest toppled off the wagon and died, he had given his life for his older brother. In those years in Kansas, their father had obviously loved Ernest above all the others in the family. The lad's death had sobered the rest of them.

Now decades later, in distant Three Hills, the mourning father recited William Cowper's hymn before he prayed.

> *God moves in a mysterious way,*
> *His wonders to perform;*
> *He plants His footsteps in the sea*
> *And rides upon the storm.*
>
> *Ye fearful saints, fresh courage take!*
> *The clouds ye so much dread*
> *Are big with mercy and will break*
> *In blessings on your head.*
>
> *Judge not the Lord by feeble sense,*
> *But trust him for his grace;*
> *Behind a frowning providence*
> *He hides a smiling face.*
>
> *His purposes will ripen fast,*
> *Unfolding every hour;*
> *The bud may have a bitter taste,*
> *But sweet will be the flower.*

Blind unbelief is sure to err,
And scan his work in vain;
God is his own interpreter,
And he will make it plain.

There was really no need for me to speak—the veteran pilgrim had given the message. However, I spoke on "The Alabaster Box of Ointment":[1]

"When the woman poured the precious ointment on Jesus' head, some of the guests asked, 'Why this waste?' It would be natural for us to ask the same question, for we needed Ernest and Freeda. David, Ruth, Mark; Father and Mother Maxwell; other members of the family—the mission, the churches in Nigeria—all needed them. Many African friends in the little village of Karu are mourning along with us today.

"While the question, humanly speaking, recognizes the value of the precious offering, it also reveals an earthly evaluation. It focuses on the material value. I don't know why God should take Ernest and Freeda when they are most needed. But that's my problem, not God's. I don't understand God's plans because I'm mortal—but I know I can trust him.

"John wrote in his Revelation: Blessed are the dead which die in the Lord from henceforth; 'Yes,' says the Spirit, 'they will rest from their labor; for their deeds will follow them.'"[2]

Thorns and Roses

For Ernest and Freeda's children, the way of the Cross was strewn with thorns as well as roses.[3]

David struggled with his low self-image before finding personal

---

[1] Mark 14.3-9.

[2] Revelation 14.13. Ernest and Freeda's grave marker was inscribed with words from this verse.

[3] See chapters 23 and 24 for further details of the family and how the Lord met their need.

peace. Slowly God brought healing through marriage and a loving family.

Ruth felt very much alone. Precious memories helped in moments of loneliness. Then I heard that a suitcase containing her mother's Nigerian jewelry—one of her few keepsakes—had fallen off a bus. By the time Ruth tracked down the lost baggage, the hand-wrought silver filigree pieces were missing.

"Lord, why did you let that happen? Ruth needs every tie with her parents!" I remember wondering. It was as if God were removing everything except his presence. And Ruth did cast herself on the One who had received to himself her parents—her most precious "possession" on earth. Later she was able to counsel others who had passed through sorrow.

"All things work together for good to them that love God,"[1] somehow kept ringing in Mark's mind. At first he didn't understand. He found it hard to mix with others and make "small talk." In church, organ playing reminded him of funeral parlor organs. Later "all things" came together in a strange way.

"I suddenly realized I no longer needed to go to church just to please my parents—but instead to please God!" Mark recalls. "That's when I made the decision to live more than superficial Christianity." In spite of the bereavement that could have left him adrift in life, he found new purpose. Whatever he did, he would do for God's glory.

Their Deeds Will Follow Them

All three knew that the seeds their parents planted in Africa continued to grow and bear fruit. As children they had played with Nigerian boys and girls who now served in the church, community, and government. Years later they received a letter from one of them, Eliazar—son of Baba, the family friend who worked in Ernest and Freeda's home for some

---

[1] Romans 8.28.

twenty years. Baba had helped raise the three children while their parents taught in the adjacent Bible school.

"I wish one of you could come back and see the fruit of your parents' lives. I'm where I am today because of your parents' impact on my life," Eliazar wrote Ruth Maxwell. He'd attended Bible school and become a missionary, eventually assisting in missionary care for the Evangelical Missionary Society.[1]

---

[1] EMS became one of the largest indigenous missions in the world. It was co-founded as the Nigerian missionary arm of SIM-related churches by SIMers Clifton and Alma McElheran. Clifton was son of the McElherans in whose farmhouse Prairie Bible Institute began, and nephew of Fergus Kirk.

Chapter 18: "For Better or Worse"

"God does not fill us to make us great,
but to make us gracious." —LEM

LEARNING TOGETHER TO THE END

"SHE SUBMITS AND I OBEY; she always lets me have her way!" LE sometimes mischievously recited when introducing his wife. But family and friends knew the love and respect he had for Pearl. He realized he couldn't have managed without her. When he traveled overseas, he brought back some memento—usually a silver broach or semi-precious stone clasp, to say "I love you—and I missed you!"[1] Fifty years after their marriage, he concluded their Golden celebration with a fitting tribute to his beloved Pearl: "To God be the glory—and to her be the honor!"

"Beyond the Price of Rubies"[2]

In the first few years of marriage, after serving as school matron, Pearl realized her husband's workload meant she needed to focus on raising their children. She knew he'd be available in an emergency, but otherwise she managed their household—and did so wisely and capably.

Earlier, some onlookers might have judged her for not sharing school responsibilities, but she quietly accepted the family role as God's purpose for her. That included starching and ironing her husband's white shirts (he always dressed immaculately) and sewing her children's frocks, shirts, and blouses from color-printed sugar sacks. In later years, she had the joy of sewing her daughters' graduation dresses—but not from sugar sacks by then!

---

[1] In keeping with their simple life style, the only ornament the Maxwell family allowed themselves at the time was a broach or clasp pin.

[2] Proverbs 31.10.

"Mother Maxwell" was conscious that although the children knew their father loved them, the demands of the school made him at times almost an "absentee" father—whether home or not. She knew he could not have developed the school and discipled the students (among them his own children as they entered Bible school) without having that complete focus.

She also knew her husband, although well disciplined and loving, hadn't had the benefit of a mentoring father in his own childhood. ("I grew up like topsy!" he told the family.) Pearl not only became the answer to his need but also part of God's answer to her own prayer at age 15 that each of her future children and grandchildren would follow the Lord.

Pearl had never been strong. When sleep eluded her at night, she used the hours to pray for family and students. Later in life, suffering from exhaustion, arthritis, low thyroid, and sciatica, Pearl felt the toll of years meeting family needs. She became depressed.[1] In the context of Prairie's culture at the time, it was a difficult trial for her, her husband, and the family. Many Christians, not understanding the physical basis of clinical depression, felt it was a spiritual problem! Mother Maxwell spent several weeks recuperating in a Calgary clinic.

Most difficult to bear was concern over waywardness that showed up in some of the children and grandchildren. The older ones had quietly followed their childhood training. Paul turned out to be of a different personality. From his grade school years on, an independent, mischievous streak brought him into collision with school rules.

"If Paul needs a spanking, don't hesitate to give it!" LE had said to me back in 1949, when Paul was still in grade school. At the time, I was superintendent of the Sunday school Paul attended. The cherub-faced, loveable boy needed attention more than spanking, I felt. When I later heard he was nearly suspended from high school, I knew what he was going through. I could only imagine the personal pain his parents

---

[1] Medics diagnosed the cause as menopausal anemia.

experienced as they tried to understand what was happening in the life of their son.

"A Thorn in My Nest"

All the child-training principles LE had held forth on, all he'd been saved from as a youth in Kansas City, everything that the school stood for in separation from the world—his own teenage son seemed bent on trashing. Paul seemed headed for the same dissolute life that the young Leslie had been saved out of. And it felt like an arrow piercing his heart when rebel Paul commented that his father seemed more interested in the Institute than in the family (see Chapter 24).

This was the father who had preached about the laxity of Eli the priest in not effectively rebuking his sons' sin.[1] "Daddy Maxwell" felt convicted that he'd not spent the Saturday morning hour of Bible study with his two youngest children as he had with the older children. "I was wrong—period!" he confessed in one of his typical terse expressions. He thought about the Scripture, "If anyone does not know how to manage his own family, how can he take care of God's church?"[2] He even wondered if he should resign from leadership, but the Institute Board did not agree.

"The Devil would have scored a double victory if I'd resigned!" he later realized. It was not as if Paul's father had neglected to correct him throughout his childhood. Now that Paul was a young adult, his burdened father had to trust the Holy Spirit to deal with him.

The way of the Cross didn't become easier with age, the veteran found. It was as if, after all these years of teaching others, God still had lessons for him—or for us who watched from the sidelines. Was there really no respite, not even in old age, to embracing the Cross daily?

---

[1] 1 Samuel 3.13. Eli reprimanded his sons but apparently not early enough or seriously enough.
[2] 1 Timothy 3.5.

Often we'd heard our mentor pray, "Lord, if you see me becoming too comfortable, put a thorn in my nest!"[1]

We'd always remember LE's study of Jacob[2]—how this strong-spirited man had wrestled with an angel from God until he wrested a blessing—in exchange for a limp as a reminder of his frailty. Was God's angel wrestling once more with LE's indomitable spirit, until he accepted the limp?

"Trust Me with Joy"

"O God!" Paul's mother despaired one day after receiving yet another report of her son's misbehavior. "What can we do about Paul?"

"Trust me with joy!" the incongruous answer seemed to come as clearly as if from someone in the room.

"Lord, how can I trust you with joy?" wept the distraught mother. "My son's disgracing your name!"

"Rejoice in what I am able to do for Paul!" she heard within her heart. Finding peace herself, she was able to pray until Paul's life turned around. After that, he and his father spent much time conferring—the kind of time Paul had needed twenty years earlier—in preparation for the day when the Board appointed Paul President.

What healing had taken place in the hearts of parents and son! "God gave us understanding hearts for those whose children stray," LE commented.

---

[1] George Whitefield (18th Century preacher) prayed: "Dearest Redeemer, make me humble. And whenever thou seest me in danger of being exalted above measure, graciously send me a thorn in the flesh, so that thy blessings may not prove my ruin." T.C. Upham (19th C.) prayed, "Put a thorn in every enjoyment, a worm in every gourd, that would either prevent my being wholly thine, or in any measure retard my progress in the divine life."

[2] Genesis 32.22-32.

Not only did parents and son experience reconciliation, but Paul, as he grew spiritually, also became a trusted friend of his aging father. On one occasion the elder Maxwell was distressed by criticism (a student criticized the way he concluded conferences) and by the departure of several faculty members. Paul expressed concern that his father was shouldering all the blame for the departures.

"A brother has come to me to point out that I've been carrying this burden myself, instead of casting it upon the Lord!" LE told the next public meeting. Paul was touched by the humility of his father in accepting his counsel and counting him as "a brother."

A Soldier's Regimen

I can't remember LE's being ill during my student days. I don't think he ever cancelled a class because of illness. He seemed to bubble with good health and energy. His stamina was staggering to us who knew his schedule: up early for personal prayer and meditation, breakfast with the family, then off either to chapel or office to handle correspondence and business. He usually spent lunch hour with the students, giving him opportunity to share informally with us. Class teaching, message preparation, and editing filled the rest of the day.

Yet he always seemed to have time to stop on the sidewalk or in the classroom to chat with a student. We didn't know the other pressures that took his time, such as board and staff meetings and personnel problems. Overseas mission conferences took chunks of time during summer months, yet all were useful ministry.

As his own family members went overseas, he had the joy of visiting them and other graduates during conferences in a dozen or so countries. When he visited his daughter Anna and her husband Allen in the Philippines, my brother David (married to Prairie grad Beverley Erickson) remembers translating for him:

"The people loved his refreshing style—but I had to explain several of his idioms and puns! He never faltered during a hot and humid eight-km. trek to a bamboo, thatch-roofed church. When he slid into a deep ditch, he got up exclaiming, 'No problem!'"

Apart from his natural physique, LE could keep up such a pace only through self-discipline, including regular walks and occasional workouts in the gymnasium. Years earlier, he'd learned the signs of "burnout." At that time, as enormous daytime pressures left him sleepless, he'd walk four miles to a friend's farm, sleep there, and walk back early the next morning in time for classes. Exhausting himself physically helped him "turn off" his mind and fall asleep.

He knew how to make the most of a Saturday or public holiday. While summer conferences elsewhere took up much of school vacation, a few days away fishing or moose hunting were precious to him and important to his health.

Until 1978 LE continued as president, showing wisdom and patience in handling problems. "God's work, done in God's way, will never lack *trials*!" he paraphrased J. Hudson Taylor's famous statement.[1] That seemed to summarize his view of the burdens of administration. As the school grew and aging took its toll, Maxwell was glad to turn over administration to Paul Maxwell and Ted Rendall while he concentrated on writing and Bible exposition—the reason most students enrolled.

But accustomed to a tireless pace, LE was impatient with himself as aches and pains increased during the last years of his life. It was frustrating not to be able to bound along at full speed. His doctor ordered him to eat his meals at home, away from the activity of the student dining hall. Later he reluctantly cut back his teaching schedule.

Cataract surgery in the 1950s had been his first lengthy bout with infirmity, as complications delayed recovery. Ten years later a detached retina left him sightless in one eye. An infection nearly took his life.

---

[1] Concerning faith, Taylor said, "God's work, done in God's way, will never lack God's supply."

In the hospital, a nurse attempted to force-feed him. "Stop being a baby," she chided when his body, accustomed to rigorous exercise, reacted. That was most humiliating for this old soldier who'd never pitied himself. He was steadily losing strength until Pearl insisted on feeding him at mealtimes, bringing homemade meals in. The hospital dietitians were none the wiser, since Pearl herself finished off his regulation fare!

However, his helplessness during recovery taught him much. Like a spiritual general, he'd been used to leading men and women. Now, for the first time in his dynamic life, he was totally reliant on others. "To think it's come to this!" he'd exclaim.

Apart from his love for the Lord and family, his greatest love was to read the Word and other books. Even with failing eyesight, he could locate favorite verses fairly accurately—he'd replace a well-worn Bible with one having the same page format but in larger print.

Darkness and Light

During his retina surgery, he couldn't even read! At one time his head was locked between two weights in order to allow his retina to heal. This once energetic man was bound to feel each dependency as if it were (in one of his typical expressions) "another nail to keep me where I belong —crucified with Christ."

As he lay weak and infirm, emotionally drained, his years of service played across the screen of memory. Wonderful years they'd been, yet he was conscious of misjudgments he'd made and of criticisms leveled at him. Had he been too brusque, too hasty at times? All he'd preached to others seemed to return on his own head.

"O God," he groaned; "just write over me, Unprofitable Servant!" Then the Spirit reminded him of a world that was suffering even more. "Disciplining soldiers for Christ" had been his ministry, but those soldiers needed to express Christ's love to hurting men and women.

It was a dark moment, not only from the bandages over his eyes but also from the depressing exhaustion. Then a comforting Bible verse flashed into his mind: "The darkness and the light are both alike to thee."[1]

"God taught me something in hospital," he told staff at the next meeting he attended, tears in his eyes. "I've come to realize there are many hurting people around us. Above all else, they need to see the love of Christ in us." There was a new softness in the Old Soldier's withered face—not the softness of ease but of empathy.

"From here to the end of my life," he said, "I want to be kind, to be gentle to every person I meet."[2]

After he returned home from hospital, LE's interest in life slowly returned. While he could no longer keep up his former pace, LE provided an important element in the school's transition just by being there.

He so loved to teach that he continued a class in Romans into his 80s—at the end leaning on an elevated podium that brought the Bible closer to his failing eyes. Although in conversation his voice sometimes trailed to a whisper, the classroom seemed to rally his speaking voice. To students, that was a special class; although their mentor's body was weak, his spirit was still strong!

Yet he didn't try to run the school from the sidelines. Once when Paul, while president, asked his father for advice, LE said to him, "Ask Ted." At the time Ted Rendall was second in command.

A Maxwellian Tour

During this period I dropped in on campus with my son, David. Driving to the school farm (a nostalgic visit for me), we noticed a lone figure

---

[1] Psalm 139.12AV.
[2] Richardson interview, quoted by Stephen M. Spaulding, *Op cit.*

walking along the side of the road. Over one shoulder he balanced a fishing rod and a fish, and with the other hand he carried a fishing tackle box. I knew at once it was the man whose life had touched mine at so many points.

"Well, well!" he exclaimed as we stopped the car. "What brings you here?" Now 78, he was on his way home from a fishing trip. Someone had dropped him off at the corner. When he learned I was showing my son around my old school, he ditched his rod, fish, and box at home. "Let me show you around, David!" he said, jumping in the back seat.

"Wow!" exclaimed my teenage son afterwards. "The president himself gave us a guided tour!" It was very Maxwellian.

"LE" enthusiastically displays a perch he's
just caught through a hole in the ice.

Chapter 19: Coronation

The cross of full surrender leaves no odor of the tomb;
That cross is covered by a life of resurrection bloom."

—Quoted by LEM

PROMOTION FOR AN OLD SOLDIER

IN A SPIRITUAL SENSE, LE preached a lot about death and life—being dead to self and alive to God.[1] The believer's eternal hope is to be with Christ forever. It was great theology, and it had practical benefits in this present life. As "soldiers prepared for war" we shouldn't cling to the materialism of our world. We often were reminded, "A good soldier doesn't encumber himself with the cares of this life."[2]

But how did life for the Old Soldier end? How did the spiritual life-and-death teaching stack up finally?

In his eighties, Parkinson's increasingly took its toll. That degeneration of the nervous system must have been a debilitating experience, coming on top of sight deterioration. Yet his former spirit bubbled up constantly. After Sam and Margaret (Thiessen) Ratzlaff once visited him, he accompanied them to the front door. All at once he was unable to take the next step—part of Parkinson's syndrome. But he looked at them with that old twinkle in his eye. "The motor won't kick in!" he quipped.

Even if his "motor" was slowing, his mind wasn't—right to the end. Conference speaker Elisabeth Elliot recalls dropping in unannounced shortly before he died.

---

[1] Romans 6.11.
[2] 2 Timothy 2.4.

"The family brought him into the tiny living room in their tiny house. He had to be supported by two of his daughters. He stopped, peered at me, and announced: "Betty Howard, Keswick, New Jersey, 1941!" Howard had been her family name, and 1941 was the year he'd first met her, when he visited her editor father."

While he was bed-ridden he still retained a sense of God's sovereignty. He'd been very concerned to hear about a brutal mugging one of his grandchildren, Steve Spaulding, had suffered in California. Earlier, when Steve graduated, LE had told his grandson, "Remember, God's way up is down!"

After Steve miraculously recovered, he flew home and visited his grandfather, whose condition was deteriorating. Grandpa Maxwell had closed his eyes, but he immediately recognized the voice as Steve leaned over him and whispered, "Grandpa, it's Steve!"

"Spared for a purpose!" was his grandfather's immediate response. It was prophetic, as Steve went on to be a missionary in the Far East.

Looking into Eternity

"What are you learning from this experience?" granddaughter Ruth recollects asking Grandpa Maxwell while driving him into Calgary for prostate surgery.

"I've placed too much value on my life and not wanted to face death!" he replied. It was a typical, thought-provoking statement from one who'd always extracted the most from living—physically and also spiritually.

"You could have knocked me over with a feather!" Ruth says. "He'd already lived a great life, and I knew he wasn't afraid of death. But from his point of view there was still so much to do—and losing his life meant leaving undone what he could still do. God was making him willing to leave even that."

"Why did he have to linger on?" some friends asked. "The Lord could have taken him while he could still cope! Ernest and Freeda's entry to Heaven came suddenly, without suffering. LE languished in distressful weakness for months!"

Why indeed? LE had taught us from the book of Job. We already knew that God permitted Job's suffering to lead him into a closer walk with him. But there were valuable lessons to learn from the last days of this mentor who had modeled for us the victorious life so well. If God had taken him from us in prime health, we'd have only the image of the zestful warrior. We might still be wondering how his teaching and preaching would stand up to weakness and ill health. God didn't take him, Elijah-like, in a chariot of fire. He would take him from a walker, a wheelchair, a deathbed—for our instruction and encouragement.

"Daddy recognized this as an important chapter in his life," daughter Miriam later told me. "He learned to accept care and show new appreciation for Mother and others who looked after him. And the rest of us learned that external strength or vigor is not the most important thing in life. Inner strength is."

Our mentor's sense of humor was still there. His single spiritual focus was still there. His awareness of unworthiness was still there. His faith was still there. So was his "stickability" (one of the coined words he frequently polished). All these were real to the end. He put into practice what he'd often challenged us with: "God help us to be better than our body's inclination!"

"I believe the Lord permitted this so I might finish my course better than otherwise," he commented to his family after one hospitalization.

From posts around the globe, we saw that LE's message could survive the enervating scourge of failing health. His passage through bodily affliction held encouragement for us. LE was certainly unique, but he was no remote icon on some pedestal beyond our sphere of experience. He was human, limps and all, but given solely to God.

He'd been mentoring students for over half a century; now in his failing years he taught us not only that the believer's pilgrimage faces tests to the end, but also that God gives grace right to the final moments on earth. We thanked God that he could entrust LE with weakness, even as he had earlier entrusted him with strength. God knew LE would glorify his Lord.

He didn't come to the end despondent, as did Jacob, who cried bitterly, "My years have been few and difficult!"

"Even before I was saved, I dreamt about being 'monarch of all I surveyed'," Maxwell told Kathleen ("Sandy") Head[1] in an interview towards the end of his life."Yet I wasn't surveying an inch of territory! I wondered what would become of my life. But when I found Christ, I passed from death to life. Ever since, life has been the fulfillment of my boyhood dream, spiritually. To God be all the glory, because I couldn't take an ounce of credit to myself!"

In his spirit L. E. Maxwell was an overcomer. We could be too.

Rehearsal without the Hearse

Unselfishly, Pearl had prayed she'd survive her husband so she could care for him to the end. The time came when the once-sprightly president had to use a walker (with a bookbag hanging from it, of course) and eventually a wheel chair. Paul Maxwell remembers wheeling him on to the platform to share a greeting at the Fall Conference, October 9, 1982. The speaker was his friend of long-standing, Stephen Olford. LE had already asked the powerful preacher if he would take his funeral service, if Olford survived him.

---

[1]Kathleen Sandever was his secretary after the retirement of Ida Heyer, his secretary for 27 years.

"Although Daddy's voice was failing," Paul remembers, "his spirit revived as I pushed his chair up to the microphone. "In a strong, clear voice, he quoted Psalm 73.25 AV—'Whom have I in heaven but Thee? and there is none upon earth that I desire beside Thee.' As he concluded his remarks, the congregation gave the Old Soldier a standing ovation."

Ted Rendall, presiding pastor of the Tab, then asked Stephen Olford to lead in prayer. Knowing that the next time he'd be back would likely be for LE's funeral, Olford could barely contain his emotions as he thanked God for founder and school.

As Paul wheeled his father out a back entrance, LE noticed a license plate on a visitor's car: KKD.

"KKD—Keep Kicking the Devil!" he quipped.

"Then Daddy looked up at me and exclaimed, 'That service was the rehearsal without the hearse!'" recalls Paul, who told him his voice was so strong, people wouldn't realize how weak he was. "Nope!" he responded. "We're perfect hypocrites—fooled 'em all!"

At meals he had to wear a bib, to take care of drooling caused by Parkinson's. "I wear this to keep bib-lical!" he joked. But he found spoon-feeding irksome. "Daddy, you have to eat!" family urged, holding another spoonful to his mouth. "What's the use!" he'd reply. But he did ask Paul to weigh him—"so I know whether I'm coming or going."

The old warrior wondered how the end would come. He feared choking to death. One night he whispered to Paul, "Maybe God will conduct a surprise attack, in which I go to sleep and simply wake up in Glory!"

"Goodbye Daddy!"

That is more or less what happened. As the end neared, family members took turns in vigil around his bed. The final week he seemed unconscious at times. Did he hear as someone read a psalm to him or as Lois sang? His lips mouthed "Amen" after Paul prayed one evening.

At dawn on February 4, 1984, two years to the day after Ernest and Freeda's funeral, family members stood around their father's bed. "We're here," Paul told him. "Good-bye, Daddy!" Anna noticed his eye twitch, as if he understood. Pearl sat holding his hand as he slipped peacefully away. He was 88. The battle was over. Family joined together in quietly singing,

Praise the Lord, praise the Lord, let the earth hear his voice,
Praise the Lord, praise the Lord, let the people rejoice!
Oh, come to the Father, through Jesus the Son,
And give him the glory, great things he hath done!

He ended well. Remarkably, he'd taught in that Prairie town for 58 years—yet his message had been trumpeted worldwide. Prairie called his memorial service, "L. E. Maxwell Coronation Service." Stephen Olford preached from the text in Psalm 116: "Precious in the sight of the Lord is the death of his saints."

"This is a time for Celebration because of what God has done through Leslie E. Maxwell!" Olford said. "It's also a time of Consummation, or Completion, because the Lord's servant has completed the work God sent him to do. And for us all it is a time of Contemplation, to consider what God is saying to us. May God call out many others to carry on the work."

Fulfilling Vows

Olford challenged the capacity crowd with another verse from Psalm 116: "I will fulfill my vows to the Lord in the presence of all his people."

"Stand to indicate you're responding to whatever the Lord is saying to you in the words of the closing hymn, 'Take My Life and Let It Be, Consecrated, Lord, to Thee.'" Nearly the entire packed auditorium stood and sang in commitment.

The message and challenge confirmed a decision Miriam Charter had just made. Daughter of the Charters who'd been hounded out of China some thirty years earlier, Miriam had given her life to Christ for missionary service the night her mother led her to the Lord in Three Hills at the age of seven. After graduating from Prairie, she went on to university and graduate studies, earning a Master's degree in Divinity. At the time of LE's funeral, she was involved in a pastoral ministry.

But now she knew God was telling her it was time to move onward to her childhood commitment. LE's casket had been left open for a time of visitation before the memorial service. Miriam felt drawn down to the front of the nearly empty auditorium to view, for the last time, the peaceful figure of her Mentor.

"I haven't forgotten what the goal is!" Miriam heard herself announcing aloud, as if her beloved principal could hear. "I've been preparing 'the instrument' all this time—now I'm ready to go!"[1]

This was not a rehearsal. The hearse was waiting outside. But before family and friends filed out, they all stood to the finale of The Hallelujah Chorus, sung by the school massed-choirs. Tears ran down cheeks, and later, tributes poured in from many of the 5,000 alumni serving around the globe.

"The coffin can't hold him down!"

After the memorial service, the family and a few friends stood at the graveside in the February cold. Daughter Eleanor heard her mother whisper, "I can't imagine that coffin holding Daddy down!" And of course it didn't! God had long ago unfettered him from the "body of death"—from the trammels of the old nature. Now Daddy Maxwell had

---

[1] Miriam did "fulfill her vows." Communism was still in power. But at age 35 she became an itinerant missionary for the C&MA in Eastern Europe and Russia, developing theological extension studies that involved women—quite an innovation in the cultures she worked among. After 13 years she returned to Canada, earned her doctorate, and helped establish Toronto's branch of the C&MA Canadian Theological Seminary. She became its Director, focusing on preparing students for missionary outreach to Muslims.

escaped from the worn physical body he had used so well to glorify God. Over his grave the family laid a marker inscribed with the verse summing up his life: "To live is Christ, to die is gain (Phil.1.21)."

I would have given my eyetooth, as the saying goes, to be present at that "Coronation" assembly. It was frustrating not to be there. After all, I was just a hop across the Rocky Mountains, as guest speaker at a conference in Vancouver. But I asked myself what my mentor would say had I asked him if I should leave my assignment to attend his memorial service. "Stay at your post, son!" I could hear him bark in reply.

The following Wednesday, my conference over, I arrived in Three Hills and spoke at the weekly prayer meeting. There was "Mother Maxwell," mainstay not only to her husband and family but also to others of us who knew her—faithful, wise, sacrificial. Her face reflected the loss of her beloved Leslie, naturally enough. But it also shone with grace and peace.

For another eight years she had the joy of praying for her children and grandchildren, and many of "the extended student family." Towards the end of 1992 she told her nurse, "I want to be home for Christmas!"

The family knew she meant her heavenly home. And sure enough, three weeks before Christmas, on December 3 they laid Pearl Eleanor Maxwell to rest beside her husband's grave under the pines in the Three Hills cemetery. She was 92, had raised seven children and left 22 grandchildren (Lorraine Hartt, the 23rd, had already passed on) and six great grandchildren. We had seen in her the fulfillment of Solomon's description of The Virtuous Woman (NIV: "The Wife of Noble Character") recorded in Proverbs 31.10-31.

So the earthly saga of Leslie and Pearl Maxwell ended, and there began the eternal celebration of all they had taught us through the years. It was a moment for us to pause and revisit the lessons. Also, it was useful to help others understand this remarkable mentor, for there were some who had not understood him. Chapter 20 explains why.

"I may need to die daily, but I don't need continually to attend my own funeral!"—LEM

UNDERSTANDING MAXWELL

MAXWELL had many admirers, yes—but also a few critics. The latter were chiefly well-meaning people who latched on to only part of his message and misunderstood what they heard. We came to realize there were several areas in which people sometimes misread, if not completely misunderstood, him. Reviewing the issues affirms LE's "passion and power"—the man and his message.

Tools, Not Labels, for Life

"Prairie students aren't sure of their position!" That was one of the criticisms of Prairie we occasionally heard. It probably arose from Maxwell's respect for the positions held by both Calvinists and Arminians—who, he felt, had something to teach each other. But, Maxwell had no doubt about his eternal security in Christ. Few people knew that although he'd held membership in a Presbyterian and a Baptist church, he came to Christ under the preaching of a Methodist evangelist and actually was a Baptist preacher.

What puzzled some was his refusal to resort to sectarian labels. He was more concerned about our relationship with Christ, and giving us tools for studying the whole Word of God—tools to last a lifetime.

Not the Beaten Track

Maxwell realized that his teaching on Law and Grace was a puzzle to many. "The author does not follow the beaten track of this hour," he wrote in *Crowded to Christ*.[1] (That was an understatement!) He saw the

Law as "God's lariat in his great round up of sinners.... Whereas Paul's epistle to the Romans clearly sets forth salvation 'by faith without the deeds of the law,' the letter first speaks of 'obedience of faith among all nations.'"

Always ready to upset unbiblical tradition and shock us into thinking afresh, LE taught that before Calvary, believers were not saved by keeping the Law but by grace (as typified in the Temple's Mercy Seat), and after Calvary believers must not escape obedience to God by an "easy Grace." Both before and after Calvary, the Law was "our schoolmaster to bring us to Christ." In his eternal sacrifice for sin, Jesus knew no dividing "dispensation." He was "the lamb slain before the foundation of the world."

Regent (BC, Canada) scholar John Stackhouse, Jr., summed up Maxwell's paradoxical teaching: "Maxwell . . . differed from dispensationalists in his holding of a Reformed understanding of the Old Testament Law as useful in the life of the Christian, while dispensationalists saw the Law to be utterly irrelevant to the dispensation of grace."[2]

"This Is a Hard Teaching"

The early disciples told Jesus that some of his teachings were hard to hear and to follow. As Maxwell faced his listeners with the teachings of Jesus, a few felt the same way. They didn't know that before stepping to the pulpit or entering the classroom, LE spent time praying that "the words of his mouth" would not be his words, but the words of the Spirit through Scripture. Once he had done that, he spoke with the authority that Jesus had given all his disciples.

Maxwell preached and taught for results in our lives. Although he had dramatic skills in portraying truth,[1] he was not there to entertain. Nor

---

[1] *Op. cit.*

[2] Stackhouse, John G. Jr., *Canadian Evangelicalism in the 20th Century.* Toronto: University of Toronto Press, 1993, p. 75.

did he try to impart intellectual knowledge so we could complete a course academically. Instead, he sought to disturb us in our self-satisfied comfort zones.

A few critics saw this as being negative, confrontational, provocative. Certain grads tried to copy him in his forthright teaching—sometimes merely antagonizing people. "Chopping off ears!" LE called that approach, and he condemned it. The difference in his using the surgeon's scalpel on us was that we knew his heart overflowed with love and grace. He never let loose on us any "hound of heaven" that hadn't already chased him back to the Cross.

Self-discipline—Bondage?

"In dealing with the subject of self-discipline," he wrote in *Born Crucified*,[2] "it is difficult to escape being stigmatized by some as an ascetic or monk."

But to him, self-discipline was in the same category as training for the Olympics or military. Flabby muscles and soft life-styles can be turned into highly motivated athletes or democracies' defenders. Multifaceted disciplines might seem inconsequential or even irksome, but they could contribute to developing human beings physically, mentally, emotionally, and spiritually.

While it's true that a few students turned discipline into bondage, it's also true that a few on staff could turn it into legalism. That went beyond the principles that our mentor had intended to be applied with grace. While he sought to put the Old Man to death daily, he also sought to free us from the bondage of self, using the gifts that God had given each of us.

---

[1] Daniel Westfall (married to a granddaughter), felt deprived because he attended Prairie after LE had stopped preaching on Genesis (others were handling that book). Dan missed LE's graphic portrayal of Joseph "bumping across the desert on the back of a camel, lonely and depressed." It had left a life-long impression on his in-laws. .

[2] *Op. cit.* p. 127.

"Unimproveable but also unreproveable!" was one of his favorite sayings, quoting Colossians 1.22. "And here's another: 'Therefore, there is now no condemnation for those who are in Christ Jesus, because through Christ Jesus the law of the Spirit of life set me free from the law of sin and death.'"[1]

How Do You Get Strength out of Weakness?

Others, like myself at first, didn't understand Maxwell's reference to weakness resulting in power. It might have seemed ironic that a woman invalid confined to her bed in a tropical bungalow should become for Maxwell the epitome of spiritual strength, of rugged discipline. But that was the paradox. Though Amy Carmichael's body was frail, in Christ she was indomitable. It was not suffering that made her strong—an error embraced by some medieval monks and nuns. But physical weakness compelled this naturally strong-willed woman to realize she could do nothing apart from Christ. Christ was indeed her life.

Maxwell didn't draw the conclusion that we must be physically weak in order to serve the Lord effectively. As a Navy veteran, at first I thought he was teaching that tears were basic equipment for warfare. Instead, LE knew that God needed healthy, robust men and women to stand the rigors of tough assignments. His point was that our reliance must not be upon human strength but on spiritual power. After all, Jesus taught that the meek would inherit the earth. The Lord told Paul, "My power is made perfect in weakness."

But LE added a caveat about power. In a message on Pastoral Leadership, while calling for boldness and authority in preaching, he also warned: "The pearl of power, God does not cast before the swine trough of our flesh. . . Power is a dangerous thing.... Power belongs to God!. . . Our boldness cannot be that of Gentile kings who exercise lordship over their people. No. It's down the Calvary road that they have to

---

[1] Romans 8.1.

go. That's leadership. Jesus led the way to Calvary, and you and I must lead that way!"[1]

Sanctification—Pilgrimage or Heavenly Visitation?

Did Maxwell teach that we shouldn't serve until we'd had a spectacular enduement of power? In commenting on Acts 1:8, he wrote, "Enduement must precede utterance. Filling would be followed by speaking."[2] He was very strong on our having the Holy Spirit's commissioning on our lives. His favorite story was about the Southern (USA) believer who asked a new pastor, "Is you sent, or is you jus' went?"

However, he wouldn't want us to interpret our need for spiritual empowering as waiting for some spiritual lightning bolt before we started obeying God in service. He knew that in his own pilgrimage, he grew as he served—"going and growing." The rookie who arrived in Three Hills in 1922 was by no means the spiritual giant we met there in mid-century. God had used the work itself to bring him to the inner Cross—and it would be the same in our lives. We'd face aspects of the self-life we wouldn't have recognized if we'd cloistered ourselves.

Again, there was possible misreading of Maxwell's illustration of Pratt who had taken Wyatt's place in wartime, therefore making Wyatt legally dead to being conscripted again. Some people could mistakenly take the illustration to imply that if we once died to self, we could no longer be tempted—a problem of some "Holiness" teaching.

"You should never take an illustration to extremes!" LE warned us as students. "Few illustrations teach the whole truth." While he stressed that the law of spiritual death had no claim of power over us, we still needed to walk "circumspectly" in the Spirit every moment. Only then could we avoid falling to the temptations bound to surround us as long as we lived in this world.

---

[1] Quoted by Stephen Spaulding, *op. cit.* (Maxwell's message c. 1978).
[2] Maxwell, L.E., *The Holy Spirit in Believers and in Missions.* Three Hills, Prairie Press, 1982.

In a similar way the Apostle Paul had been criticized for preaching that we were saved by grace, and that where sin abounded, grace abounded. "Shall we go on sinning so that grace may increase?" he asked his critics. "By no means!"[1]

In the school's 1933 catalogue, Prairie had made clear its rejection of the Holiness concept of "eradication" of the sinful nature. Rather, the Holy Spirit living in the believer was constantly overcoming the tendencies of the Old Man. We were to "take up our Cross daily"—dying to self and living unto God.

Human or Divine—or Both?

After hearing Maxwell speak on the majesty of Christ, one Christian leader wondered if LE tended to Docetism, the heresy that nearly split the early church and figured in Gnosticism. Docetism ("to seem") taught that the sufferings and humanity of Jesus were only "apparent," for if Christ suffered, he could not be divine, and if he was God, he could not suffer.

The critic may have heard Maxwell emphasize Christ's majesty in that particular message, but if he had sat through Maxwell's exposition of Philippians 2.5-11, he'd have no doubt about LE's understanding that divinity and humanity were completely and perfectly combined in Jesus of Nazareth. "From the heights of glory he descended, from the Godhead to manhood. . . . The Christ of glory was born of a lowly maiden."[2] It was because he became truly human that the incarnate Son of God "was in all things touched with our infirmities."[3]

Louise (Imbach '54) Morris has special memories of this topic.

"I was always petrified when teachers called on me to read my written answers," she says. "I remember struggling over the difficult topic of how Christ could be completely human as well as completely

---

[1] Romans 5.20-6.1.
[2] *Born Crucified, op.cit.* Chapter 24. A personal friend of the leader told the author of this misunderstanding of Maxwell's teaching on the topic.
[3] Hebrews 4.15.

divine at the same time. You guessed it—at the next class Mr. Maxwell called on me! When I read my convoluted answer, he laughed and commented, "Just a little bit of heresy there—just a little bit!"

How Big is the World of Missions?

Certain missiologists felt that Prairie's view of missions was truncated, dwelling only on the post-Carey era (18th C.).[1] But Maxwell's missiology reached all the way back to the Abrahamic Covenant: "All the nations shall be blessed in you."[2] Old Testament characters were among his Missions Hall of Fame, as were missionaries of the early church—including 7th C. Englishman Winfrid Boniface ("Apostle to the Germans") and 12th C. Italian Francis of Assisi, who was burdened for the expanding world of Islam. Maxwell was very conscious of the heritage the church had in missions throughout the centuries. Today's missionary movement, he felt, was investing that "inheritance" in eternal profit—the lives of redeemed multitudes.

"Individualistic Pietism, no Less!"

Theological liberals found fault with Prairie's emphasis on a personal experience of conversion. "Individualistic pietism!" they charged evangelicals. With their universalist[3] liberal views, they interpreted an individual's assurance of salvation as a twisted conceit or even bigotry. They did not understand (a) the necessity of personal regeneration and (b) the subsequent responsibility of the redeemed to share with the whole world the fact that "whosoever will may come." It was this sense of responsibility as well as the overflowing joy of salvation that motivated many Prairie graduates to minister in churches or missions.

[1] Cited by John G. Stackhouse, *op. cit.*
[2] Galatians 3.8,9.
[3] As old as Christianity itself, Universalism teaches that since Christ died for the whole world, everyone will eventually be saved, even without individual repentance and acceptance.

Maxwell Anti-Intellectual?

Prairie developed during one of the most tense eras of liberal-funda-mentalist controversy in North America. Both W. C. Stevens, under whom Maxwell had studied, and Steven's own mentor, A. B. Simpson, had wanted their school at Nyack to develop into a liberal arts college to train evangelical scholarship, but their board refused. At the time, several denominational seminaries were becoming seedbeds for liberal theology, and many evangelical groups feared losing their way along the same path.[1]

Maxwell addressed the issues of his day—which included these liberal trends in theological education. Many evangelical intellectuals[2] felt the same concerns, having just passed through the bruising (and often misrepresented) "Fundamentalist Debates" of the 1920s.[3]

Although most missions of that era didn't require degree-level studies, Maxwell didn't underrate scholarship. His mentor, W. C. Stevens, had degrees earned through scholarship, although in humility he shunned academic acclaim and refused honorary degrees. Rightly or wrongly, LE himself felt that accepting an honorary doctorate might make him and his message appear "man-made." However, a number of academics would have gladly recognized his contributions in the field of missions, education, and leadership development.

Most of all, Maxwell believed in continuing education. For him, it was by self-disciplined personal study and wide reading. His personal library books reflected that—sentences and sections being underlined.

It is true that his depiction of universities and seminaries as the graveyard of faith could come across as anti-intellectual. Actually, his concern was anti-academia—not without reason. Evangelical centers of

---

[1] Conley, Joseph F., *Drumbeats That Changed the World.* Pasedena: William Carey Library, 2000.
[2] As evidenced in the scholar and linguist, W. C. Stevens, Maxwell's mentor.
[3] See Fuller, W. Harold, *People of the Mandate,* Grand Rapids: Baker, 1996, pp. 30, 98, 126.

higher learning (among them Harvard, Princeton, and Yale) had been founded to train church leadership but were hijacked by liberal theology and secularism in the name of academic freedom.

While Maxwell warned against liberal influences in "higher learning," we who knew him were awed by his intellectual worldview. His interest spanned the worlds of geography, nature, science, and politics. He condemned lazy thinking in us even more than academic liberalism in society.

"Why do you suppose the Lord gave you that bump on your shoulders!" he'd taunt us if we were slow responding to some complex question in class. And if a student was timid in giving a response, he'd say, "If you were at home calling the cows, your voice would be much louder than that!" If we seemed to be scribbling too much in our notebooks instead of thinking, he'd prod us humorously: "Use less ink and more think!" He didn't want us to learn by "rote" but wanted us to gain tools that would help us learn throughout life.

Constantly he challenged us to excellence not only in handling the Scriptures but also in everything from music to athletics. Miriam Charter was encouraged to find this outlook in her mentor.

"I was making decisions about going on to university after Bible School, rather than 'straight to the field' as some thought every Prairie grad should do!" Miriam remembers. "To my surprise, Mr. Maxwell applauded my thoughts. This seemed quite unusual for a man who ate, slept, drank, and dreamed about foreign missions.

"He and I talked at length about 'taking the Holy Spirit on to the secular campus.' He shocked me by welcoming my pursuit of a somewhat academic career. When I came home from university for a weekend, some on campus came down hard in their criticism, because I'd taken on some of the "dress code" of the university (earrings and makeup, no less!). At times I felt quite rejected, but Mr. Maxwell had only warmth and love and concern for me. One fall conference when I turned up at an Alumni event in Miller Chapel, he cornered me to ask how life at university was going. He always embraced me warmly and told me he cared—and was even proud of me!"

Perhaps LE was especially open to Miriam's post-graduate studies because he knew her commitment. Later she went to evangelize and disciple people in Communist Eastern Europe.

Missions "Coming of Age"

Preparation for Missions was one area that contributed to the accusation of anti-intellectualism, because earlier Prairie had no courses in Anthropology or Sociology. Of course, hindsight can become tunnel vision, if critics disregard context.

In the first half of the 20th century, Cultural Anthropology and Sociology were pretty much in the hands of liberal scholarship. Margaret Mead's *Coming of Age in Samoa* [1] was the accepted case study, "establishing" that societies undisturbed by missionary morals were islands of Utopia. Mead became "one of the most famous women of her generation, particularly well known for her views on educational and social issues."[2]

Amazingly, academia accepted her views without question until the 1990s when a secular New Zealand Anthropologist debunked her misleading "research." [3] Yet her idealistic but inaccurate "findings" influenced students throughout the century—and still permeate textbooks. Enlightenment and Darwinian worldviews dominated Anthropology and Sociology.

As a result, Christian liberal arts colleges had to develop their own courses. It took decades to earn the respect of secular academia. Prairie's Missions courses reflected this need, which affected most evangelical

---

[1] New York: Columbia University, 1928.
[2] Crystal, David, *The Cambridge Biographical Encyclopedia.* Cambridge: University Press, 1994.
[3] Freeman, Derek, *The Fateful Hoaxing of Margaret Mead: A historical analysis of her Samoan research.* Boulder, CO: Westview Press, 1999. First published as *Margaret Mead the Heretic: The making and unmasking of an anthropological myth.* Victoria: Penguin Books, 1996.

schools. So instead of studying courses that are now accepted as essential (and appropriate) in the preparation of missionaries, before the 1950s missionaries simply did their own "field work" by relating to other cultures through study of their language and culture. That turned out to be the right way to go about the task!

Although some academics have been critical, certain Third World Anthropologists have stated that missionaries have been among their best source for gaining understanding of isolated cultures and collecting artifacts for preservation.

"Missionaries understand our people better than many of us, because they live with them—we don't!" some of them stated.[1]

Experienced missionaries took advanced studies in these and other fields, advising Prairie and also other Bible schools and Christian colleges on the need. Prairie has incorporated such studies in its curricula.

Looking for the New Man

Maxwell's core teaching on identification with Christ's death and resurrection was most often misunderstood.

Because LE understood the deceitfulness of the self-life—its sinfulness, its disguises, and its contortions to avoid death on the Cross—at times people accused him of preaching a negative, morbid message. A few misunderstood what he meant by "the flesh." Was it a dualistic Platonic view of the human body or a Medieval Roman Catholic hatred of the body as being unspiritual, fit only for self-mortification? Neither. This was a misreading of Maxwell. By "the flesh" he meant the carnal, fallen nature—"sold under sin," in the Apostle Paul's words.

True, Maxwell had no confidence in the natural state of mankind. He was convinced about the total, irreparable depravity of the sinful

---

[1] In this connection, the curator of the Jos Museum, Nigeria, thanked me for the valuable research work of missionaries. We took each new group of missionaries for a seminar with him. –WHF

nature—even if many unregenerate people displayed graceful attitudes, good deeds, and upright behavior. But he was not a pessimist. He was looking beyond what Paul termed "the old man," fallen creation, to the miraculous restoration of God's creation in "the new man." For "if any man be in Christ Jesus, he is a new creation; old things are passed away; behold, all things are become new"![1] In "hating the flesh," he was referring to sin, not the physical person. Far from hating our humanity, LE wanted us to realize our full potential as God originally intended when creating Adam and Eve.

A Zest for Life

Maxwell's zest for life on a physical level proved he was no misanthrope. He displayed a gusto for life—whether in athletics, sports, exercise, or outdoor activities such as fishing and moose hunting. In fact, he felt that God expected every person to care for the body and mind responsibly. He enjoyed marital intimacy. He appreciated the fine arts—especially classical music and literature. He encouraged students to develop voice and learn instrumental music. His zest for life involved the five senses: touch, taste, smell, sight, hearing. His sixth sense was his spiritual insight—or did that become his all-encompassing sense?

"But how about his message of the crucified life?" other critics ask. "Christians need a positive message these days—love, joy, peace!"

In his preface to *Born Crucified*,[2] Maxwell anticipates that some readers may think he "seems spoiled for everything but to see people die."

"We are guilty, verily guilty!" he responds. "Resurrections follow such blessed deaths to self, even as day follows night." Victorious spiritual living was what LE strove to bring us into, but he knew the only route was through death to self. The resurrection life could have been his sole emphasis, given his natural zest for living. But he was well aware that self could "immunize" itself by celebrating life without ever having

---

[1] 2 Corinthians 5.17 (AV).
[2] *Op. cit.*

passed from the law of death to the liberty of resurrection. He had no illusions about human nature—even in his own Institute.

"PBI can mean 'Pretty Bad Inside'!" he told us. "Satan can appear as an angel of light; even the saints can be deceived," he warned. "Remember that the heart of man is deceitful above all things, and desperately wicked!"

Maxwell knew the Holy Spirit convicts and cleanses us by using the Word of God, as the temple priest used his knife to examine the sin offering:

"Sharper than any double-edged sword, it penetrates even to dividing soul and spirit, joints and marrow; it judges the thoughts and attitudes of the heart. . . . Everything is uncovered and laid bare before the eyes of him to whom we must give account" (Hebrews 4.12, 13).

Far from morbidly preaching a negative gospel, Maxwell looked upon the discipline of the crucified life as an encouragement, assurance that we are indeed God's children. "Whom the Lord loves he chastens, and scourges every son whom he receives," he would quote to us.[1]

Our mentor simply didn't believe "the old nature" could be patched up and made presentable to God. "Everyone has a God-shaped space in his life that needs filling," was a popular saying with some evangelists—and in a symbolic sense that was true. Secularism could never fill that space, only Christ himself. However, LE pointed out that the old nature was beyond improvement. Only redemption could save the human heart.

In the end, it was not a case of filling a hole or patching over it, but of committing the old nature to death on the Cross and receiving from the risen Christ the new nature. "You cannot work from the flesh into the Spirit," he said.

---

[1] Note the entire passage in Hebrews 12.4-13.

"I'm OK; You're OK"

LE knew that the message of the Cross is never popular. It goes against human nature. It's the opposite of "Invictus," William Henley's defiant poem: "I am the master of my fate; I am the captain of my soul." Surely people don't need a negative message! "Pop psyche" parrots the cliché, "I'm OK; you're OK!" Even some Christians question the effects of teaching that the self-life should be crucified.

"I believe that for far too long the church has promoted a psychologically unhealthy attitude toward the self," one prominent Christian psychologist wrote, citing the teaching of *The Calvary Road*. Its authors state that Jesus became a "worm and no man" for our sakes, and that we need to reckon on the same position for our self-life, apart from Christ's resurrection life. However, the psychologist wrote, "Teachings like this instill deep self-doubt and cut away at the foundation of self-esteem."[1]

There is no doubt that people can take the wrong meaning out of terminology. Narramore wanted to make a useful point: that God accepts us and we need to accept ourselves. His books have helped many readers. However, the point of Maxwell (and *Calvary Road*) was that although we indeed are "worms" in our sinful nature, God has made us his sons and daughters through the Cross. The sinful nature is fit only for crucifixion, but it can continue to dominate our lives unless we deny self and embrace the Cross in daily living. The Cross actually enables us to accept ourselves as "new creatures" in Christ Jesus.[1]

Canada's national monthly, *Maclean's* may have expected to find religious gloom and doom at Prairie, but its reporter found the opposite. In the December 15, 1947 issue, a feature on the school noted: "From all

---

[1] Bruce Narramore, *You're Somone Special.* Grand Rapids: Zondervan, 1978, page 14, quoting Roy and Revel Hession, *The Calvary Road.* London: CLC, 1950 (with reprints up to 1990), p. 15. The Scripture quote is from Psalm 22.6.

[2] Professor of Psychology Larry Crabb, presents the same core message, in essence, that Maxwell preached. In his book, *Inside Out*, Crabb teaches that the solution to behavioral problems, including depression, is to have Christ, not self, at the center of one's life.

this stress on Puritan values you could get a picture of the place that is entirely false. There is nothing humorless or dismal about life at Three Hills....[Principal Maxwell] radiates cheery good humor, and he obviously finds nothing to scowl at or be sorrowful about in the religion he preaches and practices."[1]

Maxwell stressed that God doesn't intend us to be defeated but to experience the "power of the resurrection." He applied Isaiah's reassuring national prophecy to our own spiritual state: "Do not be afraid, O worm Jacob. . . . I will make you into a threshing sledge, new and sharp . . . ." Again he cited God's purpose for Israel, to be "the head and not the tail." "Therefore lift up the hands that hang down..," he exhorted us from Hebrews 12.12.

"How are you today?" he asked in an imagined dialogue.

"Oh, not bad under the circumstances," came the answer.

"Well, what in the world are you doing under there?" he concluded. "Come on out and get on top. A Christian has no business under there!"

That is the grand objective of the Cross in the life of the believer— the victorious life, life abundant, the Resurrection life. That was what Maxwell's message was really about.

---

[1] *Maclean's* Dec. 15, 1947, quoted by Stephen M. Spaulding, *op. cit.*

Chapter 21: Holding the Torch

"Between the extremes of no fire and wild fire
there is a golden balance." —LEM

HOW DID WE RUN?

THERE WERE PUZZLED LOOKS as we scanned faces and then read nametags. Suddenly there were plenty of embraces—men and women hugging each other as we wouldn't have considered doing fifty years before! Thirty members of the Class of '50 had converged on Three Hills for the Fiftieth Anniversary of our class graduation, held during the Fall Missionary Conference. This has become a joyous tradition as each year celebrates its 50th.

Fifty-Year Pilgrimages

I was blessed by the pilgrim stories these alumni recounted, and amazed at the multiple roads they'd traveled in following God's will. Now retired, they represented a wide range of service spanned, from missionary, pastor, teacher to physician and philosophy lecturer—and much more. Some had been through horrific experiences (like the twin missionary nurses who had to hide in the jungle from marauding soldiers).

But here they were, back on campus, thanking God for the teaching of the victorious life they'd received at Prairie. And swapping memorable stories about Mr. Maxwell and Miss Dearing and so many others who had touched their lives for good. Yes, there'd been hurts and tears along the way, but also laughter and victory.

A quick survey showed that these alumni were fairly typical of Prairie graduates. They were unanimous in naming Maxwell's classes as the highlight of their years—and they enjoyed his humor (some said it made them feel more relaxed). Although most indicated that the campus revival of 1946 made a significant impact on their lives, they also described their spiritual growth as "gradual" over their time at school.

What impression did they have of the principal? Comments included: "outgoing, friendly, versatile, human, profound; his tears touched me." His most noted attributes: discipline, ability to apply Scripture, excellent teaching, common sense, example, courtesy. "Mr Maxwell lived what he preached."

How about impressions of the Maxwell daughters and sons? Comments included: "friendly, humble, fun, approachable, never assuming celebrity status—a tribute in example to Mr. M's messages, above reproach, natural, solid Christian young people; busy students as we all were."

What caused you to attend Prairie? The lives of graduates was the reason most cited.

As to the Class of '50 motto ("Prepared for War") nearly all felt that it was still appropriate and a still-needed emphasis. Only two felt it now sounded too militaristic.

Roland's Problems

Several from our class I'd personally seen in action in different parts of the world. Roland Pickering was one example. He'd gone to West Africa in 1952 and was assigned by SIM to work among the Dompago people of central Benin—at the time an "unreached people group" bound by spirit worship. The task before him was fairly straightforward: reduce the language to writing, translate the Scriptures, win and teach converts, and help them establish churches. That's all!

But he ran into three problems.

First problem: Roland had never done most of those things. Prairie hadn't given him those specific courses. But in the face of spiritual warfare, Roland was "prepared for war." Prairie had helped him develop self-discipline, obedience to Christ's commission, and a burden to share his faith with people who hadn't heard the gospel. So with his small box of personal effects, he trekked into a Dompago village, rented a mud hut, and set about learning the culture and language.

Second problem: the villagers shunned him. After all, for what good purpose would a foreigner come and live in one of their huts? Roland knew his first resource was prayer. He asked the Lord to open the hearts of the villagers to him and the precious message he carried. Still the people ignored him—even ran away from him! How could he break into their culture?

Third problem: sparks from his outdoor cooking fire set his thatch roof alight. But that problem turned out to be God's answer to the second problem, which led to solving the first problem.

Then the Hut Caught Fire!

"Fire!" villagers screamed (in the Dompago language, of course), and everyone in the village started running towards Roland's hut, pulling off bundles of flaming thatch to save the palm-stem rafters from caving in. Someone rescued Roland's little box and camp cot. In African culture, it is the automatic thing to do when a hut catches fire: don't stop to ask questions—just grab a flaming brand and beat it out before the fire spreads to other roofs!

Roland was suddenly "accepted." This stranger had now suffered as so many of them had suffered. Their coldness melted in the heat of a hut blaze. At night they sat around campfires listening to the amazing story that Jesus was more powerful than the evil spirits that terrorized them. They learned that Jesus had given himself as an everlasting sacrifice for their sins. So they didn't need to sacrifice chickens and goats anymore, or pay the fetish priest to make incantations. One by one, many Dompagos accepted this powerful Savior.

Soon Roland was compiling a dictionary and putting their

language into writing. On furlough he took a Wycliffe linguistics course, and back in Africa began translating the Scriptures. Of course, Roland had to teach Dompagos how to read these newfangled marks, but as they did, they were amazed to realize that God was talking to them in their own tongue!

The work was indigenous from the start. "OK, if you build it!" Roland told the believers when they asked him to start a Bible school so they could prepare leadership. "Then if you want, I'll gladly teach in it." So up went their own "Bible school," constructed of bamboo with palm-frond siding and roof.

Whenever Roland came across the border into Nigeria for supplies or his annual "leave," he'd stop by our house. We'd reminisce about Prairie days and discuss local things like culture and church planting. One thing I couldn't understand about this handsome, talented fellow, was why he'd broken off his engagement. Lorna and I knew the young lady he'd been engaged to—a lovely person, graduate of Prairie, and now in Nigeria. How could he do such a stupid thing!

"Well," he quietly explained, "I just couldn't ask her to live the rustic life I knew was ahead of me among the Dompagos." Most red-blooded young men would gladly have forsaken the jungle to win her hand, but he forsook her for the jungle. Whether he was right or wrong, that was his sense of commitment to taking the gospel to the Dompagos.

Another thing he gave up was playing the piano, which he loved to do. Roland was simply a "No Frills" guy!

Ten years later Roland died in a road accident in Africa. I lost a good friend, his widowed mother back in Ontario lost her only son, and the mission lost a dedicated missionary. But when I traveled to the Dompago area, I *found* something very precious. Wherever I went, in village after village, I found men, women, and children freed from superstition and on their way to being the creation God had meant them to be. I sat in their little mud-walled churches and heard them reading their Dompago Bibles and singing in their exotic five-note scale. Roland had encouraged them to write their own hymns instead of translating foreign hymns.

In thatched huts, just like Roland's that had burned down, I found Christian families—spiritual lights shining among neighbors who still "sat in darkness." The Holy Spirit had established the Church of Jesus Christ among the Dompagos.

A Solemn Paradox

Our pilgrimages as graduates illustrated what LE told us so often: *God uses crucial ("cross") points in our pilgrimage to bring us back to the Cross of Christ.* Time after time, situation after situation. Our reaction to that *crux*—that death-to-self experience—reveals whether we know the reality of being "born crucified."

LE warned us that we could embrace it or reject it. We could continue our pilgrimage in obedience or in disobedience, defeat or victory. Sadly, we've all seen the results of rejecting the Cross, in the tensions and failures that litter the fields of service.

Maxwell was right: embracing the Cross in our lives is the only route to the joyous "abundant life" that Jesus promised us.

Seeing Christian workers—pastors, missionaries, lay people—in many lands impressed on us the truth of a paradox Maxwell described. We can study about the way of the Cross. We can be mentored by those who have personally experienced the Cross in their lives, including our parents. We can trust the Savior for salvation and be born of the Spirit. We can be active in the work of God. But self is so subtle that it will try in every possible way to avoid crucifixion. It will take on every guise of godliness to avoid mortification. Certainly self cannot crucify itself—that would be contradictory, an oxymoron.

A School's Metamorphosis

And how about the school itself, 80 years after it began in a farmhouse, and now with more than one hundred buildings? As a member of the

Advisory Council in the 1980s and the Institute Board in the early 1990s, I'd seen Prairie passing through a metamorphosis of its own. The students came out of a different context than ours of the 1940s. And the world's cultures to which they returned to minister had a different world-view than ours. Overseas, governments had different requirements for missionary visas. The encouraging development of national churches and leadership meant that, in many lands, missionaries were needed with specialized skills that weren't priority when we went out fifty years ago.

I'd sat in on debate about whether Prairie should remain a Bible institute or develop into a liberal arts college. Most Bible schools were debating the same issue. Was it time to include accredited courses that would equip graduates academically, or should the emphasis continue solely on a Bible curriculum? Prairie did add more academic content and offered practical professional courses such as Aviation. The Board opened a graduate theological school in nearby Calgary.

But Prairie's central vision was discipling Christian workers through Bible immersion. With that foundation, a high percentage of Bible school graduates went on to qualify elsewhere in professional skills. And many men and women who already had professional degrees came to Prairie chiefly for the Bible immersion.

Primary Passion

The original Kirk vision was to equip men and women in the Word of God. Through the years, the teacher from Kansas City helped him focus that more sharply. As I looked back at the experiences many of us passed through, obviously L. E. Maxwell's primary passion was this:

To bring us individually and personally into a closer, deeper relationship with Christ through the Cross in our lives.

Discipling, in other words. The main value of our time in Three Hills was to sit at the feet of those who could mentor us because they had already walked that way. Further equipping and outreach to others would grow out of that process.

At the Board level I saw many contemporary pressures converging on Prairie, and realized that the school itself was passing through a painful Cross experience. What of the school's image for rugged discipleship? What would the new relaxed atmosphere do to that image?

Faithful people who had given the best of their lives felt confused and hurt as they struggled along a new, unfamiliar stretch of their pilgrimage. Several "old-timers" wondered whether the sacrifices they'd readily endured to "train disciplined soldiers for Christ" would now be in vain. Many had left homes and profession and wealth to help train "disciplined soldiers for Christ." Now some felt lost in the swirl of changing attitudes among students and in society. For them it was extremely painful. It was in fact part of their pilgrimage, the way of the Cross in their lives.

All encouraged themselves with the words of Hebrews 6.10: "God is not unjust; he will not forget your work and the love you have shown him as you have helped his people and continue to help them." I was impressed with the positive outlook of several older staff and faculty who were able to embrace change without discarding the basic ethos of the school.

"Don't Spiritualize the Physical"

The principles on which Leslie Maxwell and Fergus Kirk had founded the school had not changed, but the world had. When LE retired from leadership in 1977, the pioneer must have sensed the tensions that lay ahead.

"I wouldn't be surprised if the school doesn't last another generation!" he bluntly told his son, Paul. That wasn't an easy burden to bear as the school board appointed Paul president. Fortunately Ted Rendall was already principal, and the Board readily approved Paul's appointment of him as Vice President of Theological Education.

Still, the mounting pressures on the younger Maxwell resulted in

complete exhaustion. While Paul could easily have questioned his spiritual resources, he remembered his father's wise counsel: "Don't spiri-
tualize that which is of physical origin!"

"I knew it was true!" Paul said later. "I wasn't exercising or getting
enough sleep. I tried to carry my father's load without following his
physical regimen." Overloaded, in 1986 he resigned. The principal, Ted
S. Rendall, took on leadership as president.

A familiar prayer on Ruth Dearing's parlor wall summed up her
own attitude—and that of many others. When I last talked with her, she
had only a month to live, but on her face and in her voice was a deep
calm. This was the prayer:

God grant me the serenity to accept the things I cannot change;
The courage to change the things I can;
And the wisdom to know the difference.   (Anon.)

The Millennium Project

Through membership on the Prairie Board, I was able to watch the
school's changes from the sidelines. But a key player was the young
Scot who became such a close colleague of LE and also of his son
Paul—and ended up as the school President and later Chancellor.

Ted Rendall's own story was one of embracing the Cross. Adding
to the pressures of the school was another burden—the ill health of his
wife, Norline, who suffered debilitating multiple sclerosis for over
twenty years.[1] Although staff took turns in being with her, few students
realized the tremendous pressures on their teacher-president as he
hurried home to help care for his wife between classes and administrative meetings.

Rendall ("TSR" his colleagues called him) was an academic scholar
in his own right—a factor that earned him (and the school) a part

---

[1]Years after Norline's death, Ted married Hester Dougan, a missionary evangelist of the Faith
Mission of Canada. Free from school responsibilities, they continue a fruitful revival ministry.

during the Millennium Project of the Provincial Museum of Alberta, Edmonton. The Museum chose the theme of "Anno Domini—Jesus through the Centuries." Unique among museum Millennium projects, it was partially funded by the provincial and federal governments and sought to show the influence of Jesus on western culture. Rendall read the Beatitudes during the opening ceremony and took part in a forum as one of five representatives of "faith communities."

The other forum members were a Jewish professor, a Muslim scholar, a Liberal Protestant theologian, and a Roman Catholic nun. Rendall was invited to represent evangelicals. All five were asked to reply to Jesus' question, "Who do you say that I am?"

"It was a great opportunity," Rendall related. "I simply told what Jesus meant in my life, as my personal Savior. The other speakers knew nothing of such a relationship—only an historical figure. And the Liberal was a member of The Jesus Seminar, which has questioned the authenticity of much the Bible tells us about Jesus!"

Chapter 22: Embracing Change

"The Christian life is not a goal—it's a road."—LEM

ON INTO THE FUTURE

A T PRAIRIE, "TSR" introduced changes in culture and administration that paved the way for further change after he retired from office and became Chancellor. In a keynote message to staff and students, he pointed out that, in the midst of change, Prairie continued to maintain its core values:

"We can respond to our past in different ways," Chancellor Rendall told the student body and staff. "We could reject it, revise it, or reverence it in an unhealthy way.

"Finally, we can receive our past with thanksgiving, looking at it to learn abiding lessons. That way we make our past a pedestal to look into the future, and not a prison where we are bound. That's what we want to do.

Maintaining Core Values

"If Mr. Maxwell, the founder along with Mr. Kirk, were here, what would he ask us about Prairie? I don't have to guess. In *Prairie Pillars,* a booklet he wrote, he discussed the issues that were of importance to him. These were the core values of Prairie as he saw them:

1. Is Prairie still true to the great fundamentals of the Christian faith as set forth in our doctrinal statement?

2. Does she perseveringly adhere to those original standards on which 'wisdom has built her house'?

3. Is Prairie still distinctively a Bible school? Is the Bible still at the heart of her curriculum?

4. Does Prairie remain true to her motto, Training Disciplined Soldiers for Christ?

5. Does she continue to emphasize the spirit-filled life of Christian victory?

6. Is Prairie's focus still on the most needy and neglected areas of the world?

7. Does she maintain the principle of separation from the world, from alliance with modern religious liberalism?

8. In the face of our mounting Sodom and Gomorrah society, can Prairie continue to uphold her unusual social regulations?

9. Does Prairie continue with the distinctive search question method of Bible study?

"While the school and the world have greatly changed since our founder wrote those words, I believe they all fit under the four categories set forth in 'the Evangelical Quadrilateral: Biblicism, Activism, Conversionism, Crucicentricism.' The author, church historian David Bebbington,[1] saw these as the core values of evangelicalism, and I believe they are still the core values of Prairie."

New Atmosphere on Campus

In 1991 the Prairie Board had commissioned three of us to find a successor to Ted Rendall as president. After several interviews of prospective presidents and much prayer, we felt that Paul W. Ferris, Jr., filled the list of skills and experience that the faculty and administrative team had given us. A Hebrew scholar on the faculty of Columbia University, SC, Ferris was well recommended by his students and fellow faculty, and also was an active deacon in his church. A plus was his personable wife, Lois, raised on the Canadian prairies. The entire Board interviewed him and unanimously appointed him as President in 1992.

---

[1] Cf. Bebbington, David. *Evangelicalism in Modern Britain.* Grand Rapids: Baker, 1989, pp 2-19.

Ferris brought with him helpful academic insights during a transitional time for the school—difficult for both president and faculty. Six years later Ferris moved on to Bethel College in Minneapolis, and Richard E. Down became Prairie's fifth president. Having gone through Prairie's schools as a student, Down had been VP for General Education before taking on the reins of PBI. His wife Naomi complemented his leadership with her gifts of hospitality and organization.

Interviewing Rick Down half a century after my own time at Prairie, I was surprised that he as a student had discovered forms of mischief I somehow missed. But of course, he started in earlier grades than I had! His "experience" endeared him to the hearts of the oncoming generation and gave him understanding of their needs in a new era.

Now campus visitors, even though unaware of the "Good Old Days," still find an atmosphere for community as well as personal discipleship. The mood is definitely more relaxed, less regimented, however. While eating in the student dining room during a visit to Three Hills, I discovered that.

"Today is Becky Stollinghouser's birthday," boomed a student leader over the loudspeaker. "Would Becky please stand up!" When Becky, in jeans and polo shirt, stood to her feet, the fellows and girls around her insisted she stand on top of a table, while everyone serenaded her with "Happy Birthday!" It was a contemporary Prairie student rite—far removed from the mealtimes of my era, when LE's table marked the sacrosanct dividing line between the Wilderness (the boys' tables) and the Promised Land (the girls' tables), according to the boys. The dining hall had a different atmosphere, but undeniably it was a healthy one, I decided.

Walking across a much different campus, I passed fresh-faced girls and boys chatting together. And now the girls looked up at me, smiled, and even said "Good morning!" (Was it because they realized I was a visitor, or did they greet everyone they passed?)

Pizza Parties and Skateboarding

The old Gym was still standing (overshadowed by an Olympic-standard sports center), but put to a use unheard of in my student days: skateboarding! Town youth came for pizza and skateboard workouts.

On campus I came across Dan Thomas. His grandfather, a sawmill foreman in the Rockies, had invited me the summer of 1948 to be a student missionary among the logging camps. One of my "parishioners" was Hazel, the foreman's daughter. She married, and her son Dan later attended Prairie's Aviation Department. When I was on the Board in 1991 and joined in the decision to open the Department, I had no idea that Dan would become one of the instructors.

I noticed renovations in progress on a number of campus facilities. A "Concert Hall" addition to the Maxwell Memorial Tabernacle would house a music fine arts center. That was an answer to prayer for the music faculty, who for years had made the best of inadequate space and facilities while meeting professional standards. Its Academy of Gospel Music Arts cooperates with the faculties of other Christian colleges and universities in North America and has hosted "Academy on Campus" conferences for the fine arts.

In nearby Calgary, some 60 minutes away on a smooth divided highway, Prairie's Graduate School of Theology attracts mature postgraduate students who want to build on their experience in churches and missions, equipping themselves to meet growing demands. The Grad school works with a consortium of theological schools for greater effectiveness and sharing of faculty and facilities. A Distance Education Department connects, by telephone line and computer, several hundred students who may never set foot on campus.

"Internationals" now make up about 10% of Prairie's enrolment. Students from Africa, Latin America, Europe, and Asia have enriched the lives of North American students. In particular, Chinese and Koreans bring new vitality to the Bible Institute. And Oriental faculty members find significant opportunities to carry the gospel with them as visiting lecturers in "limited access" countries. One recent example occurred when the Chinese government invited Prairie Graduate School professor Chris Chung to lecture in China. Another faculty member has performed a piano recital at the Taiwan National Concert Hall.

God's Sense of Humor

I tracked down Phil Callaway and his assistant Pat Massey working on the next issue of the school's magazine, *Servant.* The award-winning quarterly informs PBI's wide-spread constituency about the school's vision. It also ministers to readers through top-level interviews of "servants" God is using today.

Servant is successor to *The Prairie Overcomer* and its predecessors. Early in his ministry in Three Hills, Maxwell published *The Prairie Pastor* (1928), establishing a wide network of praying friends. Then followed *The Prairie Overcomer* in 1944, *The Young Pilot* for children in the 1950s, and *Servant* in January 1989. *Prairie Harvester* keeps alumni in touch with the school.

A graduate of Prairie's grade school, high school, and Bible school, Phil got into editorial work very naturally, since his father, Victor, had been Prairie's Director of Public Relations for many years. In demand as a conference speaker, Phil has written 14 books and hosted three video series being used in some 80,000 churches worldwide—which he sees as his missionary outreach. Phil's reply to my request for personal details is typical of the creative humor that adds zest to his ministry:

"My involvement came at Ted Rendall's request on a frightful day in 1988," he wrote. "I'd been in the offices of a few school principals, so when Dr. Rendall called me into the president's office, I knew it couldn't be good news. I was about to be fired for who knows what! Instead, he asked me to help start *Servant*—and to write my own job description! It was an exciting moment for a 27-year-old. I guess God had prepared me as a staff kid with a special love for the people here and a desire to tell the world what God is doing through the school.

"Looking back, I realize not just how good God is, but how good his sense of humor is. I almost flunked French class at Prairie High School—yet now my books are being translated into many languages! God often seems to use the most under-qualified to do his work, perhaps because they know they can't do it alone and they never doubt who gets the credit!"

"Still Stretching"

The man on whose shoulders the load of president fell in 1998 was Richard E. Down (HS '65, B '69). A practical, down-to-earth leader, Rick spoke quietly but purposefully as he answered my questions about his vision for the future.

"Today at Prairie," he began, "we are still stretching the boundaries of a deepening faith and a faith in action. Our key value statements[1] based on principles laid down from Scripture by our founder, still recognize that first we must know Jesus Christ, his Word, prayer, learning, and discipling as a community.

"This natural foundation will provide the boiling pot that can only bubble over into a life committed to missions and ministry, that is committed to servant leadership, self denial, and a simple lifestyle.

"We do all this through the power of the Holy Spirit and with God's supply. Praise the Lord for L. E. Maxwell and those around him who built a community of faith so that we can go forward in this new millennium, not without need but without the drag of a debilitating debt.

"At Prairie, we are seeking to fulfill the vision of grounding our people in the knowledge of Christ and his Word so that the message will

---

[1] See Appendix A: Core Values of Prairie Bible Institute.

overflow from the hearts of the young people to their Jerusalem, Judea, Samaria, and the uttermost parts of the world.

"We are recognizing that they must first have that grounding of a deep work of Christ in their lives, and then find ministry platforms for life on which they will demonstrate and share the love of Christ with the world, wherever that is for them.

"As Mr. Maxwell said to a group of students visiting on campus, "You need to find, follow, and finish God's will for your lives." May we individually, and as a community, do that.

"Please pray and partner with us!"

A Continuing Story

While tracing the history of the gospel in lands around the world, I've noticed that the test of effectiveness is not in the memory of the founder of a mission society, institution, or movement. The test lies in its con-tinuing effectiveness.

Has the original vision been passed on? Has today's generation grasped the torch to light their own world?

During one of my visits to Three Hills, Prairie grad Wesley Davidson (earlier mentioned as raised in Three Hills), showed me sur-rounding villages he and his evangelistic teams visit. Students from PBI help make up those teams, contacting homes across the plains in a radius of two hundred miles (300 km.). But they do it on a courteous friendship basis—not high-powered evangelism. Many lonely and hurting families welcome their visits. Meanwhile each graduating class provides recruits for churches and missions across North America and in other lands around the globe.

Prairie is very much alive. Faculty, staff, and students are still liv-ing L. E. Maxwell's message of the Cross. On those wide, wind-swept plains, the analogy of the grain of wheat seems to say it all: "Unless a grain of wheat falls into the earth and dies, it remains by itself alone; but if it dies, it bears much fruit." It was all part of Maxwell's paradox—an ancient truth applied to his contemporary world, still relevant today.

But Why Prairie?

"I still haven't read anywhere why Prairie 'happened'," LE's son-in-law, Bob Spaulding, once told me. He didn't mean the history—the Scottish homesteaders who moved to Alberta and called Leslie Maxwell from Kansas City to teach their children; the sacrifice of many farmers and artisans and other friends; the prayers of God's people. Spaulding knew that God's plan had brought all this together. But only the Sovereign Lord knows all the currents, the tides, that he used!

Perhaps surprisingly, Prairie was an indirect outgrowth of the mid-1800s revivals[1] in Britain and North America. A young Irish evangelist, H. Grattan Guinness, preached during those revivals and went on to encourage the formation of several missions to spread the gospel in other lands. A supporter of J. Hudson Taylor,[2] he had wanted to serve in China, but Taylor encouraged him to consider preparing others instead. He later became active in the Keswick "deeper life" movement, which emphasized the Cross in the believer's life. That led people to commitment for service and missionary outreach.

Guinness preached in Canada and greatly influenced young Presbyterian Albert B. Simpson, who later patterned his Missionary Training Institute[3] along the lines of the East London Institute for Home and Foreign Missions (often called the Missionary Training Institute) founded by Guinness in 1873.

Simpson founded two mission societies in the 1880s, and these

[1] Called the Second Evangelical Awakening of 1858.
[2] Founder of China Inland Mission, now Overseas Missionary Fellowship (OMF).
[3] MTI began in 1882, was formally organized in 1883, and moved to Nyack, NY, where it eventually became the C&MA's Nyack College.

merged in 1897 to form the Christian and Missionary Alliance. He deeply impressed another Presbyterian, William C. Stevens, whom he appointed principal of his growing schools in Nyack, NY. Although originally from a mainline denomination, like Guinness they both felt missionary training should be on a non-sectarian basis. Stevens later founded Midland Bible Institute, at which Leslie Maxwell and Pearl Plummer studied. Presbyterian farmers in Alberta, challenged by God's Word and the missionary needs of the world, called Maxwell to Three Hills.

We have to keep in mind that Leslie Maxwell, with this mix of Cross-centered teaching, didn't arrive in Three Hills as "instant" principal of Prairie Bible Institute. Three Hills became the crucible in which the vibrant young man from Kansas City grew into a prophet for his day. In turn, PBI grew around him and his team. Christians responded to his message of discipleship, of spiritual warfare, of soldierly endurance, of missionary vision.

True, his was a unique personality, but he had a single focus: identification of the believer in the death and resurrection of Christ. His goal was to see that paradoxical message produce response in our lives: worship, discipleship, obedience, service.

So a number of streams—revival and missionary, Calvinistic and Holiness—contributed to what became Prairie Bible Institute. Why did they converge in the insignificant granary town of Three Hills? Perhaps for the same reason that the grand prophecies of the Messiah's birth found fulfillment in tiny Bethlehem. The prophet Zechariah asked, "Who has despised the day of small things?" The Apostle Paul stated the paradox: "God chose the lowly things of this world—and the things that are not—so that no one may boast before him" (1 Corinthians 1.28).

"From House to House"

But Spaulding had something further in mind when he asked, "How did Prairie come to be?" He was thinking of "LE's tireless travels and preaching around the country." He compared this with Andrew Whyte's chapter on the Apostle Paul as a Pastor:

> **"And from house to house warning every one night and day with tears. The whole of Ephesus was Paul's parish. And not once in a whole year, like the most diligent of us, but every day, and back again every night, Paul was in every house. Paul was never in his bed. He did not take time so much as to eat. As his people in Anwoth said about Samuel Rutherford, Paul was always working with his hands, always working with his mind, always preaching, always visiting . . . . The sun and the moon and the stars all stand still in order that some men may get sufficient time to finish their work."[1]**

"LE was such a man," Spaulding continues. "His tireless visitation created such confidence in the school that conservative country people —Mennonites especially—were willing to entrust their children to him. I'm sure that in subsequent years it was those same people that helped support the school with their small but regular offerings.

"Of course, those were the early years. Recently, I visited two elderly women living on a farm nine miles north of Three Hills. They told me LE used to visit their father by horse and buggy. And as I visit churches around this part of the country, people invariably say, 'Maxwell preached in our church!' Or if I stay in a home, 'Maxwell stayed here!'"

So from an insignificant western village—no, rather, from the hearts of believers discipled there—flowed spiritual streams that watered and nurtured other Bible schools and missionary training schools, even missions and churches, around the world.

New Era—Ever-New Message

But what kind of future should Prairie Bible Institute expect?

Prof. John Stackhouse, Jr., cites Prairie Bible Institute as one of

---

[1] Whyte, Alexander, *The Apostle Paul.* London: Oliphant, Anderson, Ferrier, 1903. p.69.

three Canadian institutions that most affected Canadian Evangelicalism in the 20th Century.[1] But how relevant to current society is the concept of "Training Soldiers for Christ"?

During the first half of the 20th century the West led in two World Wars against tyranny. Christians could relate to such concepts. That era was followed, for the United States of America, with politicized warfare that alienated the younger generation. The British, weary of war, rejected as Prime Minister the very PM who had led them to victory over Hitler and his allies. Pulling itself out of the ashes, Europe reacted against the idea of war—although it has been disheartened to see continuing strife between nations.

Recently 31 evangelical mission groups agreed not to use military terms (such as crusade, target, army, conquer, enemy) in their literature to avoid misunderstanding by non-Christians (Consultation on Mission Language and Metaphors, Fuller Theological Seminary, CA, 2000). Ironically, some other faiths talk of war against their enemies, and urge the faithful to join their "crusade."

In the aftermath of the massive terrorist attack on the World Trade Center in New York City and other targets, killing several thousand people, USA struggled with its own terminology. Headlines declaring "War on Terrorism" raised images of tanks rolling across deserts and "smart" missiles destroying targets. But for the most part, "America's New War" would often have to be conducted covertly, fought on the invisible line of "security intelligence."

The West's military leaders realized that in order to keep up the resolve of their people and allies, they would need to develop a new vocabulary to describe the conflict. But the current enemies still had the same objectives as the more easily defined enemies of the two World Wars and subsequent conflicts: the destruction of democracy and human freedoms.

---

[1] John G. Stackhouse, Jr., *op.cit.* The other two evangelical organizations were Toronto Bible College (now Tyndale Bible College and Seminary) and InterVarsity Christian Fellowship.

Embracing Change

So in the spiritual war, while the enemy of souls is the same, his tactics may not seem as readily identifiable. Vocabulary, not truth may need to change. In a few decades a strategic term may become a cliché. Over-familiar language can become like radio static, drowning out the message.

While preserving its purpose and ethos, Prairie has re-phrased its slogan through the years. The earlier slogan of Prairie was "Training Disciplined Soldiers for Jesus Christ." In the 1970s the slogan was, "To Know Christ and to Make Him Known." In 1983, the school defined itself as "a Bible Institute that teaches discipleship to the Cross of Jesus, his resurrection power as the key to fruitfulness, and a disciplined lifestyle that stresses holiness in the Christian walk."[1] In the 1990s the slogan became, "Shaping Lives to Change the World for Christ and His Kingdom."

*   *   *   *

School slogans are useful, but the truth they represent is best shown in the lives of men and women. In the following "Family Reminiscences" Leslie and Pearl's own children –members of an out-standing but also very human family—tell their on-going story. Their honest and touching memories comprise a rare and delightful case study of a Christian family, with lessons for all of us pilgrims.

---

[1] *Prairie Overcomer,* May 1983 (insert).

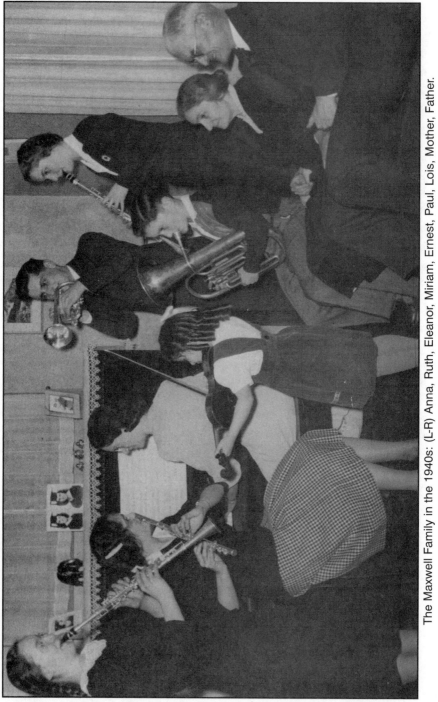

The Maxwell Family in the 1940s: (L-R) Anna, Ruth, Eleanor, Miriam, Ernest, Paul, Lois, Mother, Father.

Chapter 23: Generations

"His children are blessed after him." [1]

MAXWELL FAMILY ALBUM

GOD ANSWERED the childhood prayer of Pearl Eleanor Plummer about her future choice of husband. Yes, but how did God answer her prayer that her children and grandchildren would follow and serve the Lord? What about "Daddy Maxwell" (as his children call him to this day) and his strong convictions? How have the lives of family members reflected his principles?

"The proof of the pudding is in the eating thereof," my Welsh mother used to quote—and not just about plum pudding. How far is this true concerning the families of Christian leaders? In every family each adult eventually has to make his or her own decisions, and parents should not blame themselves for influences outside of their control. Yet sons and daughters of high-profile parents—in both the secular and "religious" world—have to process unusual motivation and cope with an imposed load of expectations.

Christian Family Syndrome

In the case of Christian families, sometimes the Devil gets blamed for the aberrations of children. But the cause may be a lot closer to home (literally). Did the context of the Bible school in Three Hills impose even greater family pressures?

    1. A large conservative Christian institution.

    2. Father as principal, publicly prescribing (in earlier years) how to raise children.

---

[1] Proverbs 20.7.

3. His own children living in "goldfish-bowl" dormitories with other students.

4. A large community of retired staff and faculty looking on.

5. Expectations that the family would model everything the principal and school stand for.

6. Sophisticated Scripture knowledge not yet processed by experience in the world.

7. Tension of reconciling parents' fame to one's own adolescent struggle for identity.

8. Parental leadership unconsciously motivating achievement, positively or negatively.

9. A child's intimate family knowledge of parents' "practicing what they preach."

10. Parents' concern that they not be perceived as favoring their own children as students—a valid concern but sometimes disconcerting to young children who are, after all, "family."

There's another factor in the syndrome that sometimes turns up among second—and third—generation Christians. Parents converted from sinful living clearly know what they've been saved out of. They develop strong convictions about the Christian life because they've made an intentional and often revolutionary 180-degree turn-around in behavior.

Their children have a godly family heritage and grow up loving God. But sometimes they don't share their parents' strong convictions (they may even see them as intolerant) because they've "grown" into acceptance of their parents' faith. That needn't imply their faith is any less genuine; they simply haven't been saved out of an openly sinful background. Leslie Maxwell, saved from a careless and dissolute life, often proclaimed the need for us "not only to love good but also to hate evil."[1] Parents require great wisdom in handling this "second-generation" syndrome.[2]

The stories of the Maxwells' immediate family and their grand-children result in a fascinating and encouraging study of this syndrome. They also help complete the story—or rather, help tell us the ongoing saga: how the family worked out the core message that L. E. Maxwell learned in his own pilgrimage from teen rebel to farmhouse Bible teacher to noted spiritual leader. In the following mosaic there are tears, laughter, and a few surprises.

God's Grace in Human Instruments

When biographers write about an outstanding leader, the result may easily lead to hagiography—uncritical adulation. That may make the leader seem unreal to younger generations. "I could never serve God like that!" they may despair. On the other hand, people who have been blessed by a leader may consider criticism as next to sacrilege. In bygone days, it just didn't seem proper to reveal anything that might be considered negative about a respected leader.

The attitudes of the era may have influenced James Hudson Taylor's son and daughter-in-law, Howard and Geraldine Taylor, to omit "the warts" from the biography of Howard's parents. (Later, two biographers, John Pollock and Roger Steer, provided a more "human" history, to the encouragement of readers who also have "limps.")

Dohnavur Fellowship's Director (now retired), Nesaruthina Carunia, told me that veteran Indian staff members walked out of interviews about Amy (Amma) Carmichael, when Elisabeth Elliot was updating her life story. They were upset that the interviewer even asked about the "human side" of their spiritual "Mother."

---

[1] Psalm 97.10.

[2] My observation of my parent's family, of our own family, and of families within my responsibility as a mission Director have led me to see these factors as key reasons for the aberrations of children of Christian workers. I hear people saying, "The Devil especially targets the children of Christian workers to discredit their parents." I think that is simplistic, although the Devil certainly uses all means available to undermine Christian testimony. There are quite understandable reasons for second-generation defections from the teaching of Christian leaders. At the same time, the heritage of godly, active parents is priceless, and God does answer prayer. The rebellion and restoration of Billy Graham's son, Franklin, is an outstanding example, as is Paul Maxwell's pilgrimage.

Like Taylor and Carmichael, Maxwell would have rejected any hint of becoming an icon. One of his grandsons, Stephen Maxwell Spaulding, wrote a Master's thesis on his grandfather's leadership style, interpreting it "through the rubric of Leadership Emergence Theory" (LET).[1] Some friends took the analysis as unduly critical of Prairie's founder, because LE failed to fit the ideal in some aspects of the LET formula. But Spaulding refers to "a moment in which I knew that [God] was truly the author of this life under study." LE's leadership had its own charisma, even if it didn't include all the textbook requirements of leadership theory. Perhaps that proved (as the saying goes), "God threw away the mold" when he made Leslie Earl Maxwell!

The Founder and His Disciples

There's truth in that—which may have escaped some of his colleagues. Others who joined his team admired his disciplined life and wanted to see us students emulate it. As is often the case, "disciples" may apply principles more rigidly than "the founder" intended. Years of personal self-discipline tempered with trials shaped the man who became the L. E. Maxwell we knew. He was able to pour himself from that personal mold into many of our lives. But some students and staff enshrined the rules rather than the principles, not realizing the misuse and misunderstanding to which rigid rules sometimes led. In some cases, they turned godly self-discipline, the work of the Holy Spirit, into regimentation.

The following family reminiscences reveal that "Daddy Maxwell" was more flexible than Prairie's rigorous environment might suggest. He had been able to embrace each student with one arm and apply the discipline of the Word with the other.[1] He also knew he had to leave the fall-out in the Lord's hands; it was God's work, after all.

But as the Founder declined in health and leadership, some

---

[1] Stephen Maxwell Spaulding, *op. cit.*

students saw in the Institute only rigid control. They reacted accordingly. My contact with LE's successors and the Board convinced me they realized the problem and sincerely sought to combine grace with law. The question was how to change the external formula yet achieve the inner objective: disciplined soldiers for Christ. The changes that took place were themselves the painful means God used to "crowd" many faithful faculty and staff to the Cross in their own lives once more, even as they aged. Inevitably, however, there were personal hurts.

Interviewing the Maxwell family, I've appreciated their openness in sharing early impressions. Their collective memories help describe the family mosaic and give glimpses of remarkable yet "human" parents trying to maintain normal family life while leading a rapidly growing Bible school. Their own words express the nuances of family dynamics more poignantly than could any observer-journalist. The fact that they have been able to share their personal feelings is an indication of their own spiritual growth. Their lives demonstrate in multiple ways the message that Prairie is all about—being dead to self and alive to Jesus Christ, the Cross in the life of the believer.

'Home Sweet Home' It Was!

LESLIE AND PEARL'S FIRST HOME in Three Hills was the McElheran farmhouse, where they welcomed their first baby, Eleanor, in 1926.

Shortly afterwards, the family moved into the first dormitory built for the infant Bible school—men on the third floor, women on the second, classrooms and chapel on the first (ground) floor, with kitchen, dining room, and laundry facilities in the basement. The Maxwell family lived on the second floor. Eleanor's mother became school matron, while her father taught classes and administered the school. During harvest season, he was often out with farmers, "stooking" sheaves of grain.

---

[1] Maxwell often described God's two-fold dealings with his people in the words of Deuteronomy 33.2-3 (AV): "From his right hand went a fiery law for them. Yea, he loved the people; all his saints are in thy hand . . . ."

With the arrival of their third child, the Maxwells moved into a tiny house, not insulated against the extreme Alberta cold. Father piled straw and snow around the foundation, and Mother, shod in boots, tried to occupy the children as they sat on the table in the kitchen—the only warm room. When LE received his US Army discharge pay, he used part to purchase land for the Bible school and the rest to buy lumber for a larger house, which Jack McElheran generously constructed without charge.

Life at home was fairly typical for a family on the Prairies in those years, coming through the Great Depression. Although at subsistence level, it was rich in family relationships. In winter, the kitchen was the center of activity—from children's bathing in a washtub on the floor to father's shaving in front of a mirror hanging on the wall. While mother washed the dishes, father would towel-down the little bairns until they "glowed pink."

Although father was a disciplinarian, he also exuded mischief. The children knew if they got too close when he was shaving, they just might be lathered with his shaving brush!

Studies and household duties filled the winter months; summer added gardening responsibilities. Vegetables canned or stored from their "kitchen garden" were vital for winter meals.

Even after Maxwell became a noted conference speaker and author, on Saturdays he'd often get on his knees to scrub the kitchen floor. Perhaps only because the floor needed scrubbing and Pearl needed help? Or because he didn't want to ask for more student voluntary help? Or, someone suggested, he felt the need to practice humility.

(See Chapters 18 and 19 for further details about the Maxwell parents.)

Leslie and Pearl Maxwell had five girls and two boys. "Our five loaves and two fish," they liked to quip, adding, "Remember—Jesus used those loaves and fish to feed a multitude!" The following sketches (beginning with the eldest and continuing to the youngest) form a color-

*ful family mosaic from their own pilgrimages and personal reminis-
cences.*[1] *It is interesting to note that five of the seven married Prairie
students.*

---

[1] In chapters 23 and 24 as well as in the main story, I have limited details to the immediate Maxwell family, since the 23 grandchildren represent a wider range than the focus of this volume. The one exception is the family of Ernest and Freeda. Lorna and I were personally involved with them before and after the parents' death. As to the other members of the third generation, I have simply listed their names, for the most part. However, their pilgrimages are no less meaningful.—WHF

For Leslie and Pearl's Fiftieth Wedding Anniversary in 1975, all the sons and daughters, several of their spouses, and many of the grandchildren gathered to celebrate.

"Christ promises more but demands more!"—LEM

FAMILY REMINISCENCES

A. First in Line: Eleanor Pearl (Maxwell) Spaulding

THE FIRST BABY MAXWELL to arrive at the McElheran farm-house, site of the original Bible classes, was Eleanor in 1926.

Typical of the eldest in a family, Eleanor was serious-minded, with a high sense of responsibility and regard for authority. Her elementary schooling was at Three Hills' public school, her secondary at PBI's high school, and Bible at Prairie. As the other children came along, her mother depended on her help and said she was "a natural little mother from the start." Four of her siblings said she led them to assurance of salvation. She and an ex-serviceman named Bob Spaulding got to know each other through Eleanor's brother Ernest, who roomed with Bob one year.

Earlier as a teenage rebel, Bob had his life turned around at Prairie High School before being conscripted into the US Army. One terrifying night in a foxhole during the brutal battle of Okinawa, Bob promised to serve the Lord the rest of his life if he survived the battle. He later returned to take the Bible course at Prairie.

Fulfilling his missionary pledge, upon graduating Bob signed up for Japan under what became the Japan Evangelical Mission.[1] As he said goodbye to Eleanor in 1949, she recollects, "His eyes told me all his lips didn't utter!" She stayed at Prairie to teach piano for a year, planning to go to China under the China Inland Mission (now Overseas Missionary Fellowship). When she did leave for overseas, her mother said, "It was

---

[1] JEM, founded by Prairie missionaries, merged with The Evangelical Alliance Mission (TEAM).

like losing my right arm!" Eleanor had helped care for her younger siblings through the years.

For both Eleanor and Bob, it was a test of seeking first God's will. Getting together again seemed impossible, but during a period of testing, Bob wrote a pledge to wait for God to give him Eleanor unless the Lord definitely showed him otherwise.

Unexpectedly, in 1950 Communism closed the door to China and Eleanor was re-routed to Japan. Bob and Eleanor became engaged. When "Daddy Maxwell" set off to speak at a conference in Japan that year, his wife gave him a pillow to help him sleep on the plane. He had no idea what made it seem so soft, until Eleanor later opened the pillowcase. Out dropped a wedding dress passed on by a good friend! The marriage took place in Karuizawa, Japan, August 25, 1951. They celebrated their Golden Wedding Anniversary in 2001.

Learning Japanese, establishing and developing a Bible school in rural Japan, as well as planting an embryo church all at the same time was more than enough for the newly weds. At the beginning, every Bible school student began music lessons on Eleanor's army surplus pump organ. Some became gifted music leaders in the churches where they later ministered.

Struggling along with students in post-war penury and winter rigors, raising a family, and teaching in a totally different culture—all these kept the Cross of self-denial central in Eleanor and Bob's lives. After the first few years, Bob became JEM's Field Director, and after their third term the mission appointed Bob as business administrator for the Mission's head office in Canada.

After five years in office administration, the Spauldings volunteered to launch a new field among the nearly one million Japanese in Brazil. That meant learning yet another language—Portuguese—and facing pioneering stresses all over again. During their first few years in Brazil, they taught the message of the Cross in the life of the believer to the newly established Japanese churches.

Gradually other missionaries joined in the work in Brazil, with greater emphasis on outreach among the very responsive Portuguese-speaking population. Most of the work in the Portuguese department was directed into a thriving national church, while several Japanese congregations continue among the diminishing Japanese-speaking peoples. When the Spauldings returned to Three Hills in 1990 to retire, they left many believers, several churches, a youth camp, and co-workers who are developing a foreign missions program through the national church.

Three daughters and two sons had been born during the Japan years—"made in Japan" they joke. Eventually all five (Dorothy, Pearl, Grace, Stephen, Robert) attended Prairie Bible Institute, the four oldest having Grandpa Maxwell as their teacher. Close association with their grandparents greatly enriched their lives. Son Steve later wrote his postgraduate thesis on "L. E. Maxwell—Lion on the Prairies."

✍ ELEANOR'S MEMORIES:

DADDY PRAYED for my first breath! Apparently I didn't breathe for the first few minutes after mother gave birth. While the family doctor worked on this little "preemie," Father paced the floor praying, "Oh God! Oh God!" At last I gasped and cried. Concern changed to thanksgiving. To provide for Mother to clothe me during the Depression years, Daddy worked a few extra hours in farm labor.

Daddy was always on the move, Bible and notes in hand, but he was always ready to get down on one knee and pick up alphabet blocks in response to my plea: "Daddy build a house!" One day when I was four, after I had done something wrong, he explained how I could ask Jesus to come into my heart. I remember going around singing, "Happy day, happy day, when Jesus washed my sins away!"

After Ernest and Lois were born, Mother decided she should devote all her time to family, especially with Daddy so busy dawn to dark. Before Prairie opened its own grade school, Ernest and I attended public school in town.

Although we had to run to keep up, we loved to accompany Daddy on his walks at times—at least part way. We had our secret hand signals. Three hand squeezes meant, "I love you." Four in return responded, "I love you too!" He tried to walk every day—sometimes up to eight miles. He said it helped overcome sleeplessness, the result of intense work over long hours. Friendly drivers were inclined to offer him a ride, so when he heard a vehicle approaching from behind he'd turn around and walk towards it until it had passed—then he would continue in his original direction.

At conferences, Daddy usually introduced the speaker. We learned to gauge the speaker's effectiveness by watching Daddy's face. When a speaker failed to make his point, Daddy would follow up the message by developing the intended point, turning it into a ringing challenge.

Annual missionary conference was the time to make financial giving pledges for the coming year—often involving sacrifice and faith. Excitement mounted each day as we heard the total of the pledges. We children made our own pledges and trusted God to help us fulfil them. One year Daddy got carried away and pledged $600—it would be equivalent to ten times that amount these days! In his enthusiasm, he'd forgotten to discuss it with Mother. She was prepared to sacrifice, but she knew the pledge was unrealistic. Ernest, our family mathematician, calculated how much it took to keep five of us children in school.

We'd have to talk with Daddy—with me elected as spokesperson! Because Mother found confrontation difficult, we closed the kitchen door and talked in the living room. I began to cry as I explained the predicament. Immediately Daddy asked, "Where's Mother? We can't leave her out of this!" When she came in, he apologized, "I didn't mean to be hard on you!" He readily agreed to a revised pledge.

Always a tease, Daddy had a favorite trick, diverting our attention when Mother served our favorite home-made chocolate cake Sunday night. When we looked back at our plates, someone's dessert was usually missing. After loud protests, the culprit would return the sweet morsel amid much family laughter.

B. Vest-Pocket Edition: Ernest Edwin Maxwell

"THE VEST POCKET EDITION OF L. E. MAXWELL," people called him (born 1927). If we who met LE in his middle life wanted to know what he had earlier looked like, how he spoke, and how he disciplined himself, all we needed to do was look at "Ernie," our fellow student.

Straight as a poker, quick-witted, serious-minded, hard-playing, and brilliant—that was Ernest. (At age two he could recite the alphabet backwards, to his family's astonishment). One of his roommates was frustrated because Ernest would work out with a basketball the night before a major exam, while others were swatting at the books. But his father was concerned that extrovert Ernest didn't seem to stick at one thing for long. Remembering his own youthful lack of goals, the older Maxwell described his son as "a jack of all trades, master of none."

"Even though he was the son of the principal, he was like one of us," a classmate said. They remember him for his good nature and devotion to God. Ernest hurried through Bible school and out to Africa (1950), the youngest candidate (21) ever accepted by SIM up to then.

Language school, marriage to fellow missionary Freeda LaVon Jones (born in Kansas), and three children followed in the next ten years. Freeda had been a copy editor for Moody Press during her years at Moody Bible Institute and now along with Ernest became expert in the Hausa language. Ernest used his teaching skills to develop a Bible school in Nigeria's heartland. Being "a jack of all trades" proved useful as he handled the many maintenance tasks around the school and helped other missionaries with repair jobs. He excelled in serving others.

When LE visited Nigeria near the first of Ernest's ministry in 1951, the father explained to a pastor that Ernest was his son.

"Ah, but he's my brother!" the Nigerian promptly added.

Traditionally, Africans give foreigners descriptive names in the local language. The Bible school students soon realized Ernest could be impatient, but they gave him the Hausa name *Ayuba* (Job)—"because you're patient with us when we're learning!"

Ernest and Freeda helped edit a vernacular gospel paper. With another Prairie grad and his wife, George and Ruth Foxall, they also developed Bible teaching materials and systems used widely in Nigeria and later Africa-wide.

While God blessed the work, Ernest's brusqueness in early years of service made him appear judgmental and intolerant to some colleagues. But he saw in Freeda the gentle qualities of his mother. Pearl later said of her, "Freeda was just like a daughter to me!"

Ernest was rigidly demanding of their first son. When a friend asked him why, he replied, "That's how I was brought up!" Ernest probably reflected the fact that his "Daddy," although self-disciplined and loving, had not experienced an ideal relationship with his own father during childhood back in Kansas.

However, the Holy Spirit worked in Ernest's life, "chipping the corners off the block," as his father would have said. "I almost wept as I saw changes taking place in his life!" commented a fellow missionary, a family favorite and prayer partner.

As Ernest mellowed, his brilliant personality coming to the Cross afresh, he became a different husband, father, and servant of God. On their 30th wedding anniversary, they told their children, "We spent the first 10 years trying to change each other, the next ten years learning about and from each other, and the last 10 years enjoying each other."

After years of strained relations, Ernest's son David asked him if he should follow his father's early example in marriage relationship. "No," Ernest replied; "I hope God will help you see beyond the mistakes I made when I was beginning marriage and family life, and enable you to make the kind of decisions I made later in life." David was touched when his once-stern father worked for him in a home-painting business. "He came with a servant attitude," David recalls.

When Paul became president of Prairie, Ernest felt a typically human twinge about being bypassed by his brother—ten years junior. "God showed me I had 'the Elder Brother complex' that Jesus described in the story of the Prodigal Son," Ernest later shared. "I had to get right with God about that!"[1]

That day, Ernest once more embraced Christ's Cross. From then on he could genuinely accept Paul's role—so much so that on visits home, he'd drop by Paul's office to chat about the Institute and offer help in any way.

In 1980 Ernest and Freeda served on Canada's prairies as regional representatives of SIM. Two years later they were killed instantly in a vehicle collision on an icy Alberta highway. It was a devastating "orphaning" for their three children, David, Ruth, and Mark, but they have walked the Calvary Road spiritually and achieved excellence in their professions.

Each has chosen an effective way to follow the heritage of their parents and grandparents.

In Alberta, David manages a Logos Bookstore, stocked with Christian and other wholesome volumes. He's also active in the Christian Booksellers' Association. One of his last and most precious memories of his parents was passing their open bedroom door as they embraced each other. He knew his father had found difficulty expressing emotion to Freeda in the early years of their marriage.

Ruth has served with SIM in Liberia, Kenya, and Canada. Mark has been active on mission boards and his church's missions committee while pursuing a different path of demanding service in which he quietly models Christian principles.[2] He is active in investment management and is ranked as one of Canada's top financial analysts. Each has had to come to terms with loneliness and search for direction in life.

---

[1] Ian Hay, International General Director (Emeritus) of SIM, recalls that Ernest shared this incident at an SIM home staff devotional session. "Two weeks later, we heard that he and Freeda had died in a car collision! That left an indelible impression on us," Hay remembers.

[2] Mark Maxwell has served on PBI's Board and is a financial consultant.

Mark experienced some kind of "closure" to the tragedy of his parents' death when he returned to Nigeria a year later, to clear up their personal effects. While there, he searched for Baba, the Nigerian who had cared for all three children while their parents were teaching at the Bible school across the compound. Now white-haired, Baba was hand-hoeing his farming plot as Mark strode across the red soil toward him.

"*Lale!* [Surely!] You've come back!" Baba cried, dropping his hoe to embrace Mark. The two rocked back and forth on the freshly hoed dirt as tears trickled down their cheeks. "Now I know it's true. Your parents have really died, or they'd have come back with you!"

Over the next few hours, the aging Nigerian reminisced about his 20 happy years of friendship with Freeda and Ernest. He then told Mark something that eased the pain of losing both parents at once. "Your mother told me ten rainy seasons [years] ago she couldn't imagine living without your father!"

✍ ERNEST'S MEMORIES
(posthumously from notes):

CHRISTMAS HOLDS MY RICHEST MEMORIES. Daddy would get up at 4 a.m. to fire up the school boilers so the duty stokers could enjoy Christmas morning with their own excited children. Then he'd be back with us for a very special day together. I learned from our folk not to get "wrapped up" in material things, but to be just as happy with the three gifts I received one year as the nineteen I'd received the year before. We learned equanimity—how to live with little or with abundance.

Mother insured we also learned equity. At Christmas time she divided up boxes of chocolates and other goodies so that all nine of us had an equal amount. Daddy's sweet tooth didn't have precedence over the rest of us.

One Christmas Eleanor received a beautiful doll and carriage— first prize in a contest sponsored by the local drugstore. At the time we were attending the grade school in town. Eleanor won "hands down" because every one of the 300 Prairie students making purchases there had voted for the principal's eldest daughter! Other customers had entered the names of children they knew in town; so their votes were divided. When the contest was repeated the next year, I got the votes and the prize—a lovely red wagon. But when Daddy realized what had happened, he returned the wagon, to be given to a runner up. "We didn't come to Three Hills to play favorites!" he explained. It was another lesson in equity.

Daddy practiced self-discipline rigorously. To rest his mind from school matters, he exercised daily for an hour (whether jogging, playing ball, or shoveling snow and opening drainage ditches). He kept up on current affairs with 15 minutes of radio news at noon, at supper, and at 10 p.m. He usually carried a book around in case he had to wait a few minutes for an appointment or meal. He told us that next to reading the Bible, we should make use of a dictionary more than any other book.

Mother was the truest practitioner of Daddy's preaching. We must credit her with the success of his ministry, as far as our lives were concerned. Because he was so busy, we saw very little of him. But he did practice what he preached, including the need to keep balanced on contentious doctrines. While he wanted students to form their own conclusions straight from Scripture, in their senior year he would divulge his personal views on debatable issues in response to their requests. He had no time for rigid, unbending extremists, yet he didn't complain about the restraints his position as principal put on his own pronouncements.

I was a student during Prairie's "Victorian" era in dress and social code. So I'll never forget a family camping trip in the Rockies, when our parents encouraged my sisters to borrow trousers from the men of the family for hiking and rock climbing. It made sense and was an example of Scripture's injunction: "Do you have faith? Have it to yourself before God."[1] We knew we mustn't let our liberty be a stumbling block to people with more conservative dress codes. So we enjoyed the liberty of

---

[1] Romans 14.22.

our family rock climbing vacation, but upon return to the Institute we submitted to the regulations without reluctance or hypocrisy.

Daddy taught us discipline but also set an example of admitting errors. Gardening was his therapy—he'd raise seedlings in house boxes and in Spring transplant them into the garden. We children took part in caring for them. One afternoon my job was to weed the garden. I invited a friend to keep me company. Daddy, on his way to the office, noticed what a poor job I was doing and gave me a verbal work-over. Ten minutes later he was back to apologize for his harshness. My friend exclaimed, "My Dad would never apologize like that!" But to us children, the incident was fairly normal. We knew he preached repentance and confession of misjudgment.

C. **Blond–But Not Adopted: Lois Christina (Maxwell) Friesen**

L OIS WAS THE FIRST BLOND in the family. Until Anna, the second blond, was born, friends commented that all the others were dark, to the point that as a child Lois wondered if she were adopted! Father put that suspicion to rest by showing her a baby photo of himself with blond curls—"just like your baby photo!" However, she was like her mother in personality.

After graduation from Bible school, Lois worked for two years in the home office of the Japan Evangelical Mission (founded by people from Prairie). In 1953 she sailed for Japan. Bill Friesen happened to sail on the same ship. While they were both taking intensive language study in Japan, Bill proposed to Lois. Her parents received a letter from Bill asking for her hand—with a humorous application of Scripture: "Who am I that I should be son-in-law to the king?" After so many years of association with good, solid Mennonites from across the Prairies, the Maxwells were personally pleased when Bill with his Mennonite heritage came into the family.

A year after their marriage, they were seconded to the Pacific Broadcasting Association for three years, helping develop radio ministries. Then the JEM mission group asked Bill to take leadership, and he served for a number of years as Field Director. Besides administrative responsibilities, he often spoke in one or other of the 15 churches related to the early work of JEM.

Seeing the need to train young Japanese for the ministry, the mission began a small Bible school patterned on Prairie's teaching methods. Though Bill was not a teacher in the school, he sometimes spoke at student chapel. During a year between administrative stints, he senior-pastored a church, assisted by a young man who later became principal of the Bible school. When the Friesens were leaving for home assignment in 1989, this man, Satoshi Nakamura, took on the duties of pastor at the church they had served for three years. Pastor Satoshi feels he is a son in the faith to Bill.

For several years Lois found her hands full as mission hostess along with caring for their four children. On the campus where they lived were the mission office, Bible school, and missionary children's (MKs') school. Though not a piano teacher, Lois taught piano to MKs and pump organ to Bible school students, at the mission's request. The rudiments of hymn-playing helped students preparing for pastorates. In time Lois taught English.

A Saturday class of high schoolers held at the local church was a special joy. These girls were eager to learn English conversation, and most of them stayed for Bible study after the English class. Several of them came to Christ. One married a Christian high school teacher. Another married a young man who was attending a theological seminary in Tokyo, where he later became a professor.

The missionaries of JEM came to a decision in the early 1980s to seek a merger with The Evangelical Alliance Mission. Bill was involved in the process and was thankful for the smooth transition. Upon retiring from the field in 1994, the Friesens felt free to leave the Japan Sea coast area, where most of their efforts had been spent. The ministries started there by JEM and TEAM missionaries were in good hands. Bible school, camps, and conferences were going forward under able Japanese leadership. They rejoice that God allowed them a share in laying the foundation for that work. There is still a great harvest to be reaped in that part of Japan.

Settling back into life in Canada, they're happy to see their own family more often: Hannah, Esther, and Mary. In 1998, the Friesens experienced God's comfort as their daughter Lily "walked through the valley of the shadow of death," dying of cancer.

✍ *LOIS' MEMORIES:*

WE KNEW DADDY LOVED US, even though his actions were quick and often a little rough—including drying us off with a big bath towel after Mother washed us down in the metal tub set on the kitchen floor!

Mother was gentle and understanding. Instead of making snap judgments upon arriving home at night, Daddy left most of the family discipline up to her. "Your mother had a wonderful home and upbringing," he once explained to me. "I was brought up like topsy." Occasionally he did reprimand us in the home (such as when he sat on a stool I'd unknowingly spilled water on)—but often he'd be back to apologize. "Mother says I was too hard on you," he'd explain—and we'd get a hug.

Daddy had definite ideas on child rearing, and we didn't seem to come to harm because of his simplistic approach. However, I think later in life he realized there was more to child training than hugging, scolding, and spanking. "There's such a wealth of material out there now to guide Christian families!" he'd comment wistfully.

We weren't model children—although the rest of us thought Eleanor, the oldest, was an example of obedience! We didn't feel legalistic about the rules (we even talked to the boys at times!). In school we weren't above playing pranks. I remember one evening when Eleanor, Ruth, and I were out for a stroll and heard voices of men we recognized as Daddy, the men's Dean, and a teacher. We decided to play a joke on them and shouted boisterously before hiding in some bushes. We thought it was great fun until the Dean hailed a passing car to help locate the "rowdies." Things could get serious, so we came out of hiding and told Daddy our joke. The men didn't seem highly amused.

I don't think the fact that father was principal earned us special consideration. We never thought of ourselves as "special" among the other students—we lived with them in the dorm until space became limited. When I needed advice on my summer plans, I signed up for an appointment with the principal just like any other student. But as I was leaving, he got up and said, "I've always thought a lot of you!" Coming from my father, whom I deeply respected, that meant so much. He gave me one of his warm hugs, and I left the office with tears in my eyes but feeling ten feet tall.

Sometimes we had the nerve to try to influence Daddy! We pointed out that he lost his listeners by preaching past 1 p.m. on Sundays. In our teens we suggested it wasn't helpful for him to make fun of natural attraction between boys and girls. He was open to advice, even from his own, imperfect children. I don't think he intended Prairie to become as regimented and legalistic as it did for some. He preferred to focus on essentials.

We all understood how busy Daddy was. I don't see how he could have done what he did if he hadn't been so disciplined with his time. Even his relaxation was disciplined. He used 15 minutes of supper time to listen to the news. We knew it was important to keep up on world news for his writing and teaching. Mother would lift up a finger to silence us if we interrupted. While listening, he'd point to the salt or pepper or whatever he needed.

Once when he pointed, we mischievously passed him everything on the table—especially the tomato ketchup, which he liked to slather on his food. We all had a good laugh. We tried to lighten up things when he got home, for we could tell he was weary.

How did my folk rate as parents? Daddy loved us, prayed for us, and set us a tremendous example. Mother devoted herself to family needs. What a heritage!

D. The 'Middlest': Ruth Priscilla (Maxwell) Hartt

HER SISTERS JOKED that Ruth was such an achiever she'd probably be unhappy with herself if she received only A+ on a paper! Yet that didn't really reflect self-confidence, she says. A striking raven-haired brunette, she was definitely a Maxwell, yet in her introspective nature she was more like her mother. She called herself the family "middlest"—and in some respects she fit the "middle child" syndrome (there were three older and three younger children).

Her siblings called her "The Whiner" and teased her by singing the jingle, "Oh they grumble on Sunday, they grumble on Monday . . . they grumble the whole week through!" One Saturday morning when her father was teaching his children from the book of Acts, Ruth asked the Lord to overcome her complaining habit—and God answered her prayer. Later she was happy to hear her mother say what a change she had noticed since that Saturday morning—she had scarcely heard another complaint from Ruth.

"I wish I could say I'd never since been tempted to grumble—not so!" Ruth comments. "But even as a young Christian, about 10 years of age, I found that God could free me from a sinful habit."

Ruth was part of The Maxwell Sisters' Trio and sometimes played the flute as accompaniment. In her last year of Bible, she felt the call to missions. Unsure of herself, she asked her father for advice. He sensed she needed more time to think through the multiple choices of ministry and location that most Prairie students faced. Ever the pragmatist, he counseled, "Take the next step before you, and God will show you the rest of the way!"

The school had already invited her to join the music faculty for a year—so that was obviously the next step. (By this time she'd become an excellent pianist, flutist, accordion soloist and vocalist, and later used her musical talents overseas as well as all over North America.)

While Ruth was 'taking the next step,' Bradford Hartt, also a Prairie grad and on furlough from Cuba, appeared at her doorstep, and proposed to her on their first date! Not that they had never known each other before—by no means![1] The Hartt and Maxwell families had been friends for many years. Did the four parents dream of a match between any of their children when they planned a joint family vacation in Banff some six years earlier? There was nothing between Ruth and Brad at that time. They all had "a pile of fun together." According to Ruth, "no one could have been more surprised than I—that Brad, with all of his talent, charisma, and fun, should have thought of me romantically!"

But during the intervening years in Cuba, Brad had prayed, wept, and sought God's will for a wife. He thought of Ruth and began praying seriously that God would make it clear. Even after coming back to Canada, he didn't let Ruth know of his interest, but waited another year until one day, during his Scripture reading, God gave him the answer. He should go ahead and propose to Ruth.

Strangely enough, that very same morning Ruth got up, and wondering what the future held, seemed to sense that God had someone special in mind to help guide her future. That very evening Brad appeared at the Maxwells' door, sat down in the living room, and began talking to Ruth about the prospects of going to Cuba! Could he have an answer in one month?

"Wow! I could hear wedding bells ring!" Ruth recollects. "But I had to sift through my thoughts before giving my answer. It seemed too good to be true. I couldn't trust my own heart! After much soul-searching, I went to talk it over with Daddy in his office when no one else was around. I poured out my concerns to his hearing ear and loving heart." Her father's response confirmed that she should answer Brad with a "Yes."

[1] Brad was the son of Prairie staff electrician Roy Dave Hartt (see main story). After graduating, Brad had served for four years in Cuba with the West Indies Mission.

Years before, in a slip of the tongue, he'd already called Ruth's father "Daddy." In high school at the time, before his parents came to Three Hills, he was missing his own father. One day in the student dining room he found himself serving the principal's table. "I don't remember what we were talking about," Brad recalls, "but I called him 'Daddy'— it just slipped out! My face must have turned red, but he jokingly responded, 'That's OK, son!' Little did I dream I'd become his son-in-law!"

After the wedding[1] in 1954, Ruth and Brad headed off to Cuba with the West Indies Mission, where they taught in a Bible school. Fidel Castro came to power January 1, 1959. In the summer of 1960, Brad somehow felt convinced he should move his little family out of Cuba. As Brad and Ruth were loading the van to leave, a neighbor informed Brad that he was marked for elimination. The Communist Party could not tolerate him, a non-Marxist foreigner, as a teacher in Cuba.

Moving to Tampa, Florida, the Hartts pastored a Spanish church for seventeen years before moving to Chicago to pastor a Spanish Baptist church. They've also ministered in the US Pacific North-West and recently have spent winters in Arizona ministering among Mexicans.

Brad and Ruth had three children, Margaret, Lorraine, and Carolyn. They passed through a difficult trial in 1980 when 22-year-old Lorraine died of an inoperable brain tumor. "The Spanish have a saying," the Hartts commented; "'What does he know about life, who has never suffered?' Lorraine's passing certainly brought us and others closer to the Lord, and helped us relate to those who suffer. A Peruvian friend was so touched that she trusted in Christ as Savior."

They'll never forget their daughter's response when she realized her cancer was terminal: "I belong to the Lord. I am totally his. He can do with me whatever he wishes!" Like her grandfather, she too was an overcomer.

---

[1] Her father's humor bubbled up in the wedding rehearsal when he asked the groom, "Wilt thou take this woman to be thine awful wedded wife?" In the actual ceremony LE was all decorum.

✍ *RUTH'S MEMORIES:*

I LOVED TO HEAR DADDY PREACH. He had us laughing one moment and crying the next as he dramatized the stories of Abraham, Jacob, Joseph, and Samson and Delilah. But the sermons that left the greatest impression were given at home—such as seeing him kneeling by his bed early in the morning, or hearing him interrupt his prayers to come downstairs to apologize to Mother about something he knew had hurt her.

I'll never forget welcoming him home from a lengthy trip. We'd all be at the train station, dancing with excitement when we heard the whistle blow in the distance. We'd try to guess which train car he'd be on, and as he bounced off the steps, we'd make a dash for his outstretched arms. Once home, we kids would pile on his lap, squealing with delight and agony as he almost hugged us to death! He jokingly told others he had one and a half dozen (he meant 1+6)—"the perfect number but not perfect kids!" But we knew he loved us seven, each in a special way.

When he came home tired, we tried to take his mind off the burdens of the school. We'd play practical jokes on him, and sometimes Ernest would challenge him to a fun wrestling match on the kitchen floor. Daddy was forever teaching us. At meals, we'd play word games.

When we went for a walk, he'd talk about the clouds, winds, and crops. One night he woke us and got us out of bed to see an amazing display of northern lights. We children excitedly wondered if the Lord was about to return!

We knew Daddy was human. For instance, we'd sometimes sense that Mother longed for more of his time. But if we mentioned some weakness we thought he had, she'd respond, "I have plenty of faults too, and he loves me anyway!" We were sure of that.

Mother and Daddy's 50th wedding anniversary was in 1975. Brad and I were ministering in Tampa, Florida at the time. I wanted so much to attend the anniversary celebration, but it was an expensive trip. Was it right to spend so much money in order to be with my family? I needed the Lord's direction. On February 19, I was reading in Daily Light. The morning texts included the verse, 'The entrance of your words gives light; it gives understanding to the simple.' That certainly included me. The evening reading was very specific, although in a different context: "You shall hallow the fiftieth year—and you shall return every man unto his family." I felt reassured that I should go.

We were all together again as a family for this special anniversary—the first and only time we were able to get together in all the years since Ernest had left for Africa. The rest of us had left one by one for the far corners of the earth, and our furloughs had never all coincided. So this was a foretaste of heaven.

The celebration service was held during the Spring Conference. Daddy remarked on the contrast of this huge gathering with the modest wedding fifty years before—when only seven were present, including the bride and groom and minister. Now we were gathered with probably around four thousand—students, staff, and conference guests! Elmer Thompson, director of the West Indies Mission and close friend of our father, gave a fine message. At the close Daddy added a few remarks and his final tribute, "To God be the glory, and to the wife the honor." That summed up our parents' lives.

E. The Quiet One: Anna Elizabeth (Maxwell) Iddings

ANNA, FIFTH CHILD, was perhaps the most inconspicuous family member, as far as we students knew her—and certainly the shyest. Much like her mother in personality, she quietly went about life while her three older sisters took the spotlight as The Maxwell Sisters' Trio. (When Eleanor went overseas, Anna filled in as one of the Trio and at times accompanied them on the piano.) A product of Prairie's grade school, high school, and Bible school, she feels that the many guests in their home—some prominent leaders, some fresh from service in exotic cultures—expanded her horizons of knowledge and understanding.

Anna was very conscientious and sensitive to the needs of others. At one mission conference, as a youngster, she had no money to give so placed her simple box camera on the offering plate. Word of that got out, to Anna's embarrassment. But it stimulated many others to give liberally. One year Anna increased her pledge a couple of times but added the larger amount on top of her earlier commitment. Ernest, ever the mathematician, pointed this out to Anna, but she insisted on meeting her pledge—$72.00, an enormous sum for a little girl in those days. A year later she still hadn't been able to pay it all, but later she saw God provide for her need.

An interesting insight on the family's close relationship occurred when her father innocently used his young daughter's pledge as an illustration of giving. Tearfully, Anna told him how this hurt her, because it seemed like a "sales pitch." She had made her pledges only before the Lord. Her father immediately apologized. He recognized his daughter's child-like commitment and faith.

Anna graduated from PBI in 1956 and was in the Philippines under Overseas Missionary Fellowship by the fall of 1958; Allen Iddings (PBI grad of '57) arrived in the Spring of 1960. They met at a field conference.

"Being of a timid nature," recalls Anna, "I was of a double mind when it came to marrying Allen. My heart fell for him, but the well-meaning advice of friends proved unhelpful to making up my mind. Some thought we were meant for each other and others didn't! So I had to make up my own mind before the Lord, and He assured me to go ahead with the promise in 2 Corinthians 12:9: 'My grace is sufficient for thee.' I have often remembered this when tests have come. God is true to give His grace to us both."

Adjusting their furloughs, they married in Three Hills in 1962. After pastoring for a couple of years, they returned to the Philippines. In 1968 they returned to Alberta to serve in pastorates there. They enjoy ministering to Filipinos around them, especially young people going to Bible School.

The Iddings have two sons, Paul and Lyndon, and a daughter, Lynnette. She was the middle child and also the most outspoken. The family laugh about the time a Prairie high school teacher inadvertently called her "Miss Maxwell," asking her to keep quiet.

"I'm not 'Miss Maxwell' and never will be!" she protested. Actually, Lynnette enjoyed letting others know she belonged to the Maxwell tribe by coming up behind aging "Grampa" on the sidewalk. Knowing he didn't have peripheral vision, she'd surprise him by planting a hearty kiss on his cheek. "My little flirt!" he teased her—giving her a special attachment to dear Granddad. She has his hearty laugh and zest for the life of faith.

"Allen and I have learned (and keep learning) two valuable lessons: Christian warfare is against the powerful enemy of us all, and God supplies all our needs abundantly, the more so as we honor Him with our tithes and offerings."

✍ ANNA'S MEMORIES:

CHRISTMAS MORNING behavior for seven excited children must have been well agreed upon by both mother and father. Gifts had been stashed away till Christmas Eve, then, after we children had gone to bed, Mother would bring them out and arrange them around the big tree in our living room. It would not have done much good to wake up and dash to be first to open the door to that room to spy on the gifts, for it was a given that we were not to enter until the whole family was ready to gather together for the celebration.

On a neatly laid table, Christmas breakfast was special with dry cereal instead of the usual porridge, as well as figs, dates, nuts, and mandarin oranges. Often the time of this meal might coincide with the Speech from the Throne, when, by example, Daddy taught us to listen intently for the monarch's recognition of God, for he greatly respected their outspoken trust in the Lord Jesus Christ. After breakfast the kitchen was brought back to order.

Yet still one more event had to happen before the front-room door could be opened. That was the arrival of our jovial Aunt Kate. But dear Aunt Katherine had little understanding of the feelings of us kids to get at those pretty packages, as she seemed to take her stately time and maybe arrived at 9 or 9:30. Now we could get into the room to snoop and guess what was coming to us. No unwrapping yet, however!

We sat around in a circle while Daddy led us in singing a couple of Christmas carols. He had a good singing voice. Aunt Kate was a voice teacher. Mother, too, had musical ability; so, with Eleanor at the piano, we did well. Then, from either Luke or Matthew, we read, verse about, the wonderful story of Jesus' birth. Following that, we knelt to pray around and thank God for the coming of his Son into our humanity.

This agenda taught us that the person of Christ Jesus and the marvelous facts about his birth were of great value to our Dad—and we, too, learned to love and honor him. I recall one time, at least, being moved almost to tears at the sense of God in our midst. The opening of gifts came at last, with lots of surprises and fun.

One Christmas Daddy taught me a personal lesson in gratefulness. After three years in a row receiving a cute little black doll, I let it be known that I wanted a popular "wetums" doll next time. On Christmas morning my doll was different and beautiful, but not a "wettums baby." Seeing me sulky and pouting, Daddy was grieved by my attitude. Privately with Mother and me, he said seriously, "Anna, Mother and I got you what we could afford and we hoped you would be happy with it!" No more words were necessary to straighten me out. I loved my new doll and my Daddy also.

Later, the Prairie Tabernacle Church scheduled a brief early Christmas Day service. Daddy, of course, had to bring the meditation. As a young girl I recall how blessed and thrilled I was at the newly inspired thoughts God gave him from the fathomless wonders of the birth of our Lord Jesus Christ.

Time At Home Was Precious

Though we did not resent his limited hours at home (because we never heard Mother complaining), we certainly could have benefited by a lot more time together with our father. We were so happy when he could spend an extra hour or two in the evening at home. That usually was the result of having visitors with us. When I'd see him striding home, I'd run and meet him and hold his hand for a few yards back to the house.

He was a great walker. Sometimes we children would walk with him for a mile-and-a-half north towards the three hills—nearly running to keep pace with his vigorous pace. Just to be with our dad was great! Back in the forties he ate noon meals with the students in the large dining hall. His mealtimes were so interrupted by questions and chats that his body became over-stressed. When the doctor ordered him to eat his meals at home, we all felt happily treated.

Summer deputation tours would take him away from home sometimes two months or more at a time. He faithfully wrote Mother many letters during this time. Because he loved to have a good garden, he'd expect to find it well manicured when he returned from his trips away. Did we ever go after the weeds before he got back!

The fun part came when the bus to bring him into Three Hills was due to arrive. We'd hurry over to the south end of A-dorm, climb to the top of the fire escape, and strain our eyes to watch down the highway to see the bus dusting our way. What a scramble to hug him! How blessed Mother was to see that we loved to have Dad back—not for what he could bring us but for himself, as we were happy to get maybe a chocolate bar from him as he unpacked his bags. Then we relished sitting at the table together and hear him tell thrilling adventures as to where he'd been, people he'd met, good times preaching, and breath-taking experiences.

People may think Daddy was ready to spank us for the least provocation. The opposite was true. I remember only two spankings—and knew I deserved both. I also knew he loved me enough to chasten me. He was brusque by nature and quickly came up with advice, but sometimes we would have benefited from more leisurely counsel, because some problems take time to bring out. But we understood the pressures on him and sought to protect his time.

I always felt that Daddy, in his spirit, was very free and non-legalistic. Disciplined, yes, but not inflexible or unreasonable. Much of the increase of rules and regulations came from rule-makers, such as some of the ever-changing deans. Early in the school's history, Daddy delegated regulation-making to others, without questioning how unreasonable an end result might become. Perhaps he was too busy to oversee this area.

My husband, Allen, remembers the times especially later in life, he had with Daddy all to himself, sharing spiritual insights. He says he left those precious sessions "with my heart awash with the presence and glory of Christ."

We had a wonderful Dad who lived what he preached, and we did not mind sharing him with others—at least, most of the time! He was not only consistent but also exuberant—so much fun!

B. The Rebel Who Became President: Paul Timothy Maxwell

PAUL, SECOND SON and sixth child, marked a new era for the family. The first five children seemed to develop "by the book." They all admit to having their share of deserved correction at home and at school, but they didn't openly rebel. Paul, born in 1937, grew up in a different milieu at Prairie, with greater school enrolment and post-World War II concepts of behavior—which affected the social environment out of which other students came. Moreover, his father was preoccupied with the burgeoning school and spent even less time with Paul than with his older children.

However, the greatest burden young Paul felt came from the expectations of faculty and students: "You should do better—you're a Maxwell!" "How could you do that—you're a Maxwell!" Paul obviously decided to be himself and to prove it by non-conformity.

Harboring many personal hurts, he called himself "the black sheep of the family." The older children had responded readily to father's biblical maxim: "Spare the rod, spoil the child." The mere threat of a spanking usually corrected a wrong attitude. But Paul seemed undaunted by punishment.

When in grade six he brought home a D on his report card, his father promised punishment if his next report hadn't improved. For one thing, his father knew Paul was capable of better and was simply "goofing off." Also, LE expected Paul would respond. But next report card again bore a D, and Paul bore the promised punishment. However, the subsequent report also was branded with a D. (This time father gave no punishment, since he'd not promised any—and by then realized Paul needed something other than punishment.)

Grade school withheld his school diploma because he refused to give his testimony at the graduation exercises. He may have been a rebel, but he refused to be hypocritical in giving a testimony he knew was not genuine. Instead he "went to a far country," geographically and spiritually. Both father and son learned much during this "desert experience."[1] Paul's waywardness was not the end of the story but part of his pilgrimage back to his Heavenly Father and his earthly family.

After graduating from Prairie, Paul married Barbara Fullington, Bible school classmate. They served in Colombia, South America under The Evangelical Union of South America from 1962 to 1970. When his father had a detached retina in 1966, Paul spent a semester teaching at Prairie. The Board invited him to remain home but he had mission commitments in Colombia.

In 1970 Prairie invited him back to teach on a permanent basis. Students considered him among their best teachers—his elective classes were always full. In teaching Law and Grace (which many considered his best class), he was able to present the balance he himself had come to experience.

---

[1] See description of the final years of L. E. Maxwell in main story and Paul's "Memories" below.

In 1978 the Board appointed Paul President. Ted S. Rendall was already Principal and also editor of the school magazine. Paul respected Ted's academic ability and experience and requested the Board to approve his appointment of Ted as VP for Theological Education.

Paul's restoration and eventual appointment to succeed his father as president is a story of God's grace. Father and son came to respect each other as colleagues. Whereas in earlier years he and his father had been (according to Paul) "strangers living under the same roof, rarely seeing each other"—now precious times together helped make up for lost years. True to his middle name, Timothy, he reflected his father's mentoring in those latter years. His sisters recollect Paul's rapport was such that he could joke with his single-minded father more than the rest of them could.

But as school president he had to bear the expectations of faculty, staff, and alumni (including debates over the school's future focus). "Administration will kill you!" his father had bluntly warned. He didn't mean the workload, but the emotional drain. The elder Maxwell knew how much his son shared his mother's sensitive nature.

"It nearly did kill me!" Paul said. Seven years later, he suffered complete exhaustion. Resigning in 1986, he with his family moved to Arizona and California for three years to recuperate. In 1989, International Students Ministries, Canada, asked Paul to become their president. The dry climate back in Alberta was helpful to Paul's health, and his skills and experience were helpful to ISMC.

Struggling through his personal pilgrimage—rebellion and repentance, work pressures and health trials—Paul learned to embrace the Cross in his life. His character and his understanding of the Word deepened. As more than one friend told me, "Paul's preaching has real depth to it!"

Paul and Barbara have four children: Dan, Don, Rick, and Ronda.

✍ *PAUL'S MEMORIES:*

O NE OF MY EARLIEST MEMORIES is of Daddy kneeling at his bedside praying, Bible open before him, only the top of his bowed head visible beneath a blanket. (In winter he left his door slightly ajar to get some heat from the basement furnace.) "Oh God! Oh God," is all I heard as I slipped downstairs. He was interceding in prayer for family and school, preparing for the busy day before him.

I met God through my parents. Through them I learned something of "the goodness and severity of God." When on one occasion Daddy announced some punishment for disobedience, Mother agreed that I deserved the punishment but said she wanted to take half of it. Of course I refused to let her—but I learned something of how my Savior had taken my punishment on himself.

I later came to appreciate my father's fearlessness in the pulpit. In that sense, he was a prophet the Holy Spirit used to bring conviction of sin. But this fearlessness could become a weakness when he publicly addressed a problem he should have dealt with privately. For instance, instead of counseling one of his grandchildren about an evident weakness, he addressed it publicly at the wedding as counsel to all.

However, this forthrightness was complemented by my father's quickness to ask forgiveness when he realized he had hurt someone. This combination of strength and humility endeared him to us all.

I know my waywardness was a great burden to Daddy—he used to preach against my sins from the pulpit, while I pretended to sleep in the pew, determined not to heed. I know it must have hurt him when I once said, "Daddy, you seem to care more about the Institute than about your family." I was later sorry I said that, after I became president and discovered how difficult it was to balance work and family responsibilities. I still marvel at all he was able to handle.

In trying to deal with his rebellious teenager, my father finally came to the end of himself and cried out for divine intervention. "God, get hold of Paul no matter what it costs him or me!" he prayed in desperation. God heard him and broke my stubborn will. I in turn heard God's voice and submitted. After graduation I married Barbara and we went to Latin America, where we found blessing in church planting and teaching the Word.

Later, when the Prairie board asked me to return to Canada and take my father's classes at Prairie, I said to Barbara, "That is inviting my own failure—because how can anyone fill L. E. Maxwell's shoes?" However, I also had a strong sense God wanted me to help train men and women in the Word at Prairie—so we returned. God gave me 15 wonderful years. That's when I really got to know my father as we discussed the Word together.

As he aged, Daddy became more mellow, with a greater awareness of God's grace and love. Hearing of a "fire-and-brimstone" preacher who had similarly mellowed, he commented, "I can understand. He is nearing the Judgment!"

I'm thankful for all that my parents taught me about life and death, law and grace—mercy and truth!

G. The Precocious One: Miriam Esther (Maxwell) Carlson

MIRIAM, YOUNGEST DAUGHTER of Leslie and Pearl, was a precocious child. Born in 1942, during the height of her father's ministry she was the family "doll" with dark ringlets over her shoulders. Her sisters considered her more musically talented than they. At age four she could accurately identify musical tones. ("That floor board squeaks in middle C," she told her mother—and so it did!) She played the piano, organ, and violin, also excelling in academic studies.

Still, what her parents thought they knew about child-rearing somehow didn't produce the same responses in Miriam as in her sisters. Father usually left punishment of the girls to their mother, but on one occasion when he did spank Miriam, the older girls stood behind the door weeping along with her. However, they felt consoled when their father picked up his little girl and she laid her head on his shoulder. She knew he loved her.

As with her brother Paul, Miriam grew up in a different era of the family and school history. Her mother still devoted all her time to the family, but father, under the pressures of the rapidly growing school, had discontinued the special times he used to spend with the older children—a change he personally regretted. Like her brother Paul, Miriam also found it difficult to live with the idealistic expectations of others concerning the Maxwell name.

At times she resented being "the youngest Maxwell" and all that it implied in some people's minds.

After attending Prairie grade school, high school, and Bible school, Miriam married Norman D. Carlson from Illinois. Norm had graduated from Prairie and gone on to Greenville College, IL., for his B.A.

"When we married, I was so relieved to be called Mrs. Carlson instead of a Maxwell!" Miriam later said. "But I began to see my family and Prairie through his eyes. That's where he'd found liberty of spirit." In 1964 the couple entered pastoral ministry in Illinois and Alberta. Norman had special gifts in relating to people individually, and saw his churches (United Brethren and Conference Baptist) grow.

Norm and Miriam experienced the Cross in their lives, coping with tensions in their ministry. In 1978 they left the pastorate and, like the Apostle Paul, took up a "tent-making" ministry. Their sports equipment business in Montana gave Norman opportunities to witness to customers. "On the golf course, Uncle Norm got through to fellow golfers—including those who wouldn't have listened to a pastor," says his nephew Mark, who also plays golf. "I looked upon Norm's ministry as a market-place application of Grandpa Maxwell's teaching."

Norman's sudden death in 2000 was a devastating blow not only for Miriam but also for a wide circle—including his 84-year-old mother, his sister, other relatives, and young people to whom he had become a mentor and friend. The Maxwell sisters and spouses all traveled to Montana to comfort their "little sister" and share in the fellowship with friends and co-workers. Miriam's brother Paul led the subsequent memorial service and burial at Peoria, Illinois. He gave thanks for the special part that Norman and Miriam had played in the family.

The Carlsons' son Tim, continues to be a strength to Miriam.

✍ *MIRIAM'S MEMORIES:*

WE'VE ALWAYS BEEN A CLOCK-CONSCIOUS FAMILY. Noon hour at our house was a matter of precision timing. When we saw Daddy coming up the path at 11:58, there'd be a chorus of "Turn on the radio" and "Plug in the tea kettle!" And during conferences, Daddy was always conscious that guests should get a good night's sleep so they'd be up in time for prayers in the morning. If visitors to our house after the evening service stayed too long, Daddy would suddenly stand up and announce, "Let's pray!" End of visit!

In contrast, when I was small enough to be held on his lap, I believed that the most important thing my father had to do in the morning was to feed me. When I crept downstairs, Daddy's special porridge would be bubbling on the stove, complete with flaxseed, which we called "bugs." Dipping his spoon from the hot bowl of porridge to the cold bowl of milk (old Scottish method) and then to either his mouth or mine was a ritual that I shared many winter mornings.

When Daddy was in the house our activities revolved around him. Just after the news went off and before he went upstairs for a short siesta, we could draw his thoughts away from the load he was carrying into something lighter. World Series time was especially fun, because Daddy would listen to a few innings of the Yankees versus the Dodgers and sometimes even opt out of his noon nap.

Mother provided the calm home atmosphere we all needed.

279

Although it might have been more exciting to travel the world with Daddy, she saw her clear calling in serving her family at home—listening, caring, and teaching. She was there when we brought home a "B" when we thought we deserved an "A." After letting us explain why, she would remind us, "It's not the grade that counts, but whether you did your best!"

Sloshing up a trout stream with Daddy, trying to keep pace, made him more of a father and less a stranger in my life. Our enormous garden provided more shared moments, watching him transplant his precious asparagus plants, learning how to make straight rows, and planting seeds the correct distance apart.

I remember Daddy saying that people would know he'd lost his calling if they found him retired in a greenhouse! Gardening in itself was not sinful—rather it was enjoyable, relaxing, and even practical. However, he believed that anything that consumed you, however "harmless," could side-track you spiritually.

When going through my most difficult years, at times I resented the position I found myself in as the youngest Maxwell. As I was approaching my final year in Bible School, playing violin in the orchestra, I became aware of my feelings toward a classmate in the violin section—Norman Carlson.

I told my mother I believed I was in love and asked if she knew how Daddy felt. I was thrilled when I found out he'd already checked Norm out—and stated his approval! From then on I knew that this would be my life partner.

Norm's deep respect for his father-in-law showed itself in little ways, such as the fact he used the term "Father" rather than the familiar "Daddy." They shared a deep mutual respect and spent enjoyable hours discussing church development and doctrine. Their discourse in Heaven now has no time constraints.

When my husband took ill, I remembered how Mother had prayed she would live longer than Daddy—so she could take care of him. Daddy humbly acknowledged her devotion during this long period and was able to express his love and appreciation for her.

Even though Norman and I had no idea we'd have only two short weeks after diagnosis of his heart disease, he constantly expressed his affection and appreciation. My most vivid memory of our 36 years together was the many times he started the morning by asking, "Have I had a chance to tell you today how much I love you?"

During my growing up years, outward displays of affection were common in our family, and Daddy and Mother were our prime examples.

I'm thankful that our son, Tim, got to know his grandparents. His lovely wife, Debbie, didn't have that opportunity—she married Tim after his grandparents' death. Tim's academic ability carried him through college to a doctorate in mathematics. His self-reliant attitude and ability to show confidence without appearing arrogant remind me of his grandfather and his Uncle Ernest, with whom he enjoyed solving puzzles.

In the midst of sad family partings, we think of the Great Reunion ahead, with no distance or physical weakness.

END OF FAMILY ALBUM

"Never had the Church so much influence over the world as when she had nothing to do with the world."—LEM

DYNAMIC DISCIPLESHIP

WHAT WAS THE GREATEST contribution of Prairie Bible Institute to us as students? Students might give different answers, but I believe the most significant contribution was the spiritual commune PBI provided. Our years at Prairie gave us time and space to learn what the Holy Spirit was trying to teach us—often in different ways.

Apart from LE's unique mentoring, we could have taken much the same academic studies elsewhere. But I believe that the mentoring plus the commune (by that I mean the disciplined environment) helped to shape our lives. In a sense, Prairie amounted to an extended spiritual retreat. Today there are a number of other excellent retreat centers where one can meet with God and with those who have walked with God. Prairie provided that special opportunity on a sustained basis.

"Far Above All"

What that sense of spiritual community has meant to graduates in their ministries came to me forcibly as I was completing work on this volume. Katherine F. Wiens ('47) telephoned me from her home some two thousand miles away.

"You won't remember me, but I hear you are writing the story of Mr. Maxwell," she said. "Have you included the chorus he led us in many a time, 'Far above all'? I have a real burden that it be included."

I wondered why it was so important, but Katherine helped me understand.

A quiet girl from a Mennonite community, after graduating from

282

Prairie she served with the Mennonite Brethren in the Belgian Congo. She survived the cruel Simba uprising but had to flee Congo during the revolution in which the country was renamed Zaire. The mission reassigned her to Brazil, but eventually she returned to Zaire.

"I never was talented," she told me, "I had a hard time learning three languages in six years!"

The reason she so wanted me to include "Far above all" was that its message and the context in which she'd learned the chorus were a strength to her in loneliness, in physical hardship, during terrifying massacres, in the carnage of civil war, during the stresses of leaving beloved nationals in one continent and making new friends in another continent.

"Do you remember the words?" she asked me. "Mr. Maxwell would start, and we'd sing along in worship. Sometimes we'd be in a prayer meeting. Oh, it brings back such memories! In moments of need overseas, I often remembered the words."

Then she sang the chorus over the telephone:
> *Far above all, far above all;*
> *Jesus the Crucified, far above all!*
> *Low at his footstool adoring we fall;*
> *God has exalted him, far above all!*[1]

It's a simple chorus, but to Katherine it took her back to the spiritual commune in Three Hills where she'd learned its truth in her own life. It had stayed with her through decades of service. To her it was important to have an updated story of L. E. Maxwell, but that meant doing what he did—exalting Christ as Lord.

The chorus encapsulated the experience of Katherine's spiritual growth. She could close her eyes and hear the students responding to a Bible message, sharing concerns with fellow students, praying together, denying self, rejoicing in victory, celebrating the Lord's Supper—until

---

[1] Chorus of a Keswick hymn, psssibly by missionary evangelist Howard Guinness.

Jesus the Crucified was lifted up as Lord, far above all! The chorus was almost a theme song.

For Katherine, as for so many, Prairie had been an experience, not just a course.

Pilgrimage Lessons

As I look back on the story of Prairie and the Maxwell family pilgrimage, I see several truths of LE's life message being worked out:

1. The way of the Cross is not easy or comfortable. That has been the story of LE's ministry, of his family, of his grand-children, of the Institute itself.

2. The most spiritual believer, the finest leader, still is human and has his/her "limps." All of us—like righteous Job—can grow. LE was a man of integrity, truth, discipline, vision, commitment, devotion, repentance, confession, compassion, and faith. Yet he was able to learn from his own family about relationships.

3. The Maxwell story demonstrates that God does answer the prayers of parents and of children.

4. The family members help us understand something else—something that many parents and children presume upon: No generation can ride on the spiritual life of the previous genera-tion. Heritage is precious, but each person has to learn the truth of the Cross in his or her life. The inheritance is no guarantee of the crown.

5. But the way of the Cross, even though it passes through death, emerges in victorious living. In the pains that each student, each family, and Prairie itself have suffered, there is hope at the end of the path. In fact, there is a crown each pilgrim will receive: "Be faithful until death, and I will give you the crown of life" (Rev. 2.10).

To us who follow on, the message is: "Hold on to what you have so that no one will take your crown" (Rev. 3.11). Eleanor Maxwell told me that after she heard her father preach on that verse, she caught up with him on the campus sidewalk, hugged him, and exclaimed, "Daddy—I'm not going to let you take my crown!" He beamed.

An Urgent Message for Today

We face a different world, but in need of the same message that L. E. Maxwell proclaimed. Society characterizes the claim to truth as bigotry. Many churches preach Easy Grace instead of declaring God's Absolutes. However, the Cross of Christ is a radical statement of absolute truth: God's holiness vicariously judging sin in an act of divine love to redeem his creation.

Yet, as mentioned earlier, the concept of the Cross has been grossly distorted in some quarters. Radical Feminism rejected the Eternal Father's sacrifice of Jesus on the Cross as yet another male myth to encourage and perpetuate violence. Maoist revolutionaries and Liberation Theology portrayed the Crucifixion as their model for using violence to overthrow oppression. In view of such distortions, the Good News of Christ's Cross obviously needs to be declared, clearly explained, and demonstrated afresh in this generation.

The message of the crucified life is, in some ways, more significant today (if that were possible) than in Maxwell's day. Back then, even though theological liberalism was growing, society as a whole retained values of an earlier era influenced by the spiritual awakenings of the previous two centuries. Today, society as a whole has become permeated with liberal individualism. That is at the heart of society—in education, law, commerce, and entertainment.[1] "The world" of liberalism is so pervasive that it has become the norm, so much so that our churches, let alone non-churched society, hardly question it. Instead sometimes the church's response seems to be, "Adapt, accept, live in and of the world."

---

[1] Phillip E. Johnson, *The Wedge of Truth*. Downers Grove: InterVarsity Press, 2000.

In a subtle and ironic twist, the culture of death and the culture of life have become interchanged. The culture of spiritual death entices us, "Eat of the fruit and enjoy life!" But the culture of spiritual life still challenges us, "Reckon yourself dead to sin and alive to God!"

So the worldview of today's students is radically different from Maxwell's day. They've grown up in a society that promotes individualism and hedonism—suspicious if not disrespectful of authority, feeling little obligation to meet the needs of others. Secular author Robert Bly[1] calls them "the Sibling Society"—they and their peers are the center of the universe.

Needed but Still Resented

"Maxwell's message was needed in his day," some friends tell me. "But people aren't ready to hear about 'dying to self' and 'the crucified life' nowadays." Attitudes do change with different eras, but Maxwell's message was just as unwelcome to the hard-driving society of the Modern era as it is now to the self-gratifying PostModern era. We could go back a long way in history and say that the message of the Cross was unwelcome—resented—in Jesus' time on earth.

"Unless you deny yourself and take up your Cross daily, you cannot be my disciple," Jesus told his followers living in a self-righteous nation, in the midst of a pagan, idolatrous world. That "irrelevant" message infuriated Saul of Tarsus until he met the risen Christ and was himself transformed. From then on he spent his life as Paul, expounding to Jew and Gentile what Jesus meant. Is the truth of the crucified life relevant today? Not to the interests of the self life, but it is to all the problems of the church and to the world it should be reaching.

Is that message needed today? Of course it is—more than ever!

Jesus is still calling men and women to leave their "nets" (a very current word) and follow him. His Spirit is ready to prepare them to

---

[1] Robert Bly, *The Sibling Society.* New York: Addison-Wesley, 1996.

reach their own generation, to revolutionize them and give them the vision for their world. L. E. Maxwell is no longer with us, but his paradoxical message is still relevant. In fact it is essential to the victorious living and ministry of every believer: The Cross in the life of the believer: "I live by the faith of the Son of God, yet . . . ."

And that is the continuing story, because *Maxwell's Passion and Power* should also be ours.[1]

*   *   *

"Forget it, young man! Wait till you've got something to write about." When L. E. Maxwell told me that concerning a writing career, he had no idea I'd one day write his story. Neither did I. Now I can hear my mentor chuckle as he barks, "Serves you right!"

I did find something worthwhile to write about.

– W. Harold Fuller

---

[1] For those who may still wonder how to gain the victorious life L. E. Maxwell experienced, see Appendix F: OK—But What Do I Do Now? (page 300).

287

APPENDICES

Appendix A

CORE VALUES
OF PRAIRIE BIBLE INSTITUTE

Prairie is a place where lives are transformed through holistic biblical education which produces people whose worldview, lifestyle and ministry honors Christ, impacts their world and furthers the global mission of the Church. We want you to know the "core values" we treasure—that permeate all aspects of who we are and what we do today.

WE ARE A COMMUNITY THAT IS
CHRIST CENTERED

Without him we have no reason for being a school. Jesus is our Savior, our-model and mediator. "Jesus said to him, I am the way, the truth and the life, no man comes to the Father but by me." (John 14:6)

BIBLE BASED

We view all of life through the absolute truth of the Word of God. It is our place of reference, focus and perspective. "All Scripture is God breathed and useful for teaching, rebuking, correcting and training in righteousness so that the man of God may be thoroughly equipped for every good work." (2 Timothy 3:16, 17)

PRAYERFUL

We do it, we don't just talk about it. Staff meet daily for prayer by department and weekly as a corporate body. During the school year staff and students dedicate one day each semester for prayer, half days each month during the summer. Students continue to pray for God's work around the world through their ACTION prayer groups. "By prayer and supplication with thanksgiving let your requests be made known to God." (Philippians 4:6)

LEARNING

We need to know God's Word, understand the issues of our times and be equipped to meet those needs. We must be prepared to "give the reason for the hope that you have" (I Peter 3:15). No person should pay an academic penalty for serious Christian studies. It is possible for our students to transfer credits to many universities and colleges, both Christian and secular.

MENTORING/DISCIPLESHIP

Our passion is to model and nurture our students to spiritual maturity. Students get to be part of formal discipleship groups designed to encourage personal spiritual growth. It is not enough to "pump a head full of knowledge," we must impact the heart. "Whatever you have learned, received, heard, or seen in me, put into practice" (Philippians 4:8).

GLOBAL MISSIONS

The natural outgrowth of knowing Jesus, studying his Word and becoming a disciple is like a pot boiling over. We will overflow with the truth of Christ to a sin sick world. God calls us to be witnesses locally, nationally and globally (Acts 1:8).

SERVICE ORIENTED

Learning takes place by doing. It is not sufficient to learn academically. We must apply what we learn. Prairie students are personally involved in ministry, first discovering their gifts and then developing their skills. Formal internships (some up to a year in length) form a key component of our programs.

LEADERSHIP DEVELOPMENT

We are training those who will be able to disciple and lead others. Upperclassmen volunteer to lead and mentor first year students in the discipleship program. "…the things you have heard me say in the presence of many witnesses entrust to reliable men who will be qualified to teach others" (2 Timothy 2:2).

SELF DENIAL/SIMPLE LIFESTYLE

This is not so much a statement of what we do or do not have. It is a statement of our focus and priorities—to passionately serve Christ so that others may come to know Him. "…I have learned in whatever state I am, in this to be content. I know both how to be abased, and I know to abound…." (Philippians 4:11, 12)

GOD SUPPLIED/NO DEBT

We will be content with God's supply. We are dependent on him for our needs. We know that he supplies through the sacrificial giving of others and so we pledge to be wise stewards of what we have. We will not go into debt. Gifts given to Prairie go to meet present needs not to service debt. We're not paying for "dead horses" or "crashed computers." "Owe no man anything, but a debt of love…" (Romans 13:8).

Please pray and partner with us!

—Rick Down, President

Appendix B

TIME-LINE AT PRAIRIE

1922 L.E. Maxwell arrives in Three Hills
1924 Board formed, Maxwell as Principal, Fergus Kirk as President
1925 Leslie and Pearl marry in Boone, Iowa
1927 First class graduates
1938 High School opens
1941 Elementary (Grade) School opens
1956 Maxwell's first cataract operation, followed by complications
1957 Ted Rendall joins faculty, editorial team
1960 Rendall appointed Vice-Principal
1961 Kirk retires as President; Henry Muddle becomes President
1965 Muddle retires; Maxwell becomes President
1966 Maxwell's retina surgery
1967 Rendall appointed Principal
1970 Paul Maxwell joins faculty.
1977 LE retires; Paul Maxwell becomes President; Ted Rendall
    continues as Principal
1981 Fergus Kirk dies, age 86
1984 L. E. Maxwell dies, age 88
1986 Paul retires from presidency; Rendall appointed President,
    continues as Principal
1986 Social regulations are relaxed
1989 Graduate school opens
1992 Pearl dies, age 92
1992 Rendall becomes Chancellor; Paul Ferris appointed President and
    Principal
1998 Ferris resigns; Down appointed President and Principal

Appendix C

IS THERE NO CAUSE?

Is there no cause for which to die?
  "For what are we here?" is the searching cry;
If life is short and death is sure,
  Do I live for what will endure?

What is the cause, O friend of mine?
  For what will you die in life's short time?
Earth's passing pleasures hold many a thrill.
  Is it worth dying for their fancy and frill?

Was there no cause when Christ came to earth –
  Left heaven's glory to live in this dearth?
Was there no cause for His suffering such loss –
  Or was there a reason for His death on the cross?

There was a cause for such infinite cost:
  Men without Christ are eternally lost.
"Christ died to save" is the message clear;
  The question unanswered: "How shall they hear?"

This is God's cause, for it I will die;
  From home and loved ones I'll gladly fly.
With Christ in the Garden, the battle is won;
  I cry, "Not my will but Thine be done!"

©1966 Paul Maxwell

Written by Paul T. Maxwell, age 26, upon news of the death of fellow missionary Ernest Fowler (GMU and LAM) at hands of guerillas—"Colombia's First Evangelical Missionary Martyr," according to Paul Marshall (Hefley, *By Their Blood.* Milford: Mott Media, 1979.) A Colombian pastor said: "The road to evangelization of our nation is paved with the blood of our martyrs."

Appendix D

Quips and Quotes

Selected sayings frequently used by L. E. Maxwell, some from other sources.
From the booklet by Wentworth Pike, Action Ministries, Three Hills, AB.

1. A man all wrapped up in himself makes a mighty small package.
2. Sort them out, Lord, sort them out! (when several prayed at once).
3. Faith and life always go together. Believe and behave!
4. God does not fill us to make us great, but to make us gracious.
5. UNPACK! (to homesick and restless ones)
6. You need a backbone instead of a wishbone.
7. You can as much understand the Scripture with the natural mind as a jackass can understand musical harmony. If you find yourself in the barn, don't be offended, brother.
8. There's no sect quite so sectarian as the non-sect sect.
9. God help us to be better than our body's inclination.
10. Bless the women out there who are doing a man's job.
11. No place is too sacred for Satan to intrude.
12. Lord, save us from ourselves.
13. Wherever there is the indulgence of self, there is sin, no matter in which of the many departments of life.
14. Not do or die – do and die!
15. Liberty is not license.
16. The greatest mission is submission.
17. Did you went, or was you sent?
18. Don't let the world pour you into its mold.
19. We are always getting to live, but never living.
20. It's the small, simple things that show which way the wind is blowing.
21. A holy life is made up of little things.
22. Most people want happiness without holiness.
23. A lot of things don't need praying about, they need obeying about!
24. I may need to die daily, but I don't need continually to attend my own funeral!
25. Just a poor piece of proud pottery.
26. The cross of full surrender leaves no odor of the tomb; That cross is covered by a life of resurrection bloom.
27. Too many Christians have "pew"monia.
28. A perfectly good thing out of divine order is a wicked thing. Nor am I permitted to snatch in despair at a kind of promised relief from a miserable condition.

29. Christ promises more but demands more!
30. Oh, it's good to soar these bolts and bars above,
To Him whose purpose I adore, who providence I love;
And in Thy mighty will to find
The joy, the freedom of the mind.
31. If you were at home calling the cows, your voice would be much louder than that.
32. Lord, save us from being so right that we are rough.
33. "How are you today?"
"Oh, not bad under the circumstances."
"Well, what in the world are you doing under there? Come on out and get on top! A Christian has no business under there."
34. Our consecration is not to service but to Someone.
35. The human heart is fallen, foolish, and fickle.
36. If you have need of nothing, that is what you will get - in fact, that is what you have already.
37. If you are as dry as dust and know it and admit it, you qualify for His filling.
38. The Holy Spirit cannot guide where He does not govern.
39. Quoting W. C. Stevens: "As long as you exist to give and not get, you'll be all right."
40. Don't be so heavenly minded that you're no earthly good.
41. God doesn't comfort us to make us comfortable, but to make us comforters.
42. The Christian life is not a goal - it's a road.
43. Jesus didn't come to make bad men good. He came to make dead men live.

From *Born Crucified:*

44. Christ dying for me makes inevitable my death with Him. p. 16
45. Were we not declared righteous in Christ that we might be holy in life? p. 21
46. Self can never cast out self. p. 23
47. I must be either "dead in sins" or "dead in sin." p. 27
48. We are so worldly-minded we would rather be indecent than different. p. 37
49. Never had the Church so much influence over the world as when she had nothing to do with the world. p. 43

50. The Cross contradicts human nature at every point. p. 63
51. The flesh seeks to glory in God's very presence. p. 89
52. Quoting Dr. A. J. Gordon, "If we regard the doctrine of sinless perfection as a heresy, we regard contentment with sinful imperfection as a greater heresy." p. 22, 78
53. Quoting T. C. Upham, "Put a thorn in every enjoyment, a worm in every gourd, that would either prevent my being wholly thine, or in any measure retard my progress in the divine life." p. 93
54. We cannot live in the flesh and do the work of the Spirit. p. 8
55. Many of us would not mind being missionaries if we could be great missionaries. p. 16
56. Between the extremes of no fire and wild fire there is a golden balance. p. 21
57. In your weariest and weakest and most bewildered moment, simply say, "Now, Lord, here is my chance - and thine: my chance to die, thy chance to manifest the life of Jesus." p. 25
58. When we credit Him with goodness in having tried us, then faith immediately beholds God abundantly able to deliver us. p. 37
59. God can take no pleasure in the flesh. It is unimproveable and incorrigible. p. 204
60. Our tent is pitched not in a paradise, but on the battlefield. p. 13
61. This gospel is indeed good news, but good only to the man who gets it. p. 44
62. Christians must become convicted and convinced that missions is the first business of the Church. p. 48

==============

Appendix E

THY BROTHER'S BLOOD CRIETH
by Amy Wilson Carmichael

THE TOM-TOMS THUMPED straight on all night and the darkness shuddered round me like a living, feeling thing. I could not go to sleep, so I lay awake and looked, and I saw, as it seemed, this:

That I stood on a grassy sward, and at my feet a precipice broke sheer down into infinite space. I looked, but saw no bottom, only cloud shapes, black and furiously coiled, and great shadow-shrouded hollows, and unfathomable depths. Back I drew, dizzy at the depth.

Then I saw forms of people moving single file along the grass. They were making for the edge. There was a woman with a baby in her arms and another little child holding on to her dress. She was on the very verge. Then I saw that she was blind. She lifted her foot for the next step…it trod air. She was over, and the children over with her. Oh, the cry as they went over!

Then I saw more streams of people flowing from all quarters. All were blind, stone blind, all made straight for the precipice edge. There were shrieks, as they suddenly knew themselves falling, and a tossing up of helpless arms, catching, clutching at empty air. But some went over quietly, and fell without a sound

Then I wondered, with a wonder that was simply agony, why no one stopped them at the edge. I could not. I was glued to the ground, and I could not call; though I strained and tried, only a whisper would come.

Then I saw that along the edge there were sentries set at intervals. But the intervals were too great; there were wide, unguarded gaps between. And over these gaps the people fell in their blindness, quite unwarned, and the green grass seemed blood red to me, and the gulf yawned like the mouth of hell.

297

Then I saw, like a little picture of peace, a group of people under some trees with their backs turned towards the gulf. They were making daisy chains. Sometimes when a piercing shriek cut the quiet air and reached them, it disturbed them and they thought it a rather vulgar noise. And if one of their number started up and wanted to go and do something to help, then all the others would pull that one down. "Why should you get so excited about it? You must wait for a definite call to go! You haven't finished your daisy chain yet. It would be really selfish," they said, "to leave us to finish the work alone"!

There was another group. It was made up of people whose great desire was to get more sentries out, but they found that very few wanted to go, and sometimes there were no sentries set for miles and miles of the edge.

Once a girl stood alone in her place, waving the people back; but her mother and other relations called, and reminded her that her furlough was due, she must not break the rules. And being tired and needing a change, she had to go and rest for awhile; but no one was sent to guard her gap, and over and over the people fell, like a waterfall of souls.

Once a child caught at a tuft of grass that grew at the very brink of the gulf; it clung convulsively, and it called--but nobody seemed to hear. Then the roots of the grass gave way, and with a cry the child went over, its two little hands still holding tight to the torn off bunch of grass. And the girl who longed to be back in her gap thought she heard the little one cry, and she sprang up and wanted to go; at which they reproved her, reminding her that no one is necessary anywhere; the gap would be well taken care of, they knew. And then they sang a hymn.

Then through the hymn came another sound like the pain of a million broken hearts wrung out in one full drop, one sob. And a horror of great darkness was upon me, for I knew what it was--the Cry of the Blood.

Then thundered a voice, the voice of the Lord, "And He said,

'What hast thou done? The voice of thy brother's blood crieth unto me from the ground'."

The tom-toms still beat heavily, the darkness still shuddered and shivered about me; I heard the yells of the devil-dancers and the weird, wild shriek of the devil-possessed, just outside the gate.

What does it matter, after all! It has gone on for years; it will go on for years. Why make such a fuss about it?

God forgive us! God arouse us! Shame us out of our callousness! Shame us out of our sin!

--From *Things as They Are*, by Amy Carmichael. Copyright, The Dohnavur Fellowship. Used by permission.

Appendix F

Personal Response: **OK, But What Do I Do Now?**

AMONG THOSE WHO HAVE PERSEVERED in reading thus far, there may be a few who say, "OK–all this theory sounds great. And the stories of discipled Christians are challenging. But I've heard all that before. What do I do now?

"The way of the Cross I understand," they may say; "Christ died for me that I might have eternal life. He wants me to take up the Cross daily in denying myself. And I need to obey my Savior by sharing the Good News of the Cross with others around me—and maybe around the world.

"I'm willing for all that. But try as I might, I don't see any difference in my life. It seems that self is still at the center, influencing all I do—even when I try to serve the Lord. How can you help me to enter into this victorious life that Maxwell talked about?"

One thing I know—you don't need more words. You've already read the teaching and exhortation and examples. But I do have one simple word of advice that may help.

Enroll in God's School.

I'm not talking about Prairie Bible Institute or any other institution. I'm talking about the School of the Holy Spirit. Enroll in it.

Your problem may be that you are trying to put self to death. That's something like Easter in the Philippines. Men are actually nailed to crosses, to agonize as a tourist attraction. Some believe they'll receive special absolution for their sins by suffering in this way; but most hope that the pain will bring in enough money from tourists to make it all worthwhile.

That can almost be our problem. We forget that, with all our sincerity, we cannot crucify our self-life. It simply thrives on the attention! We know the Scriptures; we understand the teaching that the self-life must be put to death; but we aren't experiencing victory. We also forget that the process is not ours to agonize through, but it is the work of the Holy Spirit to accomplish.

Paul wrote to the Philippians, "'...he who began a good work in you will carry it on to completeness until the day of Christ Jesus."

That's why I recommend you enroll in Christ's School of Discipline. Time at Prairie gave us the space and time to do that (if we were willing), but not everyone has the opportunity to live in a commune or to take time out for a spiritual retreat. However, wherever we are, we can come to God in sincere desperation (remember Paul? "Oh wretched man that I am!") and ask him to "work in you to will and to act according to his good purpose."

But let me warn you. If you sincerely do that, be prepared for things to happen in your life. The Holy Spirit will be your teacher; he will allow things to happen that will drive you to God. Petty things may bother you as never before, to give you the opportunity to deny yourself, to place that aspect of your self-life on the Cross. You may find yourself in circumstances you wouldn't have chosen. In God's school of discipline, you will be "crowded to Christ" (as Maxwell would say). So when you enroll, be prepared for lessons to start! You can fail the class, or you can pass it and be ready for the next.

That's all you'll need—enrollment in the Holy Spirit's school of discipline. To prepare, you'll need to feed on the Word of God and spend time in prayer with your Lord, but God will choose the curriculum, the class schedule, and the assignments. He will "work in you to will and to act according to his good purpose." And, again, "he who began a good work in you will carry it on to completeness..."

So enroll now. Enroll each day. It's a school with guaranteed results.

By the way, you also might want to take the advice of Stephen Olford, in his Foreword, to study especially Chapters 10-13 of this book. But only the Holy Spirit can really teach you those truths.

God bless you,

W. Harold Fuller

BIBLIOGRAPHY

MAGAZINES AND PAPERS

Prairie Harvester. Three Hills: PBI
Prairie Overcomer. Three Hills: PBI
Young Pilot. Three Hills: PBI
"Lion on the Prairies." Unpublished thesis by Stephen Maxwell Spaulding, 1991.

PUBLISHED BOOKS

Callaway, Bernice, *Legacy.* MacCall Clan. 1987
----, and Victor, *The Spirit of Prairie.* ed: Phillip Callaway, PBI,1997
Davidson, Roy. L., *God's Plan on the Prairies.* Three Hills: PBI,1986
----, *With God on the Prairies.* Three Hills: PBI, Revised 1984
Epp, Margaret, *Into All The World.* Prairie Bible Inst. 1973
Govett, R., *The Twofoldness of Divine Truth.* Harrisburg:
        Christian Publications Inc. c1850
Keller, W. Phillip, *Expendable.* Three Hills: AB. Prairie Press. 1966
Kirk, Hector A, *Balanced Security.* Maple: Beacon Press (nd)
Maxwell, L.E., *Abandoned to Christ.* Three Hills: Prairie Press, 1955
----, *Born Crucified.* Chicago: Moody Press. 1945/1973
----, *Boy Wanted.* Three Hills: Prairie Press, (nd)
----, *Capital Punishment.* Three Hills: Prairie Press, c 1957
----, *Crowded to Christ.* Grand Rapids, MI. Wm. B. Eerdmans, Co. 1951
----, *Pentecostal Baptism.* Three Hills: Prairie Press, c 1971
----, *Prairie Pillars.* Three Hills: PBI, 1971
----, *The Holy Spirit and Missions.* Three Hills: Prairie Press, c 1957
----, *The Holy Spirit in Believers and in Missions.*
        Three Hills: Prairie Press, l982
----, with Ruth Dearing. *Women in Ministry.* Wheaton: Victor Books. 1987
Stackhouse, John G., Jr., *Canadian Evangelicalism in the 20th Century.*
        Toronto: University of Toronto Press. 1993

Index

Index

Index

Index

Index

Reader's Notes:

Reader's Notes: